SOUTH YORKSHIRE RAILWAYS

Andrew Walker and John Walker

AMBERLEY

First published 2021

Amberley Publishing
The Hill, Stroud
Gloucestershire, GL5 4EP

www.amberley-books.com

ISBN 978 1 4456 9828 1 (print)
ISBN 978 1 4456 9829 8 (ebook)

British Library Cataloguing in Publication Data. A catalogue record for this book is available from the British Library.

Typesetting by Aura Technology and Software Services, India. Printed in the UK.

Introduction

The authors of this book were born and grew up around the places depicted on page 56 of Stuart K. Baker's seminal *Rail Atlas of Britain*, published by OPC in 1977. It was this book that first enabled us to appreciate the true nature and complexity of the railway system of South Yorkshire, and to 'join the dots' to see where the multiplicity of lines, junctions, yards, collieries and stations fitted into the grand scheme. And what a scheme it was. The network resembled a densely packed web even then, and of course many of the minor branches, along with pretty much the entire Hull & Barnsley route, had already gone in the wake of the Beeching cuts and other rationalisation. The Woodhead route was still there, but its days were numbered. Around fifteen pits in the Barnsley area were still shown as having rail connections on that first edition of the atlas – and that is a fraction of what once existed.

The railways of South Yorkshire were built on the coal and iron industries, with the Victorian promoters pushing through plan after plan to extend the railways from the mines to the ports and to the major manufacturing cities that were growing at a pace never seen before. In the late 1970s, when the earliest pictures in this book were taken, it was still possible to capture the remnants of these pioneering railway ventures before the industries withered and the last of the branch lines closed. Some lines have since enjoyed a renaissance of sorts – passenger services on the Barnsley to Penistone route, the reopening of Rotherham Central station and the reinstatement of the Swinton chord stand as examples – but these are outweighed by the bigger closures, notably of the Midland main line through Cudworth, the Woodhead route and the marshalling yards at Tinsley and Wath. The East Coast main line through Doncaster remains the flagship and is busier than ever, but today's rail atlas is a pale shadow of its counterpart of forty years ago. In this book we have compiled a selection of images that span those decades, and which illustrate the diversity of rail traffic in this once most industrial of counties. Most of the images are, of course, unrepeatable today. We hope they give a flavour of the railways of South Yorkshire.

Our particular thanks go to fellow photographer Vaughan Hellam for providing many of the pictures, some featuring rarely photographed locations, from his extensive collection.

Andrew and John Walker
December 2019

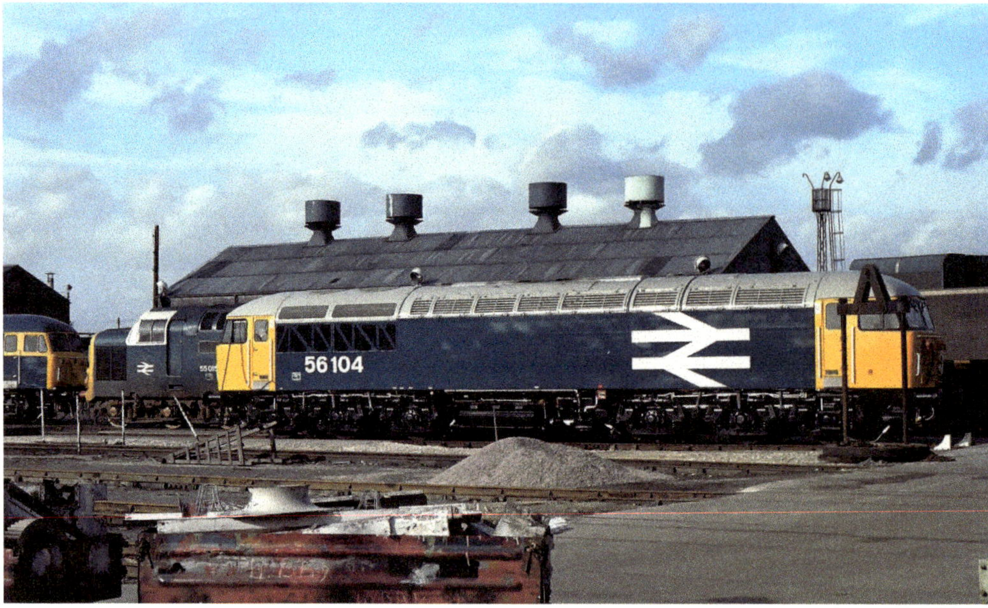

Diesel generations at Doncaster Works

The English Electric 'Deltics' were not built at Doncaster, but they were repaired, refurbished and repainted there for two decades. Here Deltic No. 55015 *Tulyar* stands alongside newly built freight locomotive No. 56104. Doncaster constructed eighty-five of the 3,250 hp Co-Co machines before production moved to Crewe for the final batch of twenty in the class.

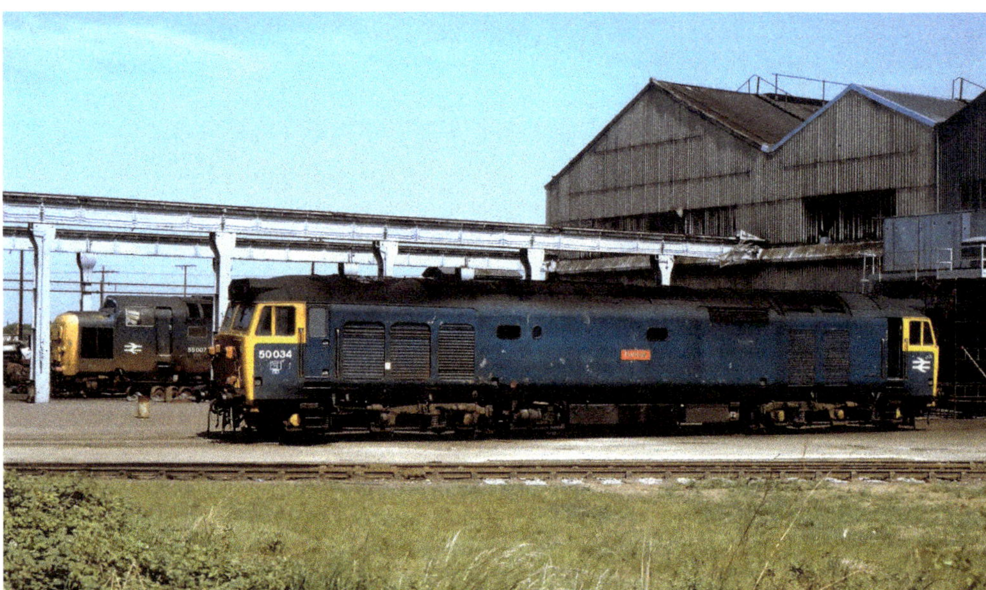

Only one will emerge...

Doncaster Works in May 1982, and two classic English Electric machines are seen at the back of 'the plant' awaiting attention. Sadly for Deltic No. 55007 *Pinza*, it is the attention of the cutting team. For No. 50034 *Furious*, refurbishment is the happier outcome, though it too would be withdrawn in 1990 and later scrapped.

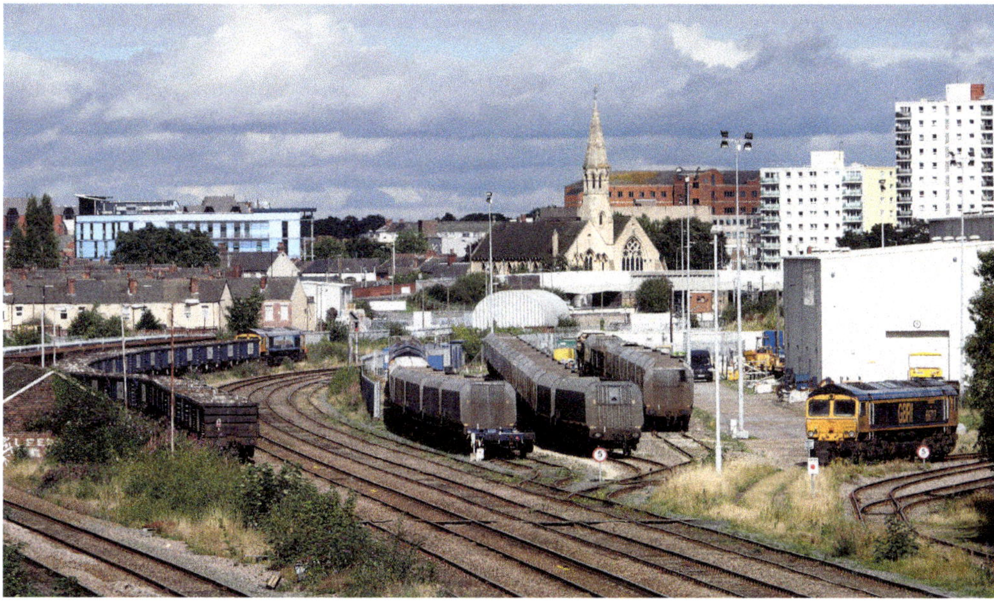

A constant presence among a changing Doncaster skyline

The GBRf facility at Doncaster Roberts Road depot plays host to Class 66 No. 66717 and several rakes of hopper wagons in this September 2016 view. New high-rise buildings dominate the horizon, but St James' church – 'the railway church' as it is known – built in 1860 for the shareholders of the GNR, is a constant.

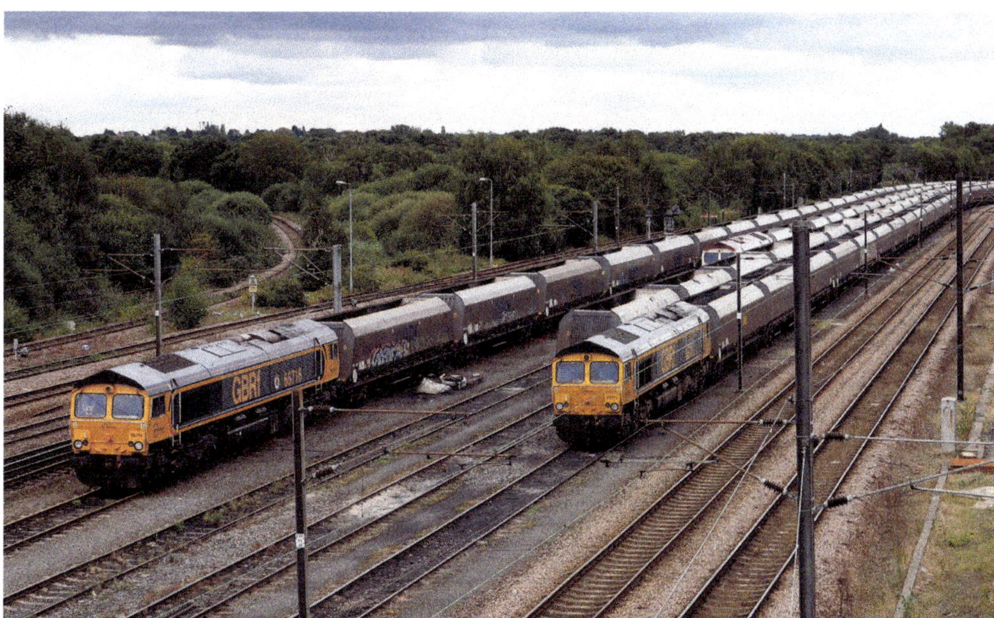

High capacity wagonloads dominate at Decoy Yard

A view of Doncaster Decoy Yard, taken in September 2016, with the now-uniform rakes of high capacity coal wagons very much in evidence. GBRf machines Nos 66716 and 66712 are nearest the camera. Biomass loads are now in the ascendency as coal declines.

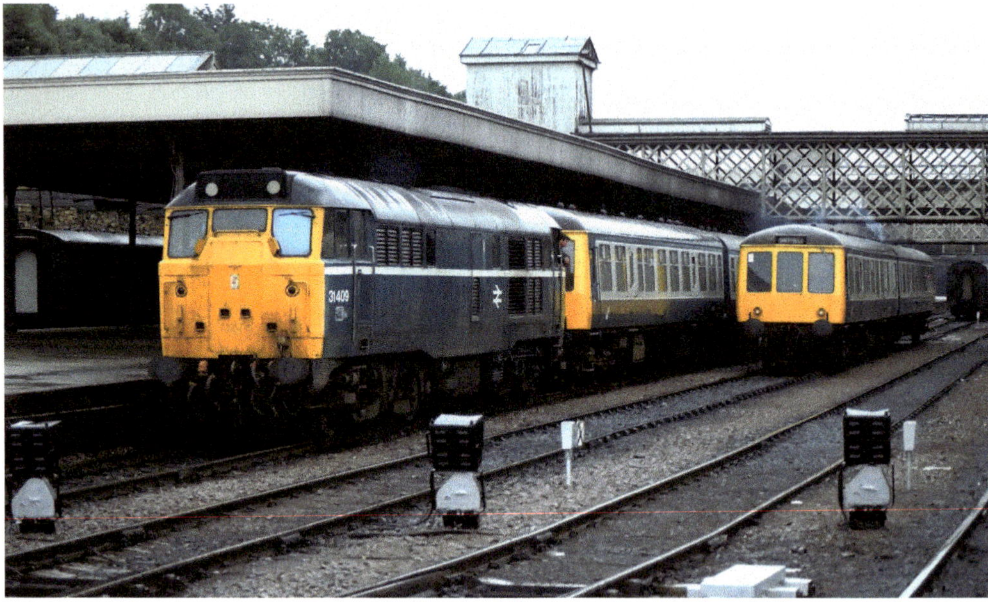

Type 2 rescue for failed DMU at Sheffield

In pre-Sprinter days, Sheffield station was always busy with multiple units and coaching stock. Here Class 31 No. 31409, with a white bodyside stripe that will have been applied at Finsbury Park depot, gives a helping hand to a failed DMU in September 1983.

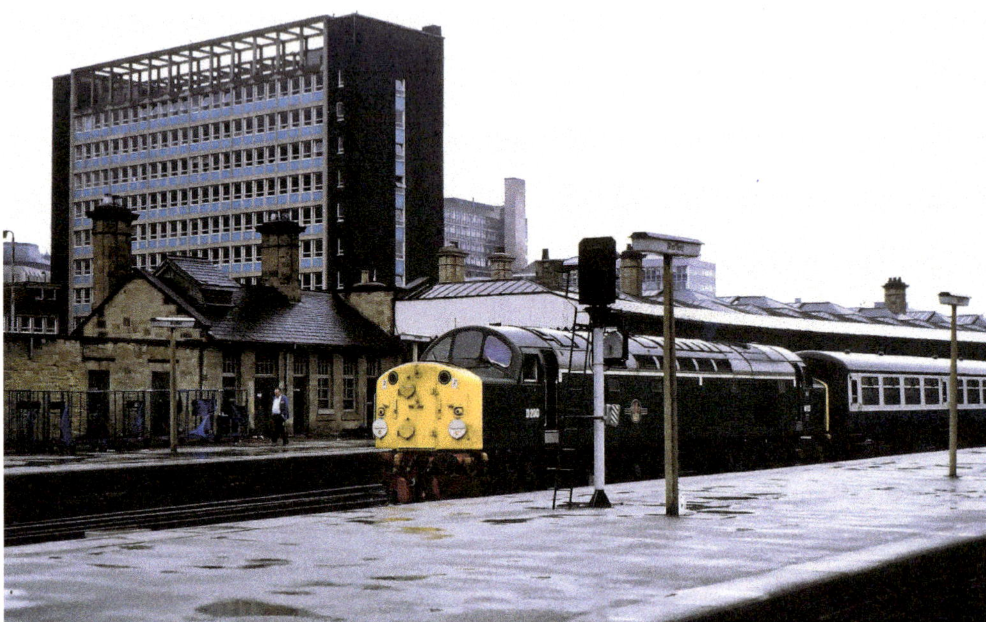

Muted colours of an English summer

There is little to indicate that this picture was taken in summer, but in fact this is August 1984, and celebrity Class 40 No. D200 stands among the puddles at Sheffield station with empty stock. The tower of BR's Sheaf House divisional office looms overhead.

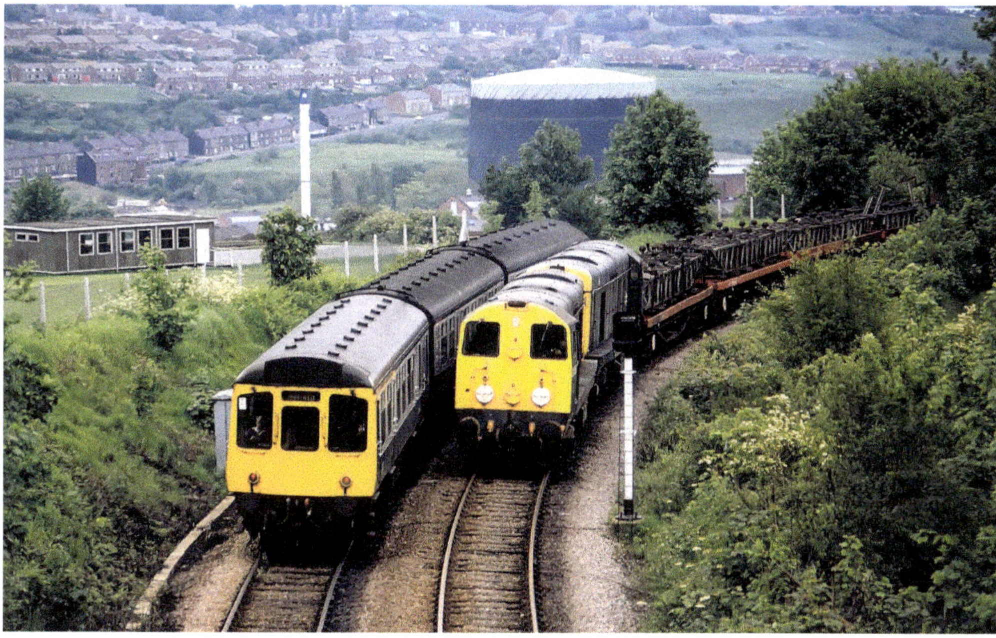

Woodhead remnants are taken to Penistone

A pair of Class 20s waits at signal BY9 at Barnsley in June 1983 while a Huddersfield to Sheffield DMU passes. Somewhat ironically they are taking a trainload of dismantled Woodhead route gantries to Penistone for scrapping.

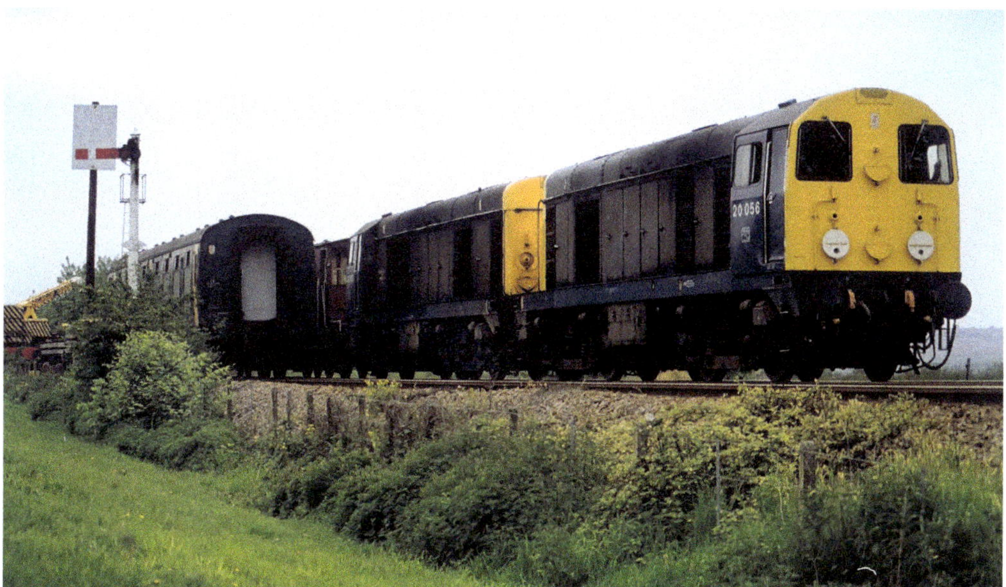

Engineering work on the Wakefield to Barnsley line

Standing adjacent to the school fields at Honeywell, Class 20s Nos 20056 and 20032 are in charge of an engineers' train engaged in track laying in May 1983. The sighting board behind Barnsley Station Junction's semaphore signal was a familiar feature here for many years.

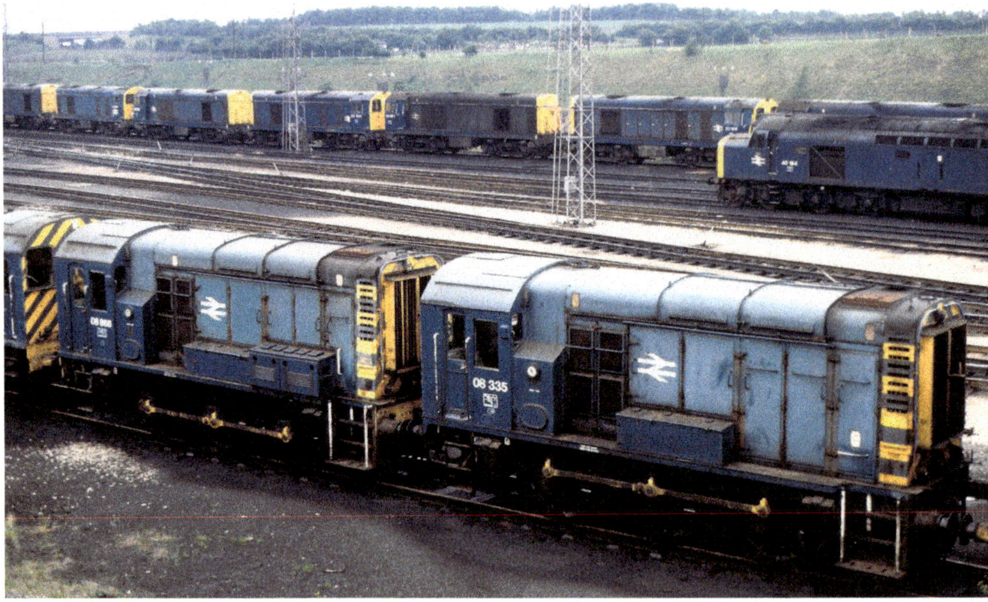

An English Electric show at Tinsley depot

Tinsley was the largest diesel depot in South Yorkshire, and there was always an impressive array of motive power on shed at weekends. Here in the summer of 1982, a line of Class 08 shunters keeps company with a Class 40 and the obligatory entourage of Class 20s, all in the uniform rail blue of the era.

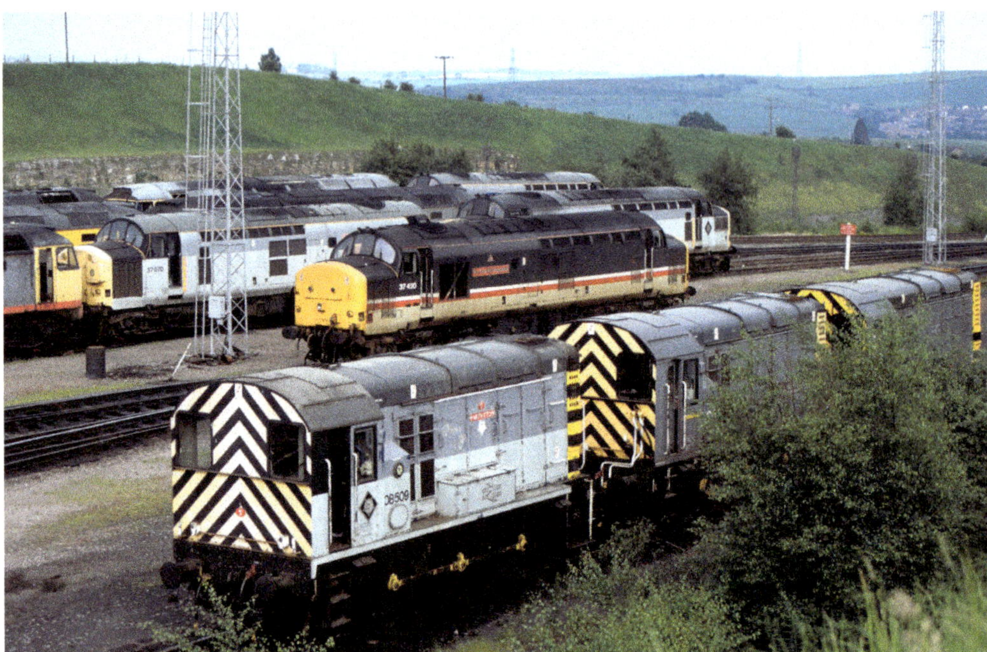

Tinsley machine recognises another long-gone depot

Class 08 No. 08509, carrying the unofficial nameplate 'Wath ETD' along with its cast Tinsley crest, is seen at the depot in June 1993. Behind are two Class 09s, Nos 09013 and 09008. Among the Class 37s visible are Nos 37420 and 37070.

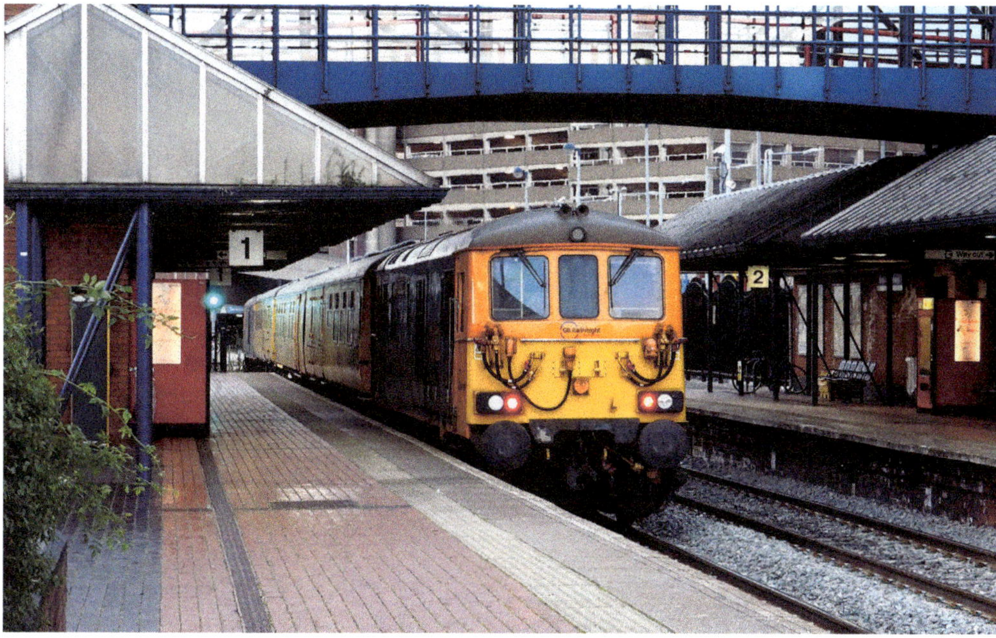

Unusual motive power for the Barnsley area

A Network Rail inspection train is seen passing Barnsley in October 2016 with GBRf's No. 73962 on the rear of the top-and-tail formation. Class 73s would have never been seen at Barnsley in BR days as they were exclusively deployed in the former Southern Region. Now the surviving Class members travel far and wide.

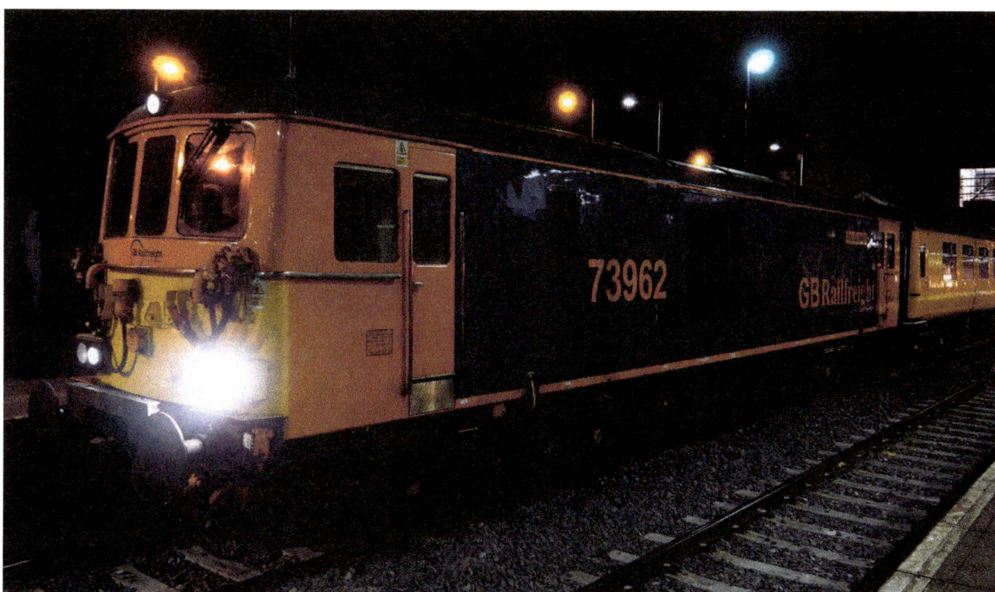

Night-time duties for GBRf's No. 73962

On the evening of 9 October 2016, one of the refurbished 'Super Electro-Diesel' Class 73s, No. 73962, pauses at Barnsley station while working a Network Rail test train. Re-engined at Brush Traction in Loughborough in 2014, No. 73962 now has a more powerful diesel engine, but retains its third-rail electric traction capability.

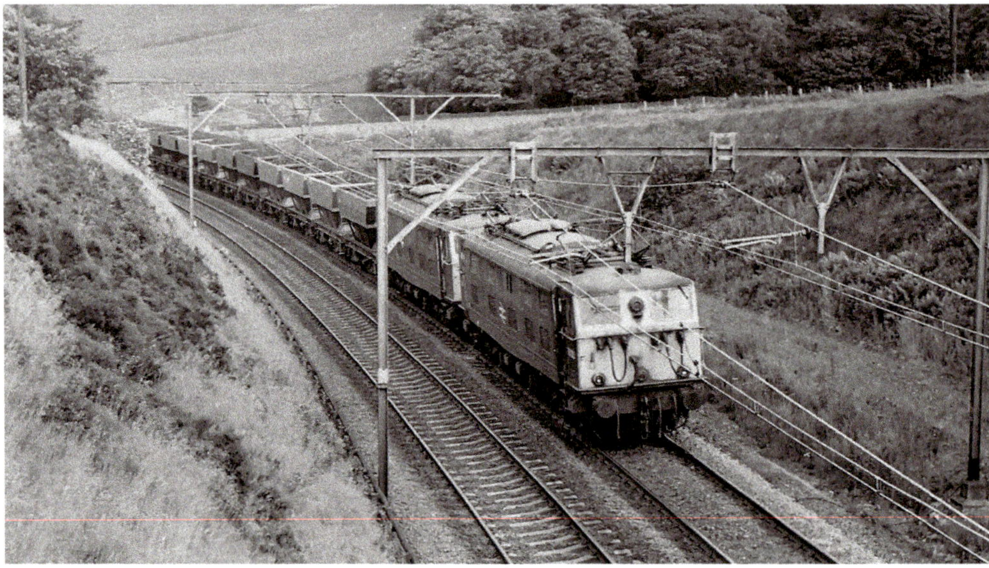

Westbound hoppers on the Woodhead route

A load of 21-tonne hoppers makes a change from the routine MGR rake for Class 76s Nos 76021 and 76026, seen here heading west at Millhouse Green between Penistone and Dunford Bridge, in June 1981. On the right is evidence of the former electrified goods loop here.

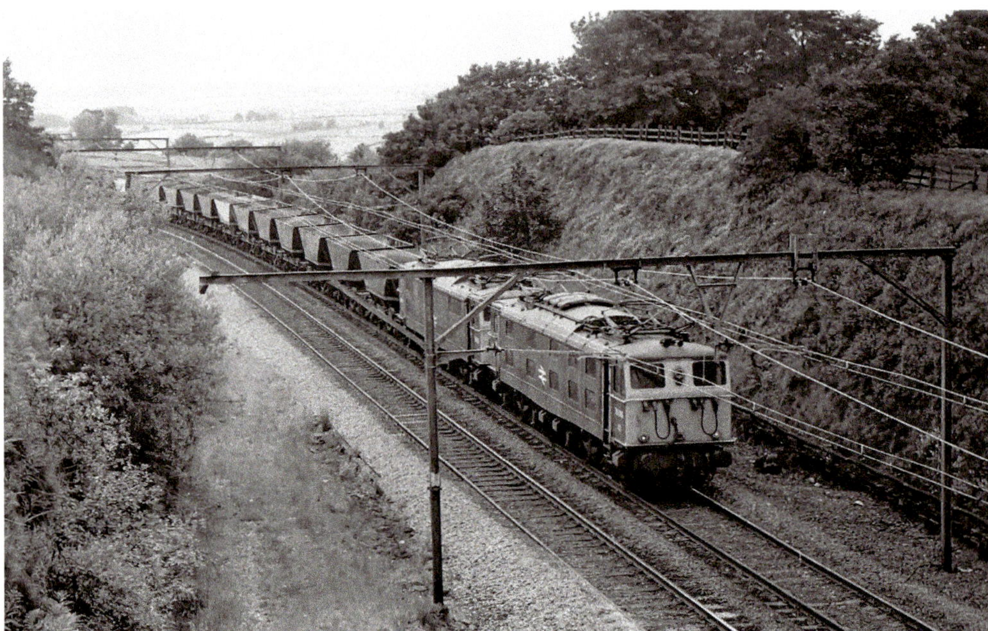

Away from the bustle of the city

Out on the moorland beyond Penistone there were many places on the Woodhead line where the silence was only disturbed by the passing of the occasional train. Here a pair of Class 76s head through Millhouse with empty MGR hoppers returning to Yorkshire from Fiddler's Ferry power station. This was in late June 1981, a mere three weeks before the line closed.

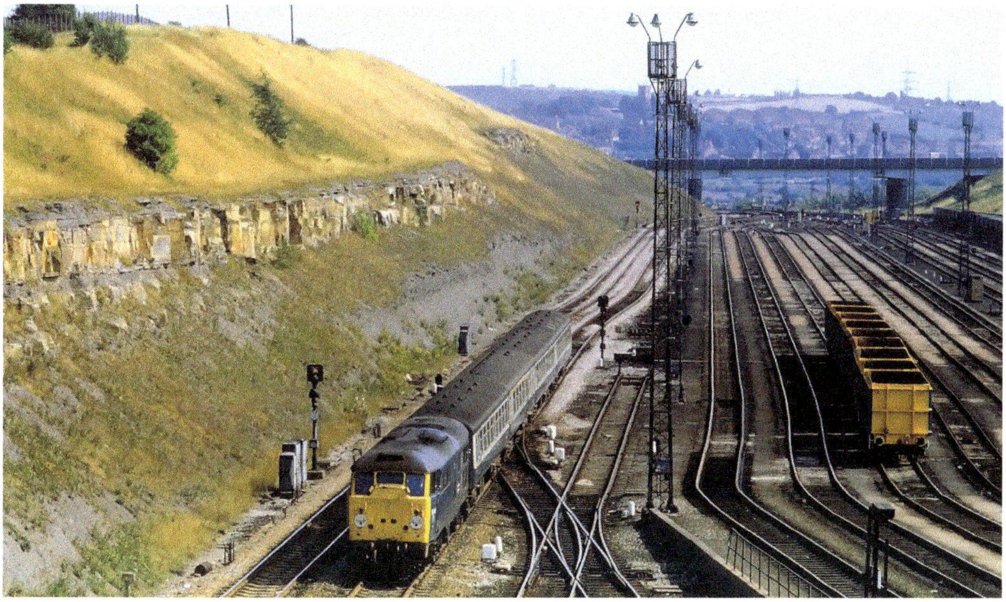

Tinsley landscape dwarfs No. 31141

Engineering work in the Sheffield area led to the diversion of trans-Pennine passenger services in the summer of 1984. One such working from Hull to Manchester threads its way along the perimeter of Tinsley Yard with Class 31 No. 31141 in charge. The yard was still fairly active at this time, but its decline and fall was not far away.

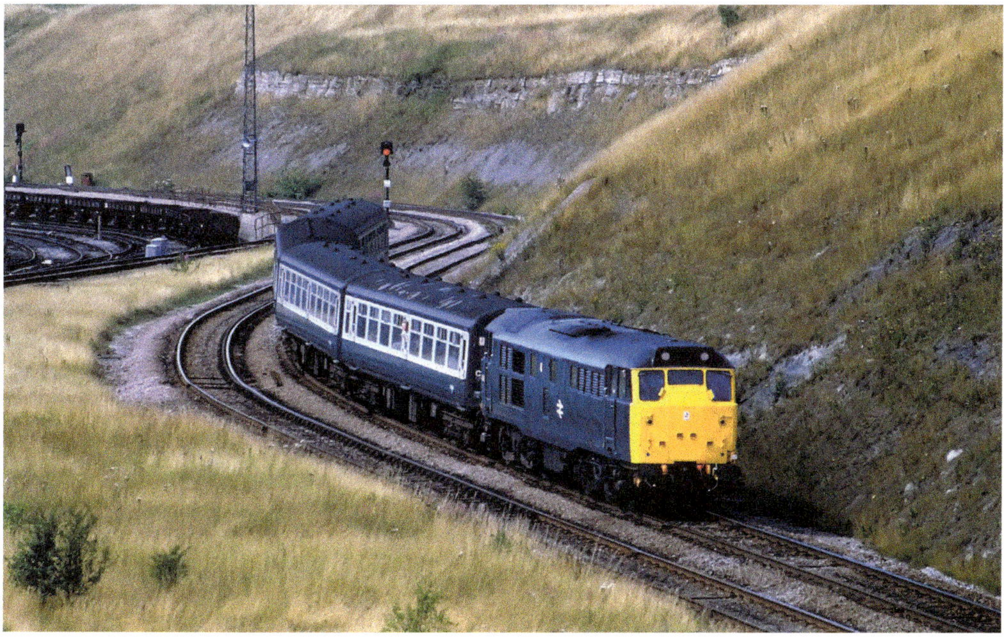

Enjoying ex-works haulage on an unusual diagram

Thanks to engineering works, trans-Pennine passenger services were diverted through Tinsley Yard in August 1984. Here, ex-works Class 31 No. 31445 looks smart as it winds around the perimeter of the yard on an eastbound service. Such a diversion would be impossible today due to the truncation of the lines here.

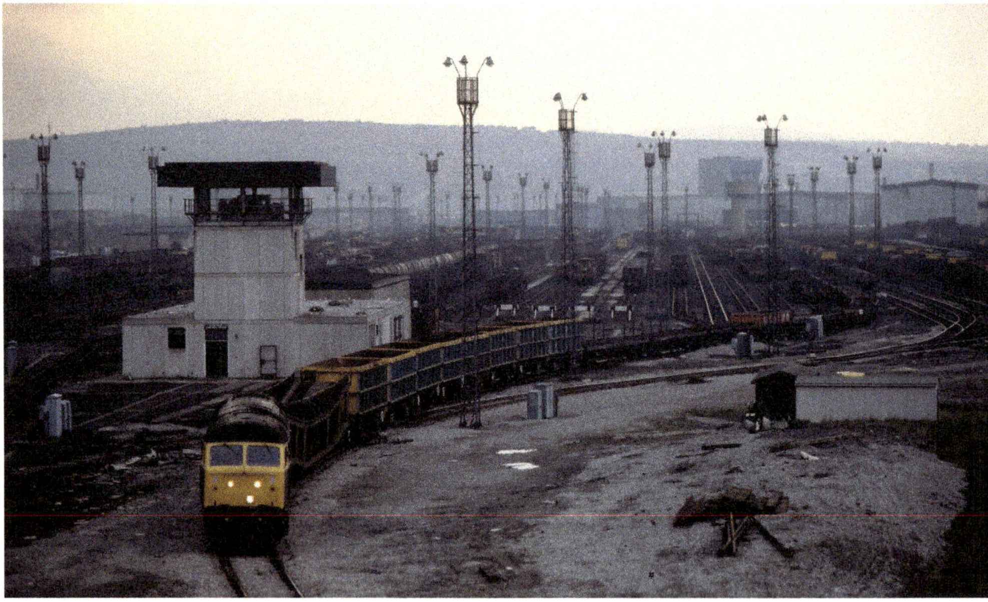

An evening departure at Tinsley Yard

This view of the control tower and yard at Tinsley was taken on the evening of 9 April 1985. The yard looks fairly busy as Class 47 No. 47128 departs towards Treeton with a mixed freight. The Tinsley complex was only twenty years old at the time of this picture, but had sadly already outlived its original purpose.

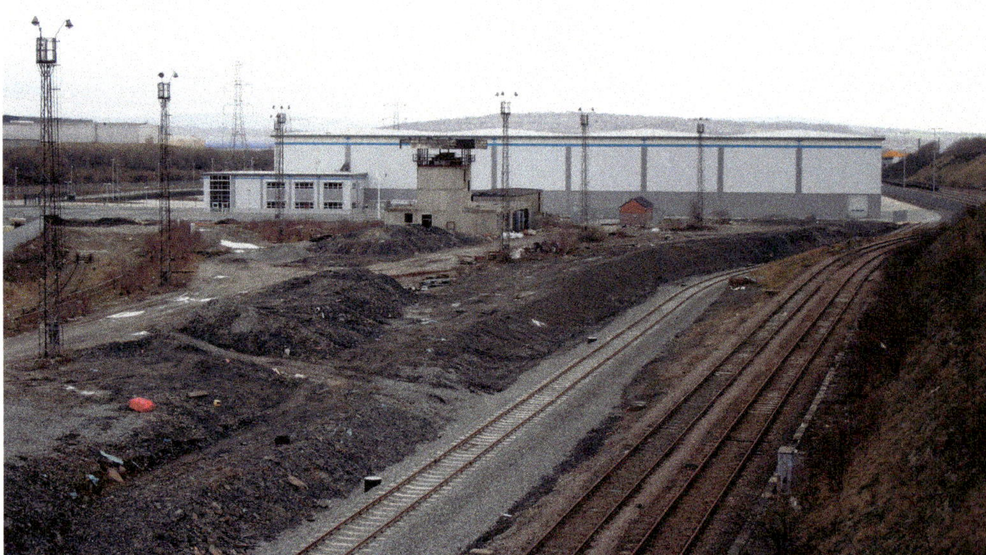

The changing face of industrial Britain

The former marshalling yard control tower at Tinsley is dwarfed by the construction of a new commercial building on the site of the once extensive sidings, seen here in 2008. Surviving floodlight towers are a stark reminder of the original purpose of this site, where the railway is now, in every sense, marginal.

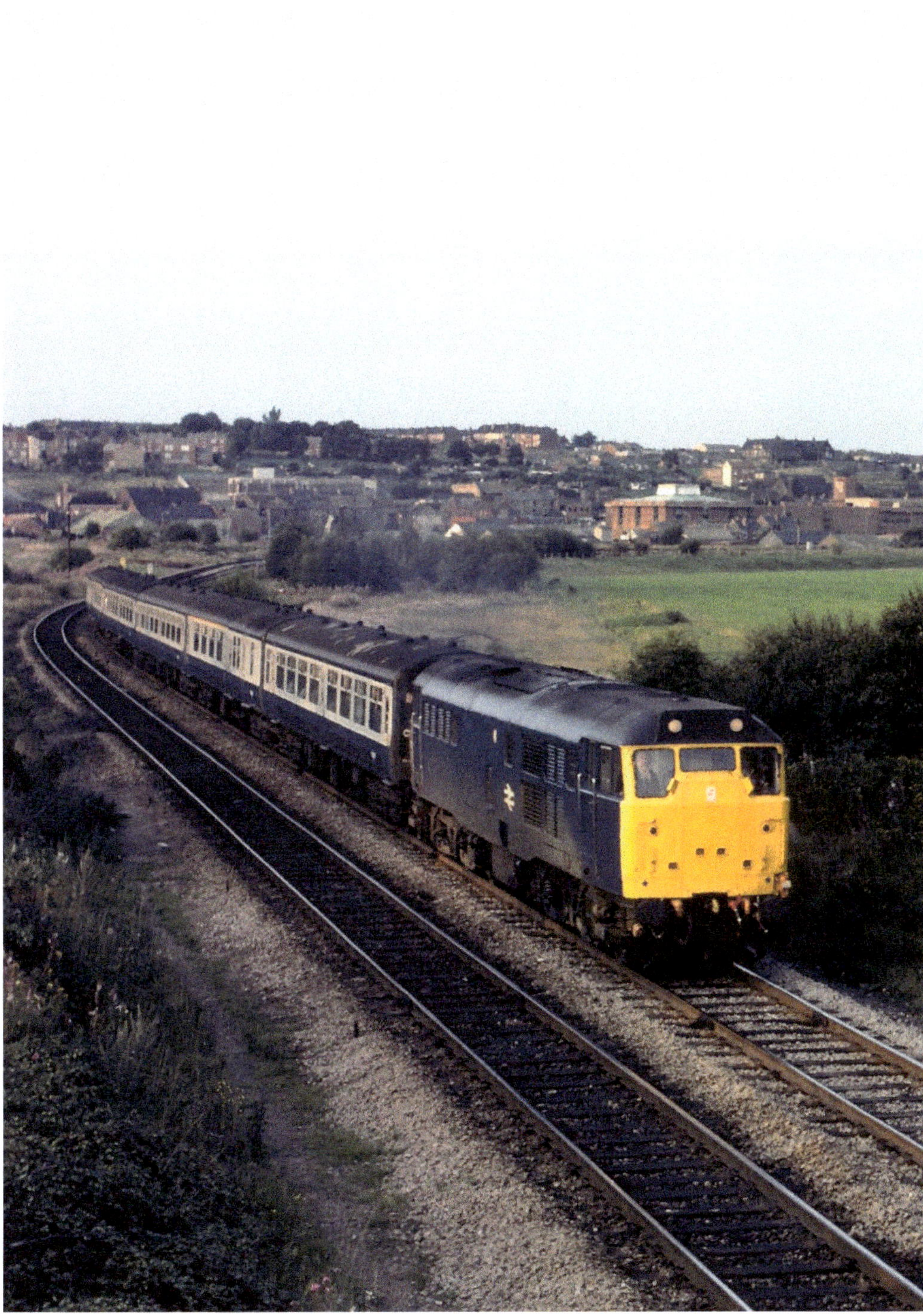

Evening passenger duty for Type 2 No. 31439

A sunny August evening at Mexborough in 1984 sees Class 31 No. 31439 pulling away from the station with a Cleethorpes–Manchester service. Just beyond the back of the train was Mexborough No. 3 Junction, where a chord diverged around to the Wath route.

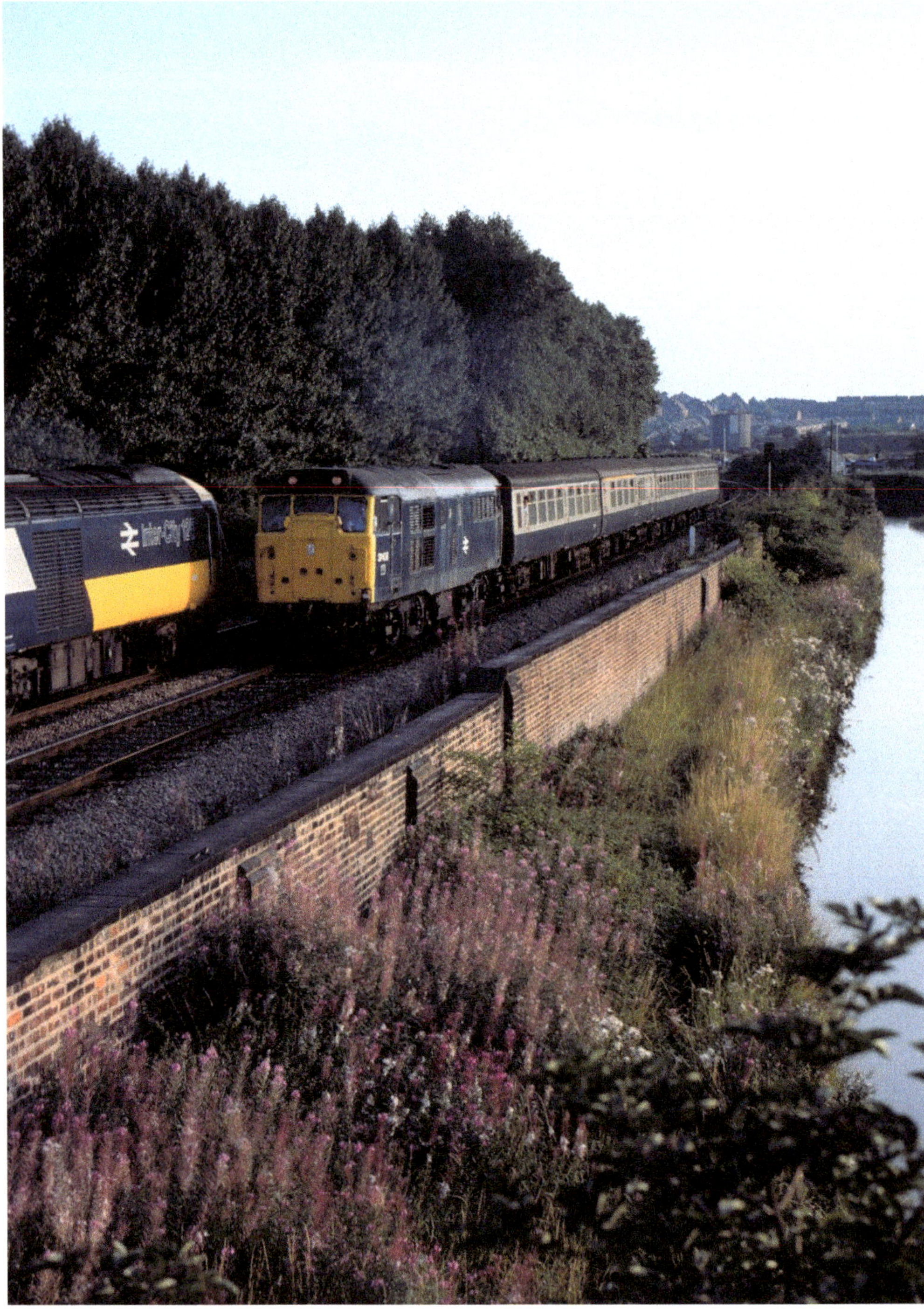

North and south at Kilnhurst

An eastbound Cleethorpes service approaches Mexborough at Kilnhurst on Saturday 18 August 1984, as an HST heads towards Sheffield on a section that is now freight-only, following the reinstatement of the Swinton chord. The Class 31 on this occasion was No. 31438, on 1E52 – the 17.38 from Manchester.

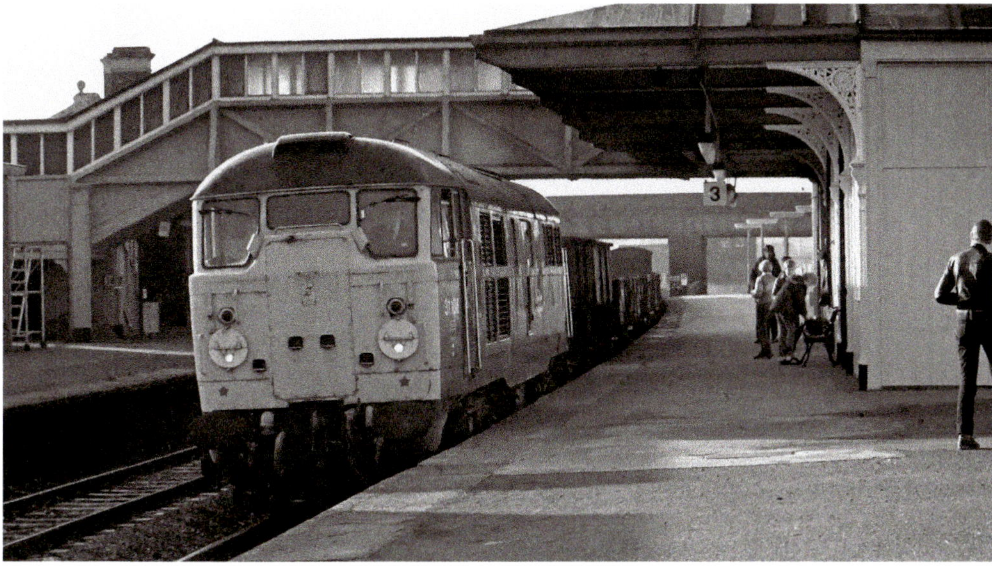

Northbound freight turn for No. 31106

The now-closed Masborough station at Rotherham always provided a good vantage point to watch freight traffic. Here in October 1983, Class 31 No. 31106 goes north through platform 3 with a mixed goods. At this time Masborough had five years' life ahead of it as a passenger station.

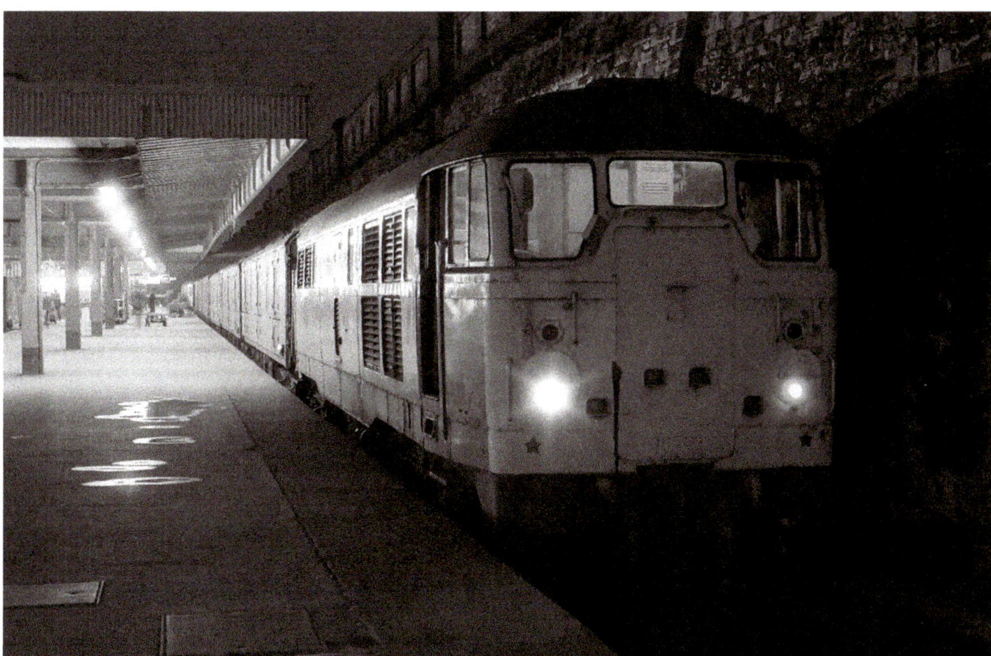

In the days of rail-borne parcels traffic

Overnight parcels and newspaper traffic were once a staple of the British railway scene. Here at Sheffield, Class 31 No. 31129 waits while its vans are loaded in October 1983, in a scene that will be occurring elsewhere at many key hubs across the network.

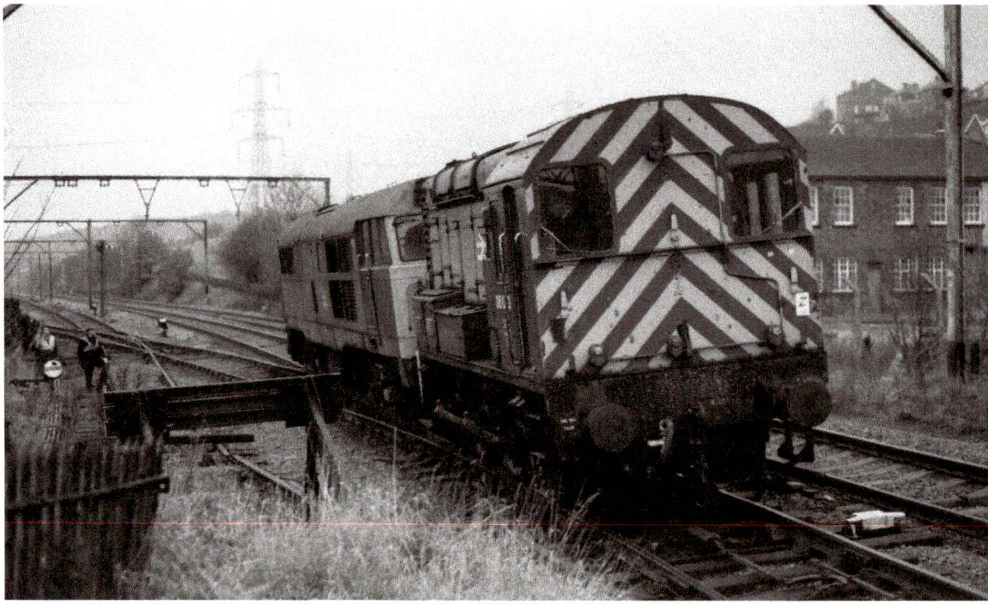

On the former Woodhead line at Wadsley Bridge

This is Wadsley Bridge, on the former Woodhead route to the west of Sheffield. In December 1983, Class 31 No. 31281 tows Class 08 No. 08033 in the direction of Stocksbridge steelworks, the terminus of the now-truncated line. It would be some years before the overhead gantries were all finally dismantled. (Vaughan Hellam)

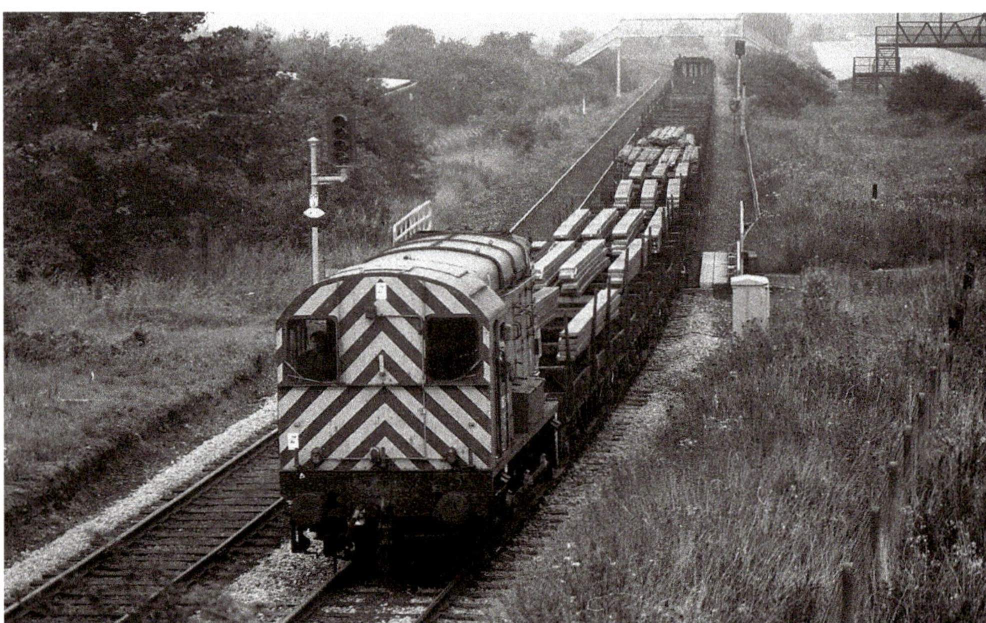

Steel trip working for Tinsley Class 08

An everyday sight across the Sheffield region at the time – this is Class 08 No. 08244 heading through Rotherham on its way to Tinsley Yard with a trip working of steel from Aldwarke in the summer of 1984. The train is approaching Rotherham Road. (Vaughan Hellam)

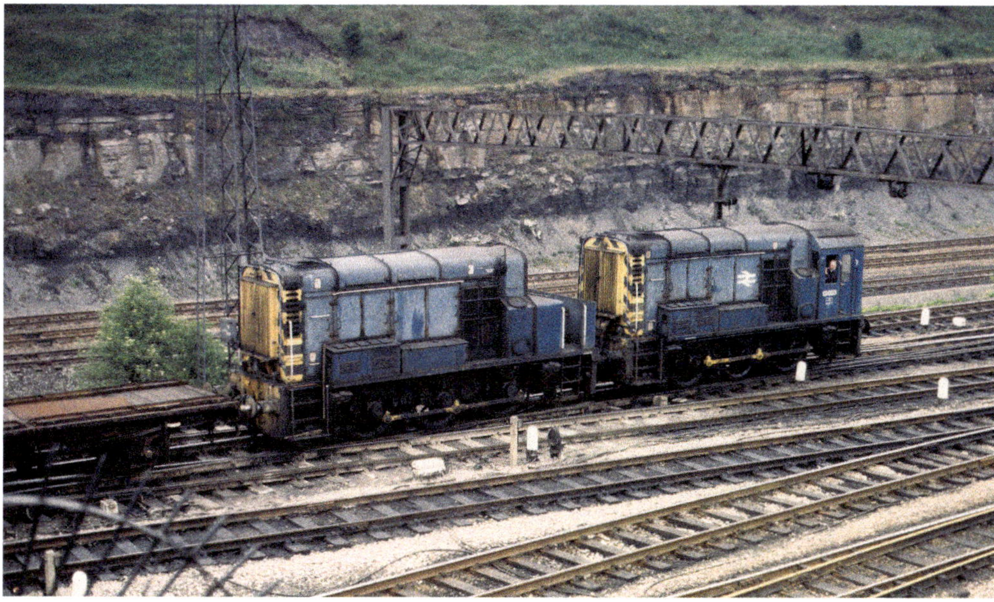

Heavyweight shunter at Tinsley

The challenge of providing sufficient tractive effort for hump shunting at Tinsley Yard was met by the creation of the three Class 13 'master and slave' units, converted from six standard Class 08s. Weighing in at an impressive 120 tons, they were very effective at their specialist job.

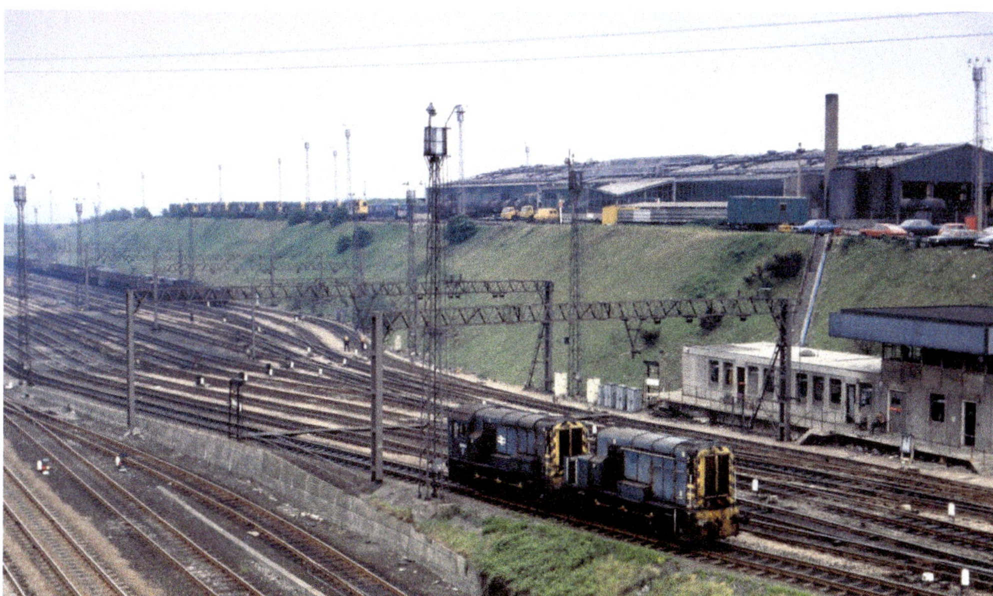

The high and low of it at Tinsley, 1982

The classic view of Tinsley depot, seen from the approach road above the sidings. Down in the yard, 'master and slave' Class 13 shunter No. 13003 awaits its next task beneath the recently de-energised Woodhead route gantries, and up on the embankment, a line of Class 20s is stabled outside the shed. All this railway infrastructure has since disappeared.

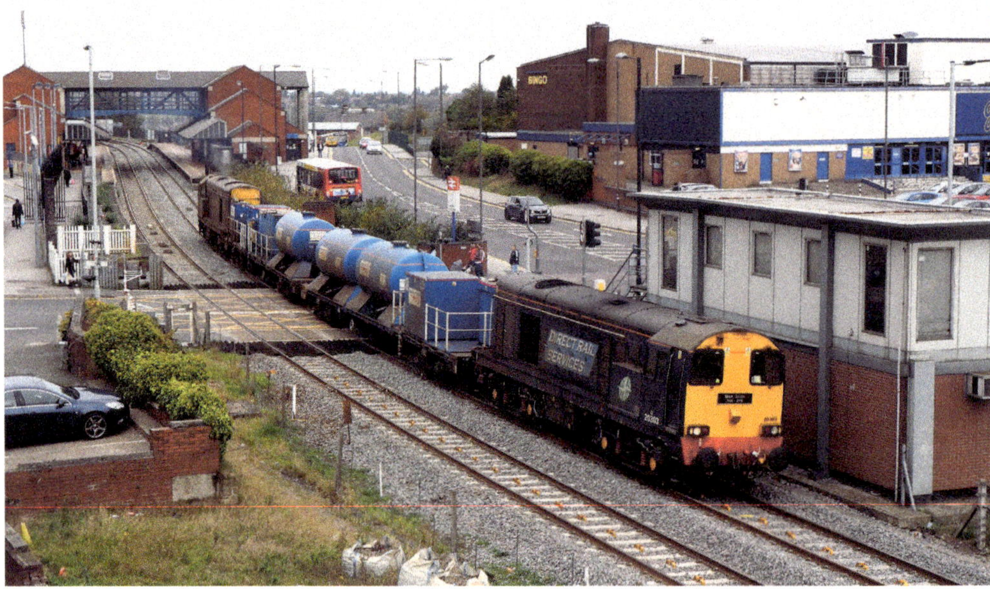

Class 20s keep the lines free of leaves

Autumn 2016, and one of several Rail Head Treatment Trains, or RHTTs, passes Jumble Lane level crossing at Barnsley with Class 20s providing the top-and-tail motive power. No. 20303 *Max Joule* is leading, with No. 20305 *Gresty Bridge* at the back.

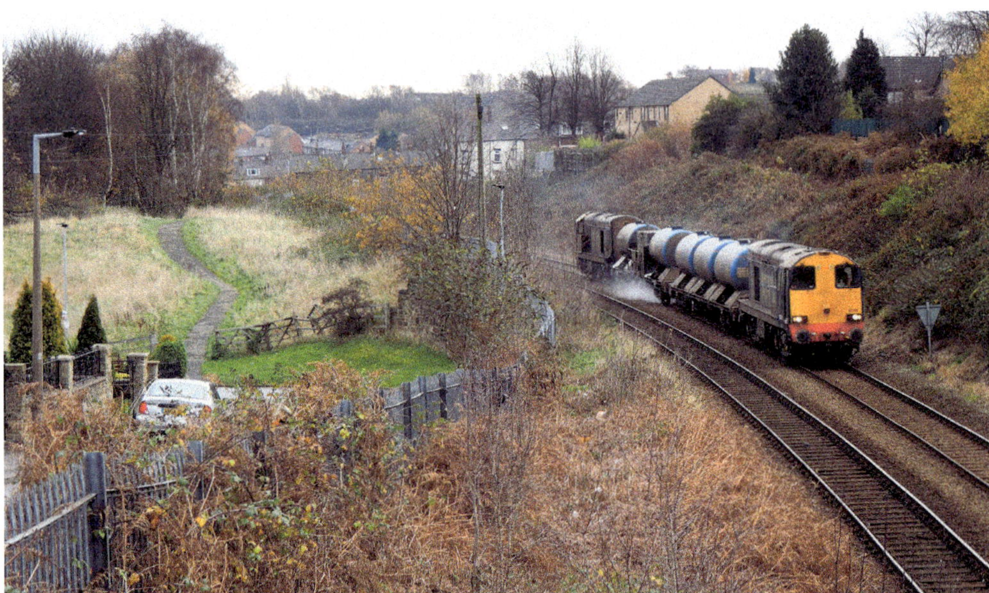

Tracking the old Midland route at Barnsley

A railhead treatment train approaches Barnsley from the Wombwell direction in this view from December 2017. The Class 20s are on former Great Central tracks that once formed part of the route to Mexborough via Stairfoot. To the left is part of the embankment that carried Midland lines to Cudworth and Chapeltown.

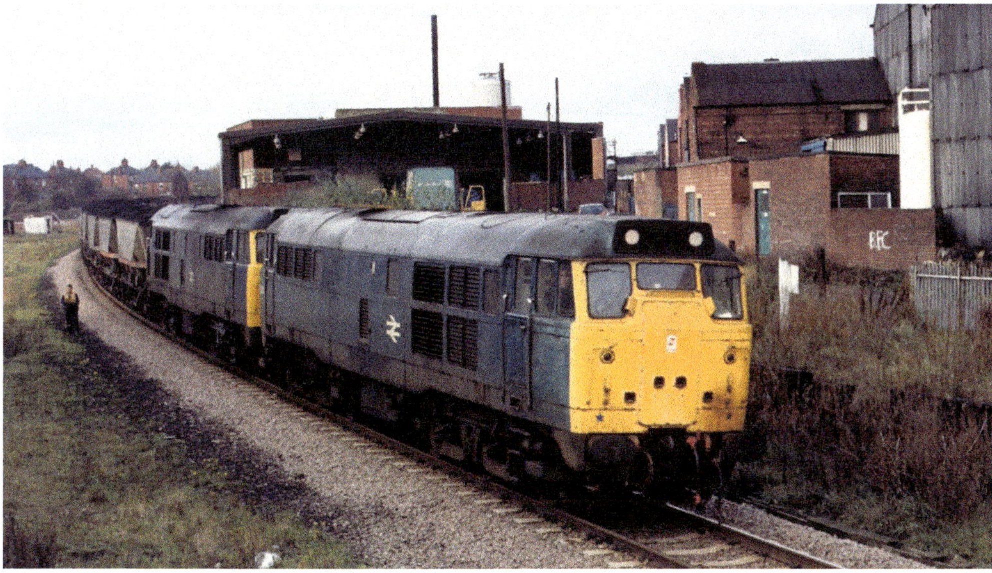

An unusual pairing for Dodworth MGR service

Pairs of Class 37s formed the routine motive power for MGR services from Dodworth colliery in the brief post-Woodhead period prior to the closure of the pit. Here in November 1982 though, a pair of Class 31s has been rostered for the run to Wath Yard. The train is seen approaching the site of Summer Lane station with Nos 31302 and 31221 in charge.

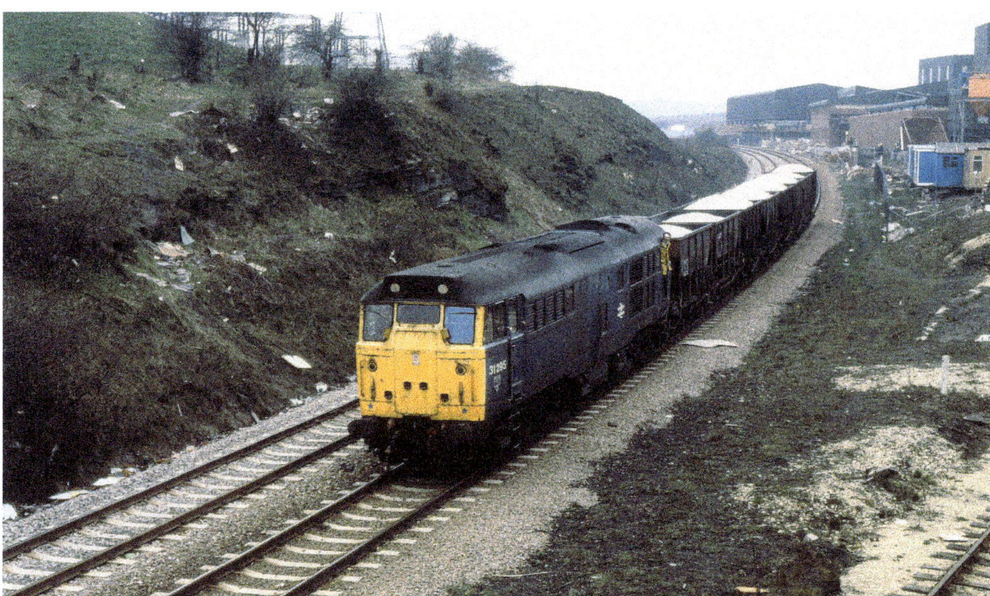

Sand delivery for Stairfoot glassworks

The Beatson-Clark glassworks at Stairfoot on the outskirts of Barnsley was a regular recipient of sand deliveries by rail. Here, Class 31 No. 31295 approaches the works in March 1983. It will reverse into the factory site where an industrial shunter will transfer the wagons to the unloading bay. This was one of the last rail freight-served locations to survive in the town. (Vaughan Hellam)

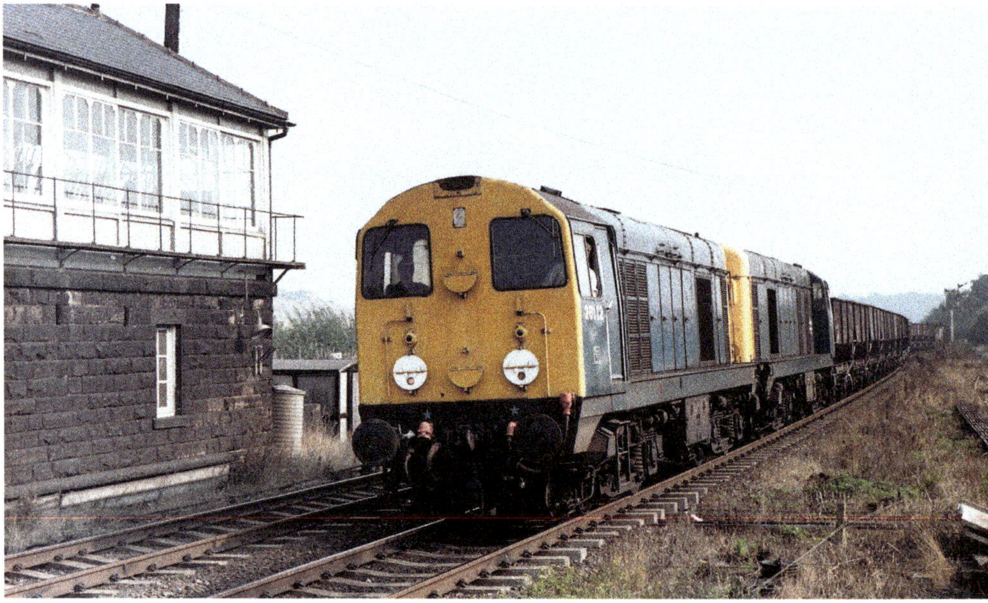

Class 20s power north at Cudworth

A lengthy train of hopper wagons trails behind Class 20s Nos 20112 and 20210 as they accelerate away from the Stairfoot branch at Cudworth in the summer of 1981. The stone-built Midland box here was one of the most substantial in the area. (Vaughan Hellam)

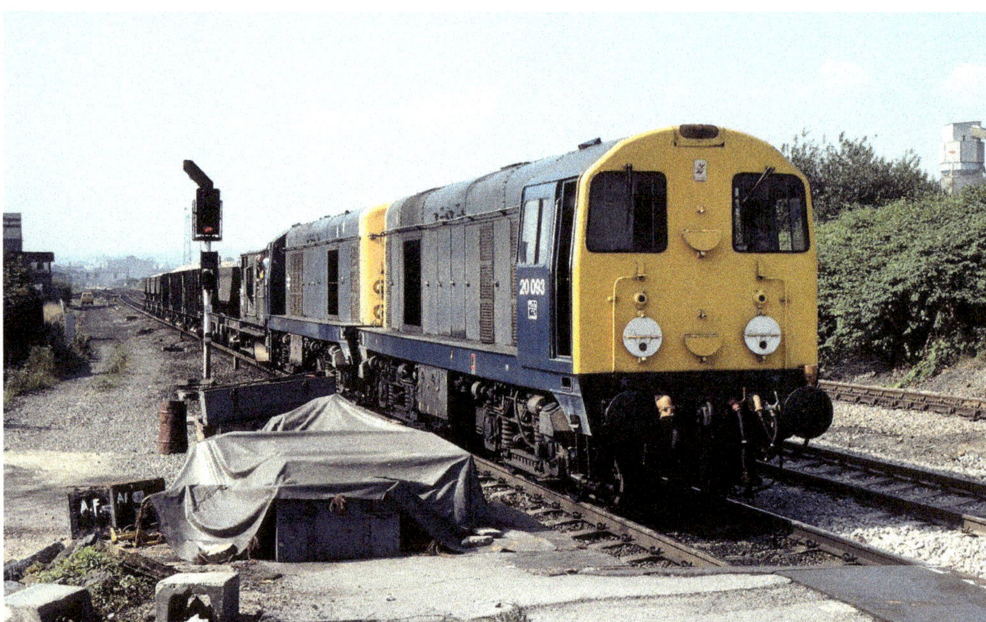

Engineering work at Brightside

Photographed from the now-closed Brightside station on the main line north of Sheffield, a pair of Tinsley-based Class 20s is seen on ballasting duties in August 1984. Brightside Junction signalbox is just visible on the left. A line once diverged here to Tinsley Yard via Shepcote Lane.

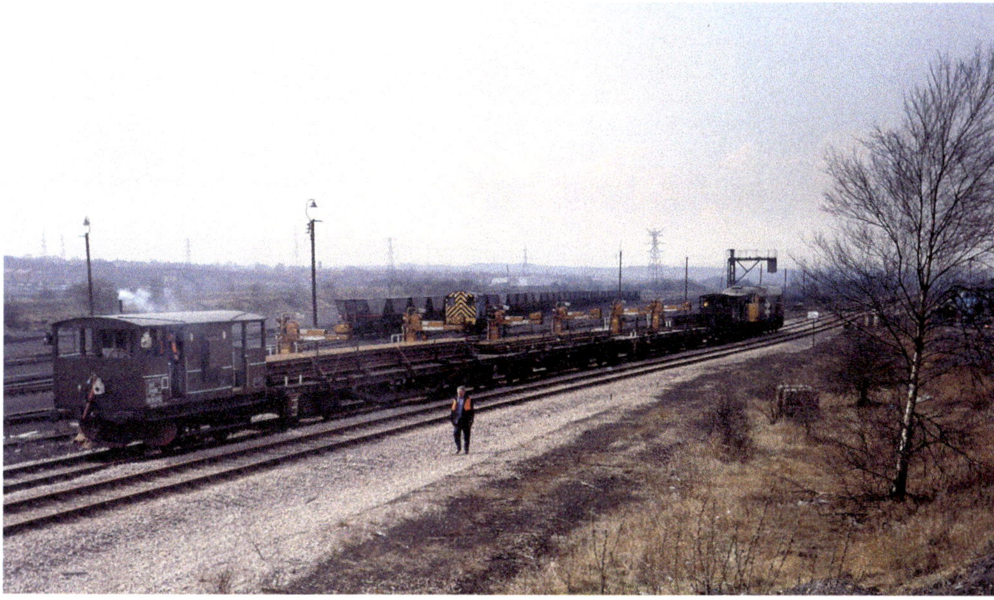

Wath Yard, near the end, 1986

A Class 31 stands at Wath in April 1986, during operations to recover track from the section of line between here and Dovecliffe, which had recently closed along with the line via Stairfoot to Quarry Junction at Barnsley. Soon the yard at Wath would itself be no more. (Vaughan Hellam)

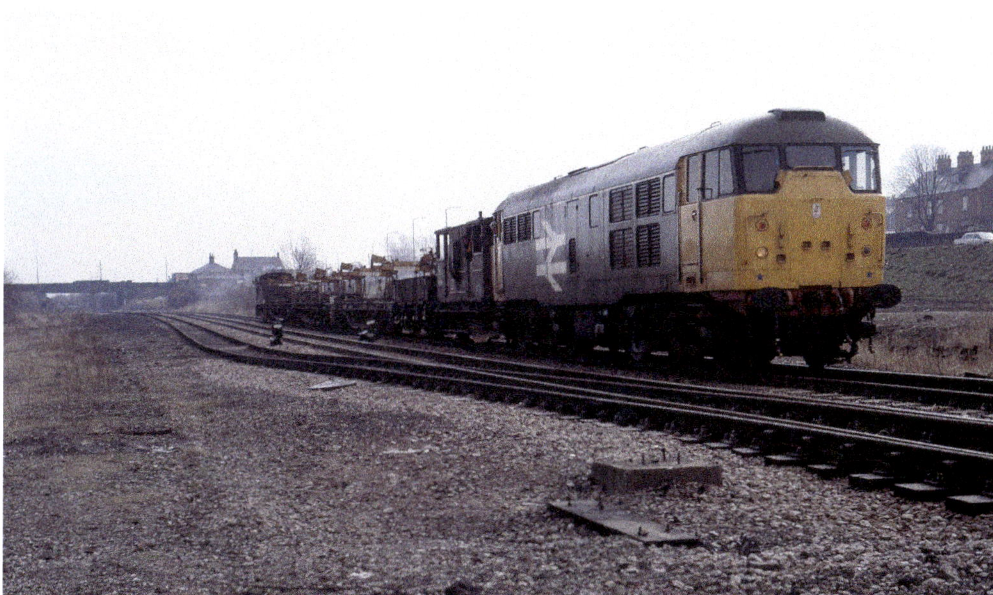

Track recovery operations on the former GC line at Wombwell

A Class 31 stands with a recovery train at the site of the former Darfield Main level crossing in Wombwell, on the section of line between Wath and Aldam Junction that once formed part of the Woodhead route electrification. This image dates from April 1986, when the line was no longer carrying any regular traffic. (Vaughan Hellam)

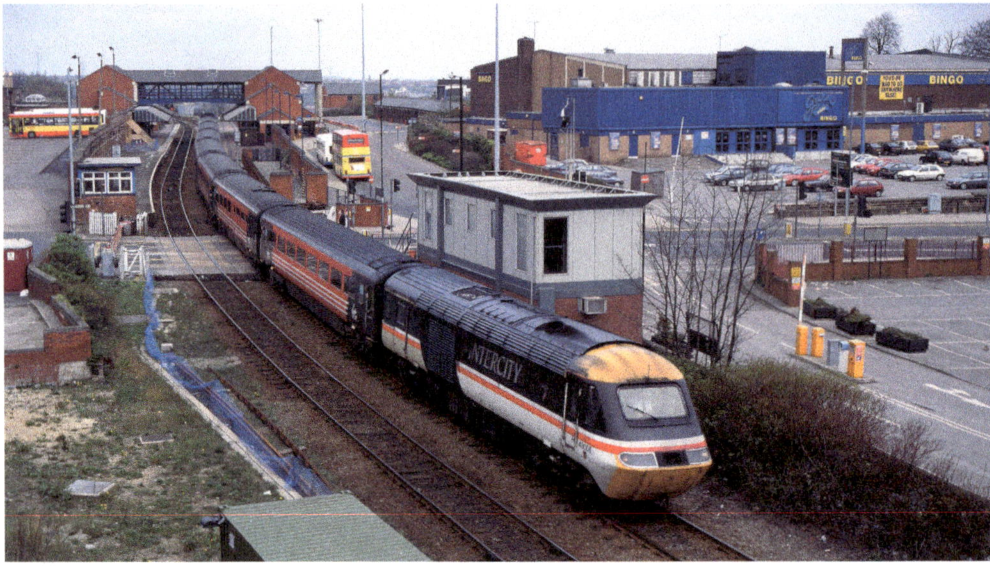

Cross-country diversion passing Barnsley

A diverted Virgin cross-country service from Berwick to Penzance heads through Barnsley on Easter Day, 4 April 1999. HST power car No. 43006, still in its old InterCity livery, is leading as the train crosses Jumble Lane and passes the new signalbox.

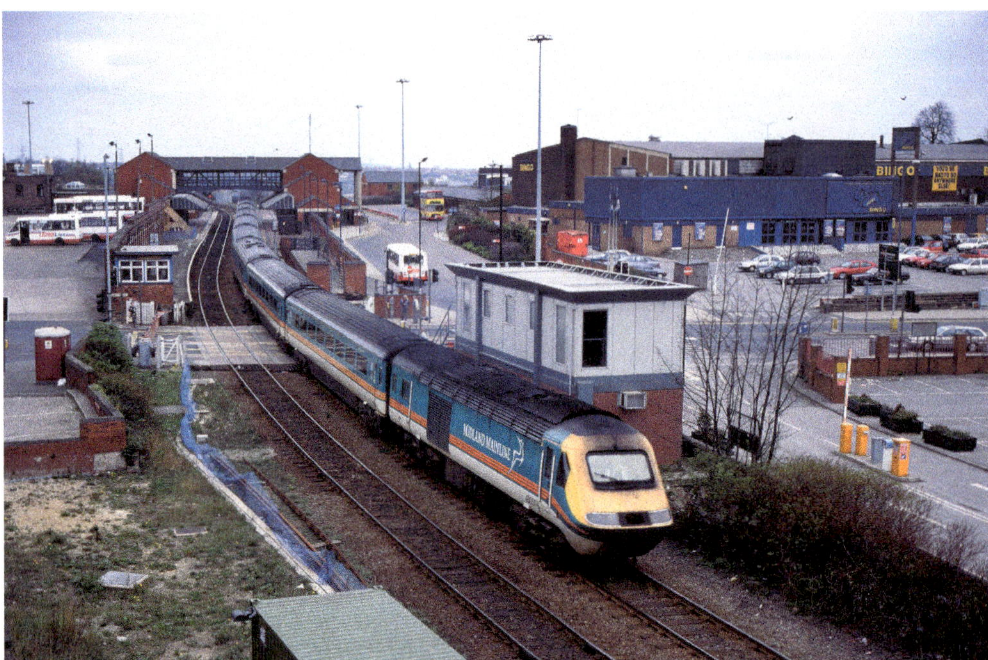

Easter diversions at Barnsley

The closure of the Moorthorpe line led to numerous diversions via Barnsley over the Easter weekend of 1999. Here a Midland Mainline-liveried HST unit, with power car No. 43051 leading, passes Jumble Lane level crossing on 4 April.

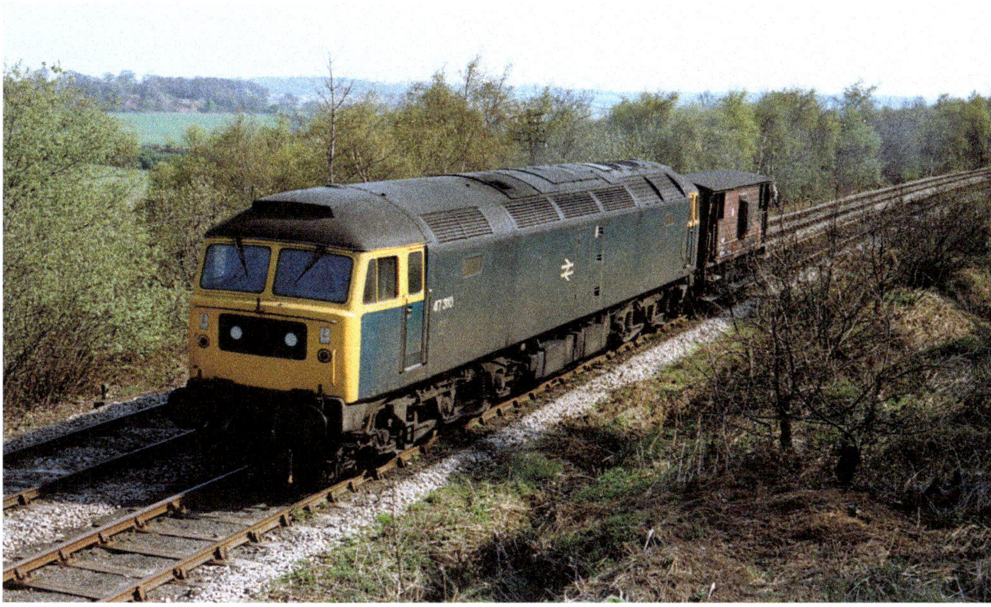

Tranquility of a rural branch line

The industrial nature of South Yorkshire is juxtaposed with much tranquil countryside, and here at Dovecliffe near Wombwell, there is little to indicate that this is a coal mining and coke-smelting region. Class 47 No. 47310 is captured on a trip from Wath Yard to Barrow Colliery in April 1982, on a stretch of line rarely photographed. (Vaughan Hellam)

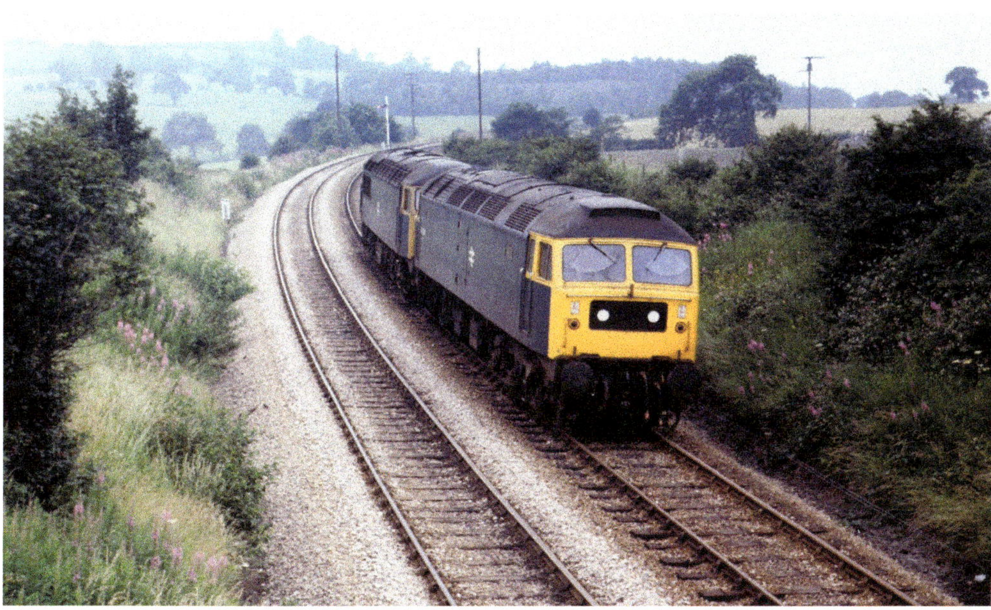

A helping hand for No. 56001 at Dodworth

Looking from Dodworth towards Penistone in July 1980, Class 47 No. 47304 tows dead No. 56001, presumably destined for Wath. At this date the line between Barnsley and Penistone was freight-only, a status that changed in 1983 with the diversion of the Sheffield to Huddersfield passenger service.

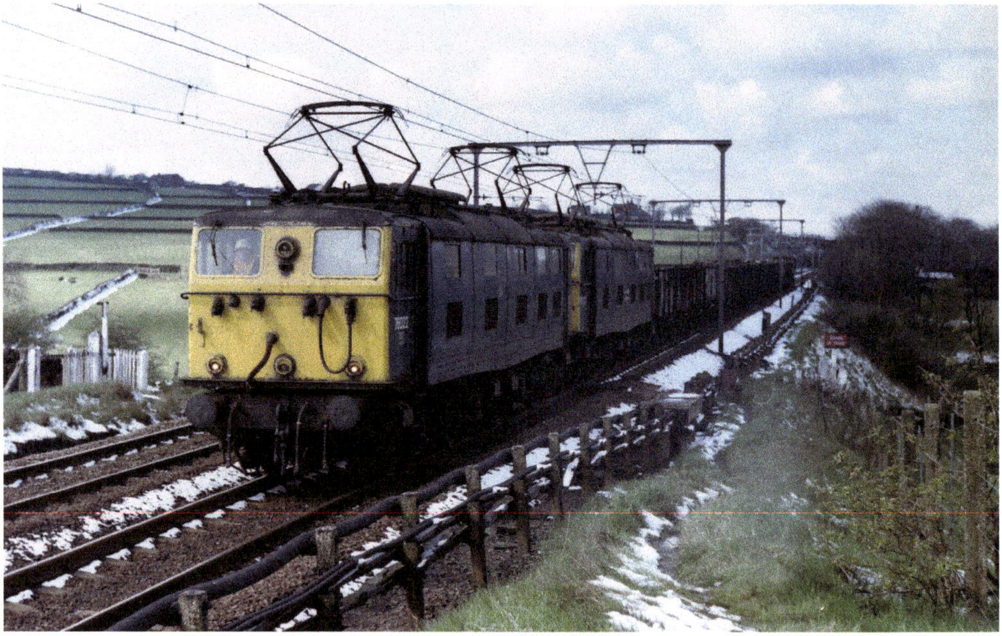

A sprinkling of snow in the hills

Away from South Yorkshire's industry, the open hills and fields to the west of Penistone have received a dusting of early spring snow as Class 76s Nos 76022 and 76023 head for Sheffield with what looks like a scrap metal train. The date was April 1981. (Vaughan Hellam)

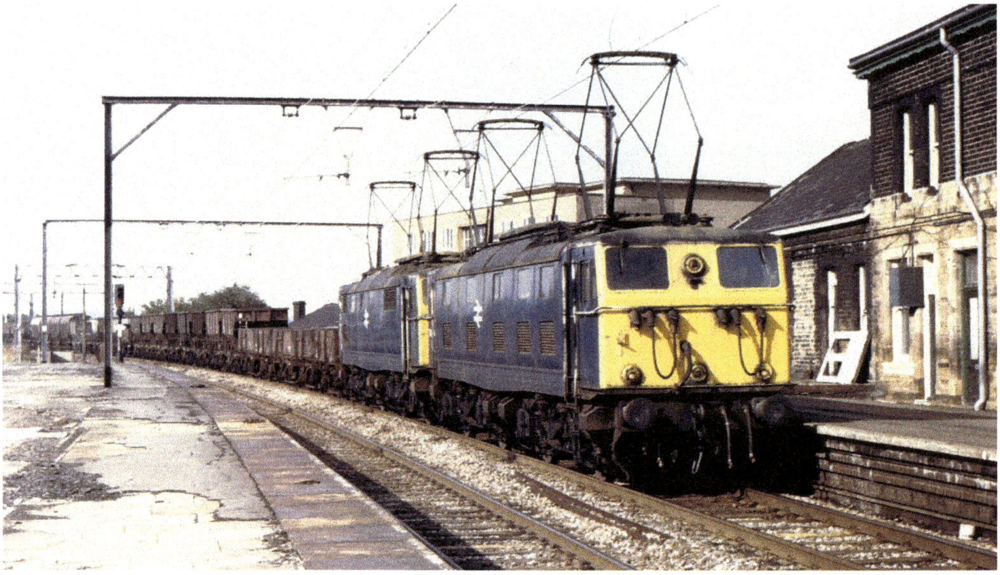

It's not all coal traffic over Woodhead

A bright morning at Penistone in October 1980 sees dual-braked Class 76s Nos 76014 and 76027 heading for Tinsley with a mixed freight. The majority of traffic on the route at this time was in the form of MGR coal services to and from Fiddler's Ferry power station, but the mixed wagon load seen here provided some welcome photographic variety. (Vaughan Hellam)

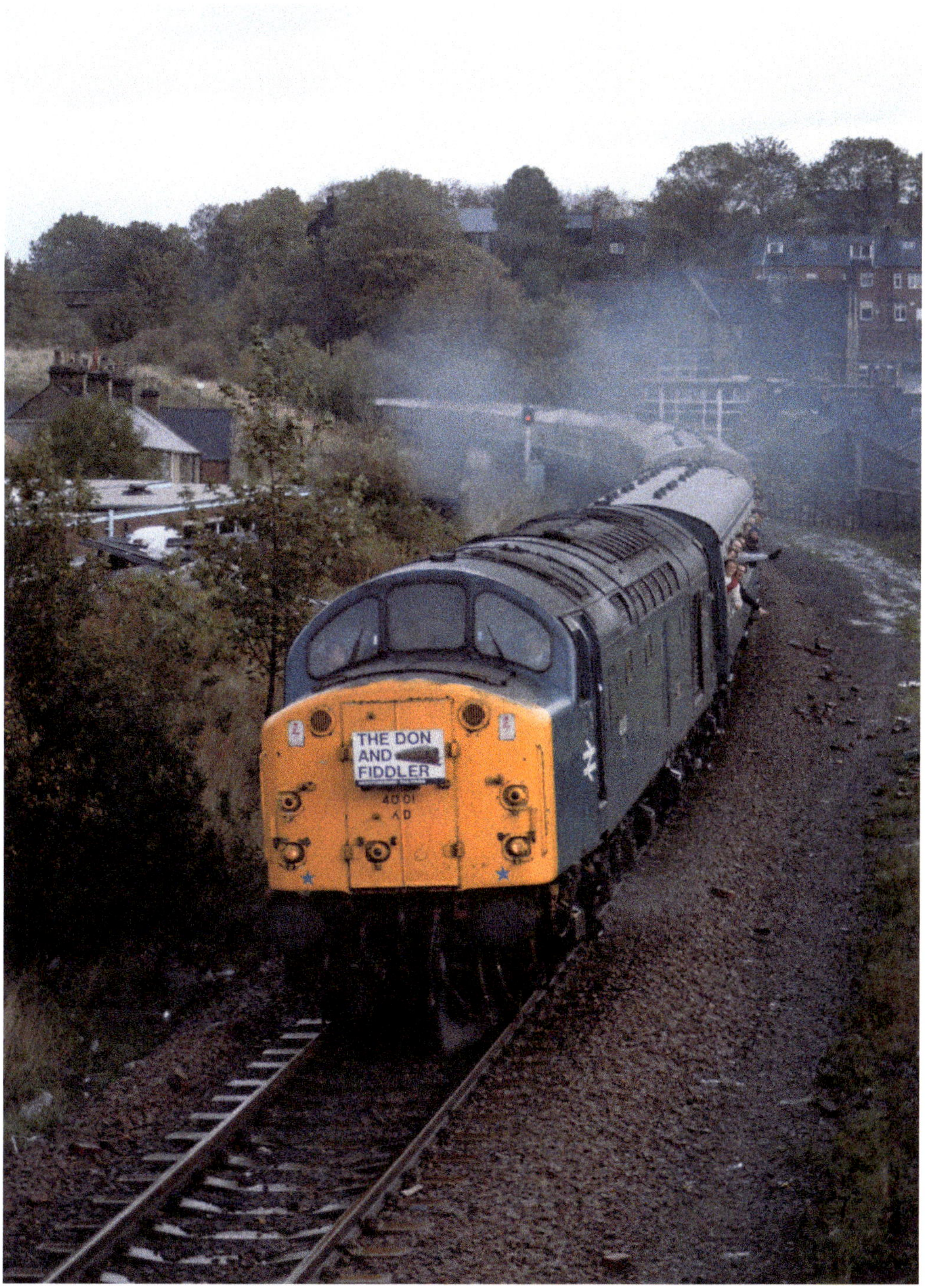

A rare visitor to the Penistone branch

A Class 40 was very rare motive power for a railtour traversing the Barnsley to Penistone line, as the *Don & Fiddler* did in October 1984. Here No. 40012 *Aureol* storms past the site of the former Great Central station at Summer Lane. Class 47 No. 47316 is providing banking assistance on this steeply graded section.

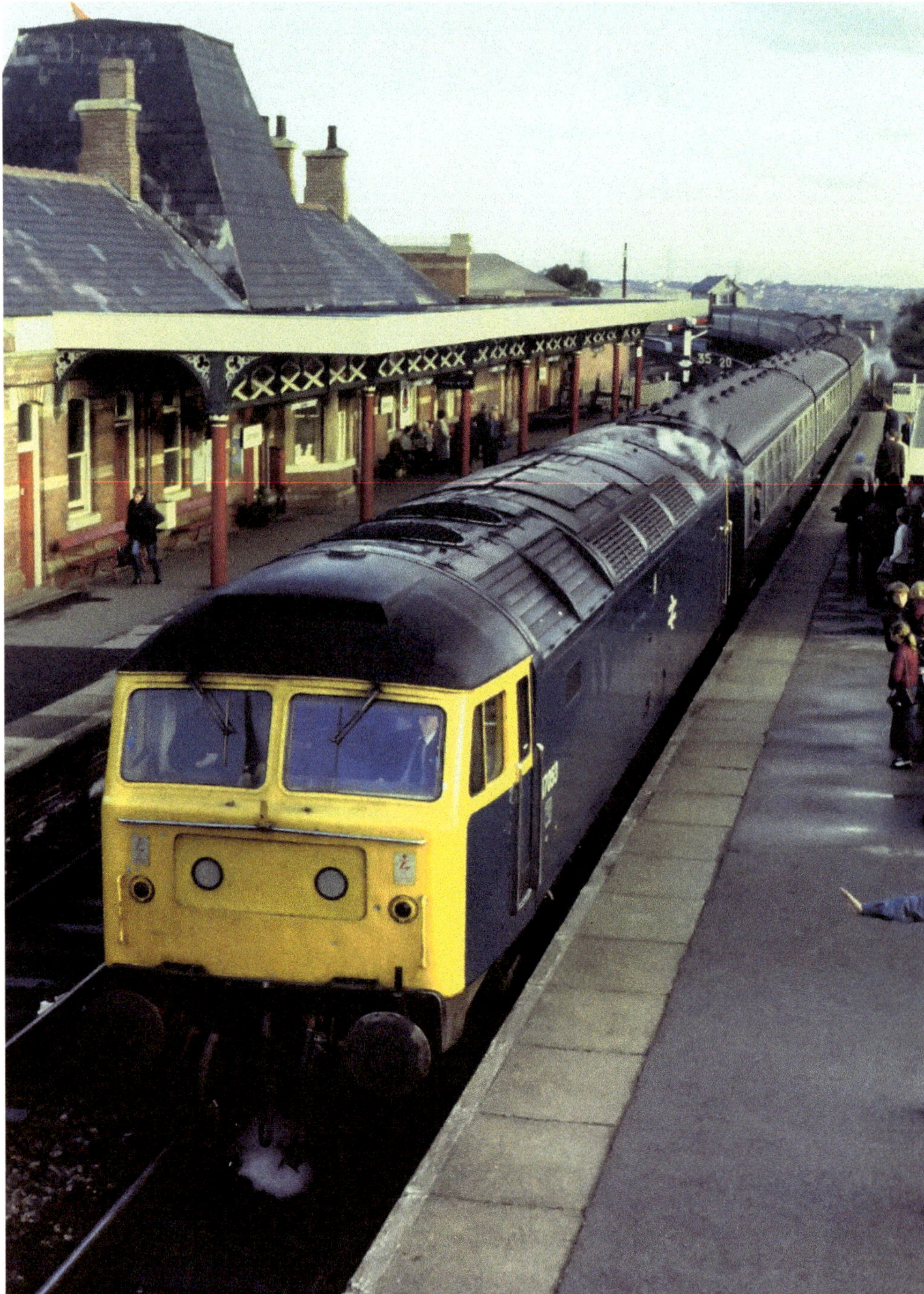

Bound for the sunny south coast

As the summer season draws to a close, Class 47 No. 47053 pulls into Barnsley station with the Bradford to Weymouth service on 17 September 1983. The steam-heated locomotive failed shortly after this on the approach to Sheffield station, necessitating a rescue mission by Class 56 No. 56017.

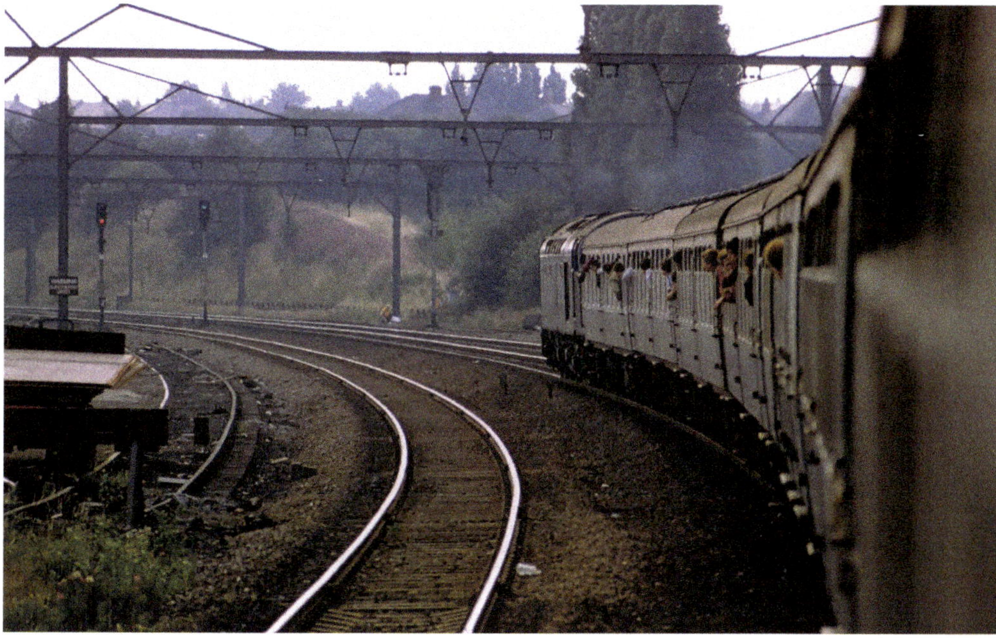

On former Woodhead route lines to the seaside

A summer Saturday service for Skegness heads through Darnall on the outskirts of Sheffield in August 1983. The sought-after haulage on this occasion was Class 40 No. 40085. The gantries from the Woodhead electrification, spanning multiple tracks at this location, are still standing, though the wires have gone.

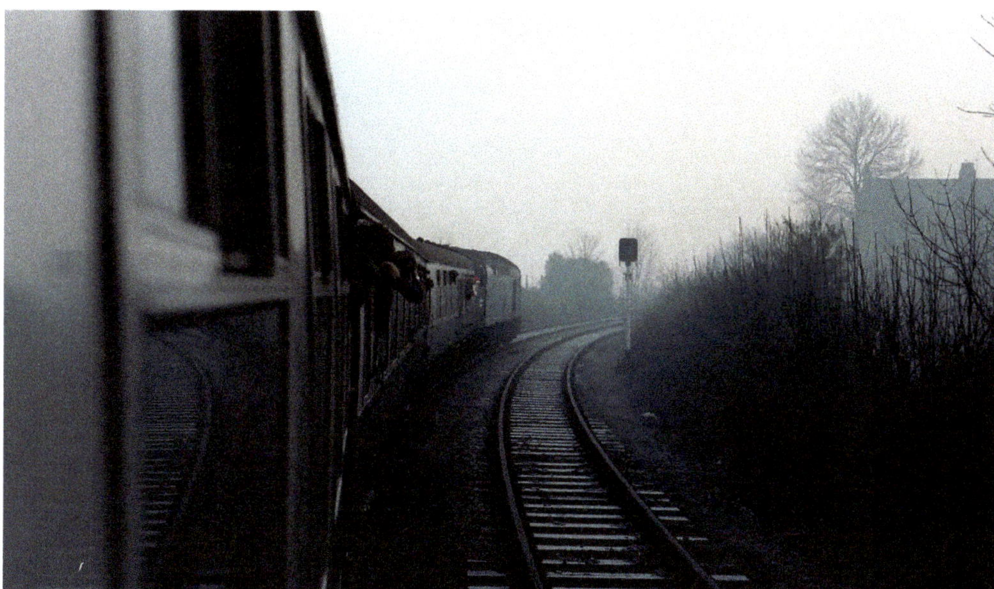

Rare Class 40 mileage

On a rather grim December morning in 1984, the *Christmas Cracker III* railtour makes its way down the steeply graded line from Penistone to Barnsley, with Class 40 No. 40118 in charge, bound for Bristol. This was the last time a Class 40 visited the former Great Central branch.

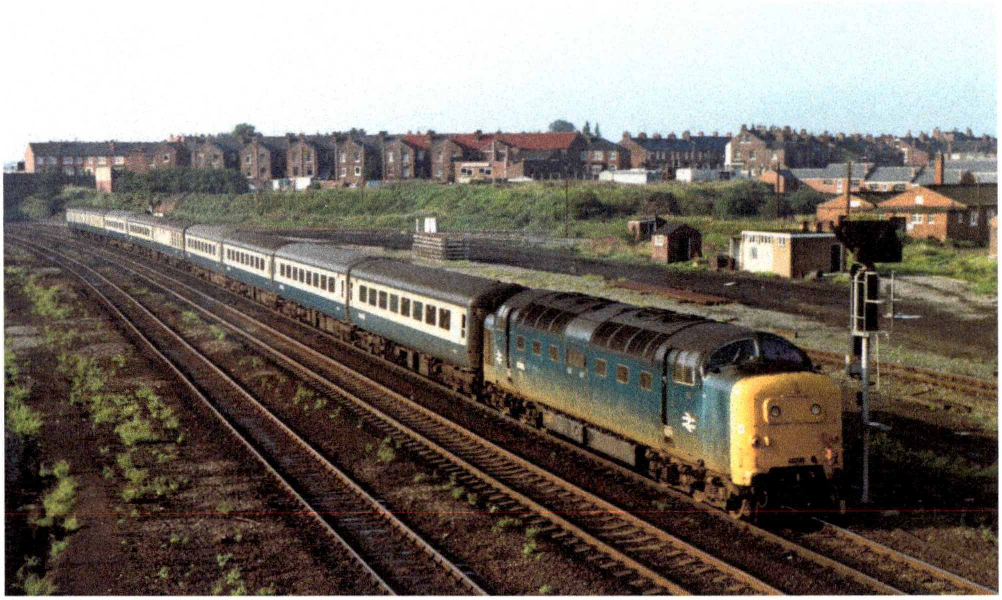

Anonymous Deltic approaching Doncaster

Very much an everyday scene in the summer of 1980, a Deltic-hauled service from King's Cross to the north approaches Doncaster and is seen here from the vantage point of Hexthorpe Road bridge. The locomotive is No. 55010 *The King's Own Scottish Borderer*, which has lost its nameplate on this side. (Vaughan Hellam)

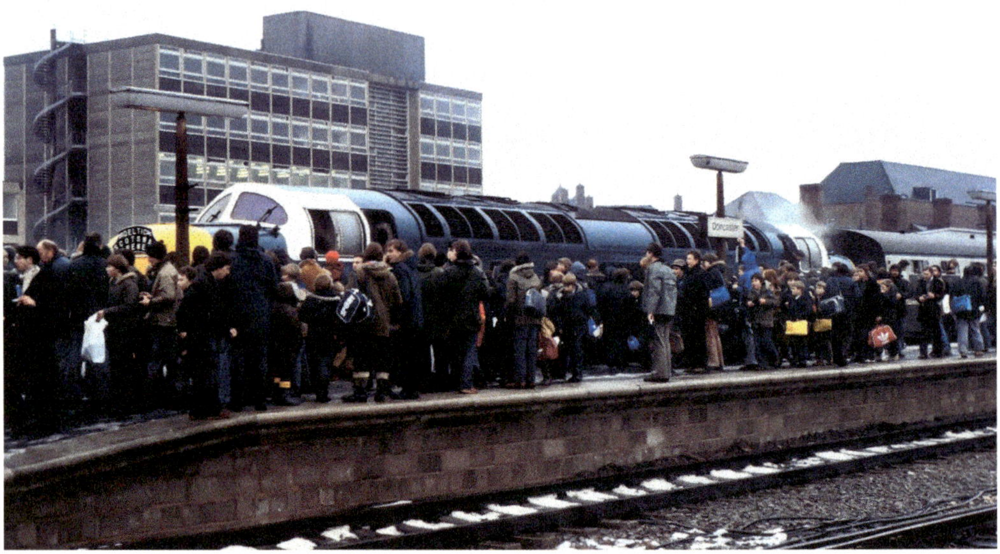

Farewell to the East Coast racehorses

After an all-too-brief career of a mere twenty-one years, the Deltics were retired from main line service in January 1982. The finale saw No. 55015 *Tulyar* heading the 'Deltic Scotsman Farewell' from King's Cross to Edinburgh on a miserable Saturday morning. Crowds throng the platform at Doncaster as they savour the familiar Napier engine note.

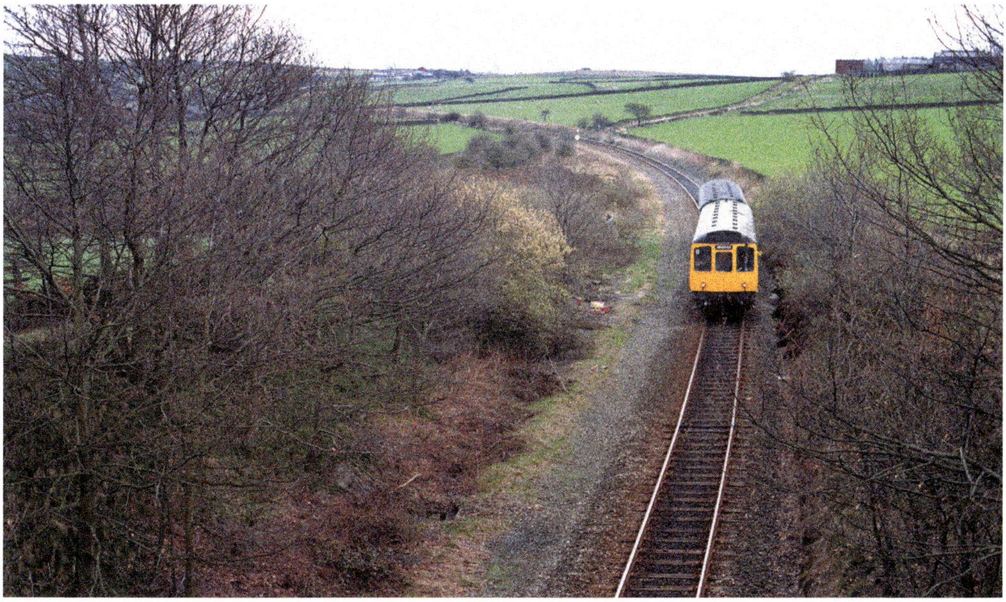

Through South Yorkshire farmland

The Penistone to Huddersfield line is one of the most scenic in the county and runs through tranquil rural countryside for much of its length. Here near Gunthwaite, between Penistone and Denby Dale, a BRCW DMU heads towards West Yorkshire in 1987.

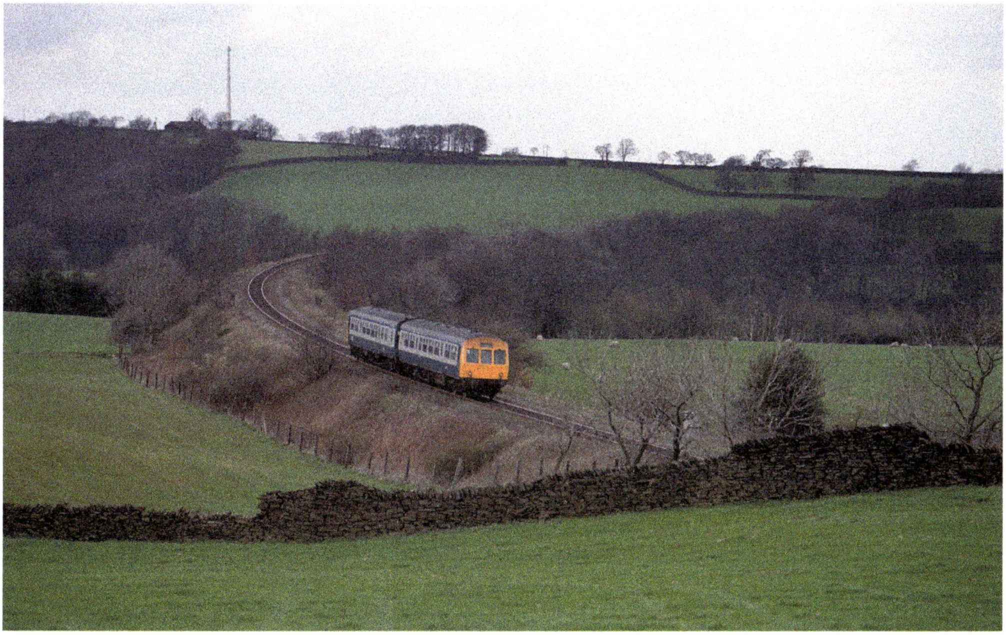

Heading for Penistone

Another view of the rural surroundings of the Huddersfield to Penistone line, with a two-car service heading east in 1987. The somewhat unloved 'Pacer' units would soon displace the solid DMUs on this route. The TV transmitter at Emley Moor is visible on the horizon.

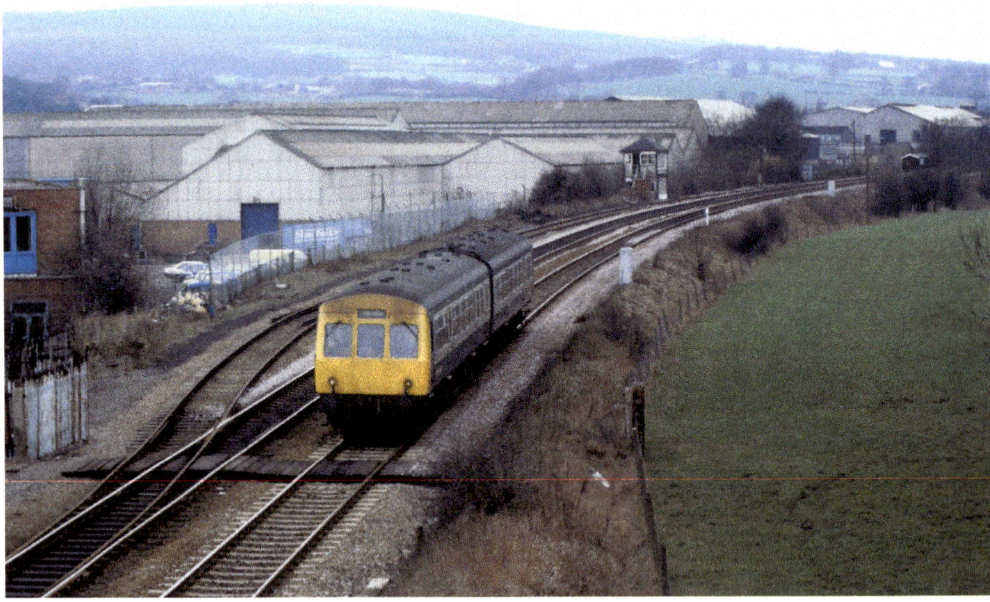

Passing Ecclesfield West

A Leeds to Sheffield service passes the Midland Railway's Ecclesfield West signalbox in April 1985. The box controlled access to an oil terminal here, the entrance to which can be seen on the left. Just out of shot to the right was the former Great Central line, which ran parallel here.

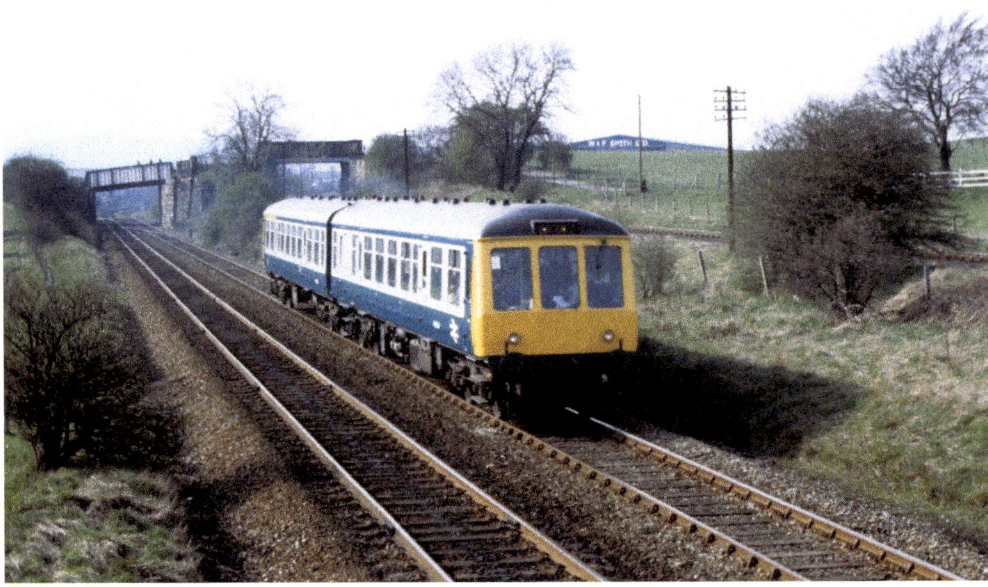

Parallel lines at Ecclesfield

Former Midland and Great Central lines came within a few yards of each other here at Ecclesfield. A DMU from Leeds heads towards Sheffield on the MR route in May 1982. The freight-only GC route, which at this time terminated at the nearby Smithywood coking plant, can be seen on the right.

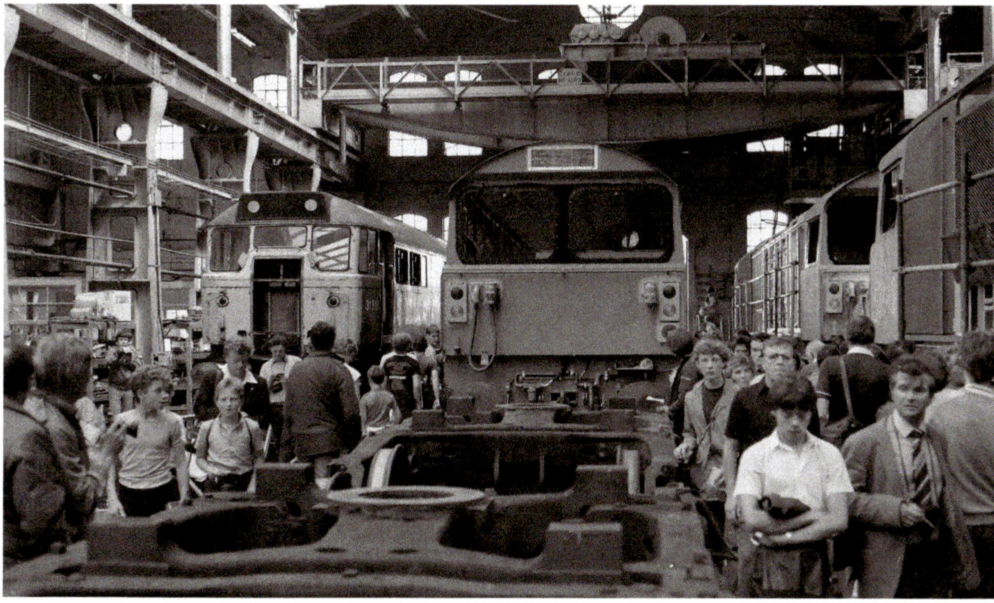

New builds and refurbs at 'the Plant'

Doncaster's 'Plant' was very busy in the summer of 1984, as this image shows. Three new Class 58 Co-Co freight locomotives, Nos 58017, 018 and 019 are nearing completion, while Brush Type 2 No. 31318 undergoes conversion to No. 31451 on the left. Open Day visitors throng the Crimpsall shops.

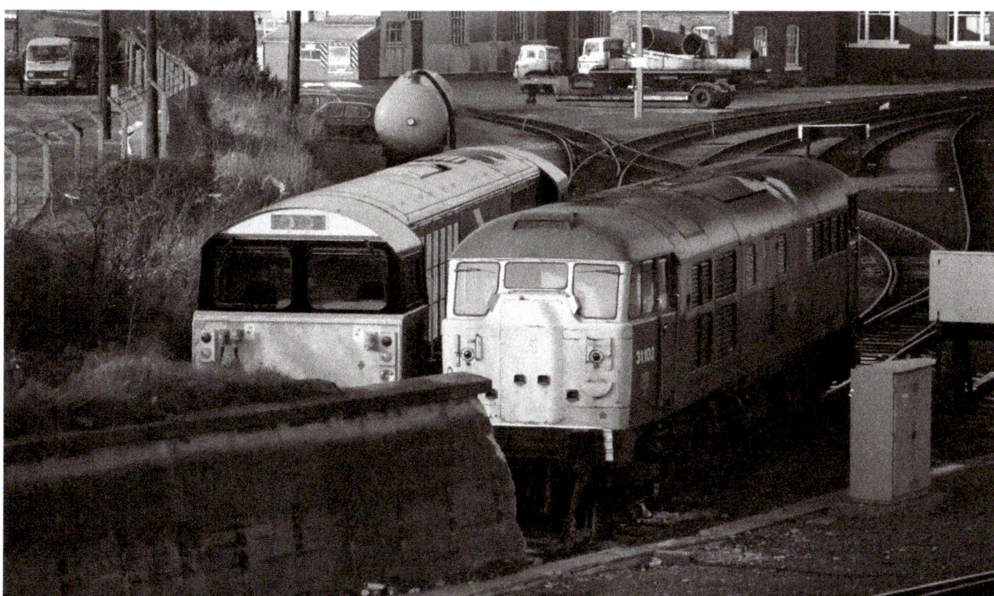

Old and new contrasts outside 'the Plant'

In January 1984, Class 31 No. 31102 stands on the works headshunt at Doncaster alongside newly built Type 5 No. 58010. The 58s were all out-shopped in large logo 'Railfreight' colours, but thereafter the Class went through a series of livery changes, including the grey 'Coal Sector' style, in which guise a number of them also received names.

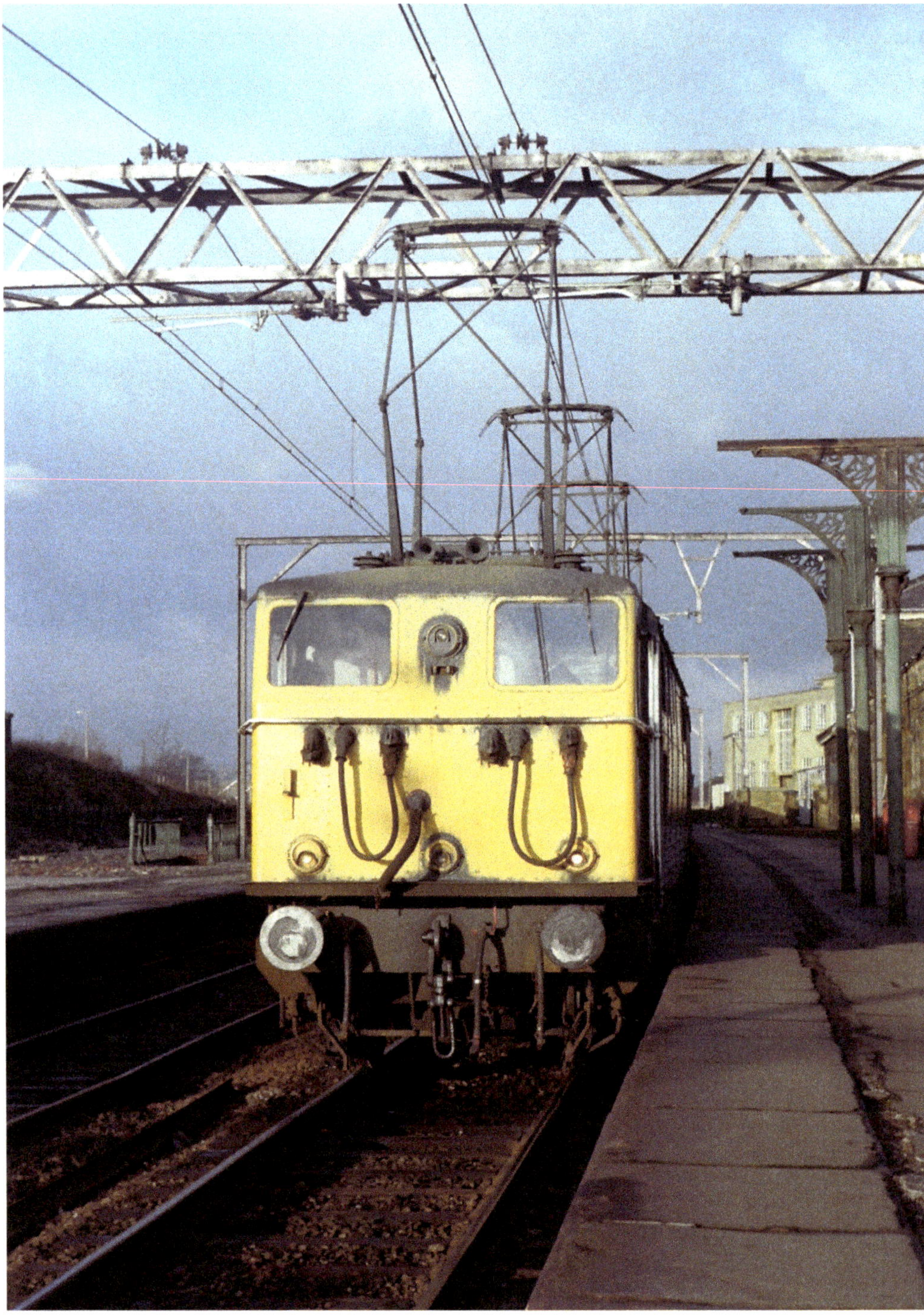

Class 76s wait at Penistone

Brilliant winter sunshine illuminates a pair of Class 76s waiting at Penistone's signal No. HJ10 in December 1979. The redundant canopy on this platform had recently been dismantled, but some of the original MS&LR cast-iron stanchions remain.

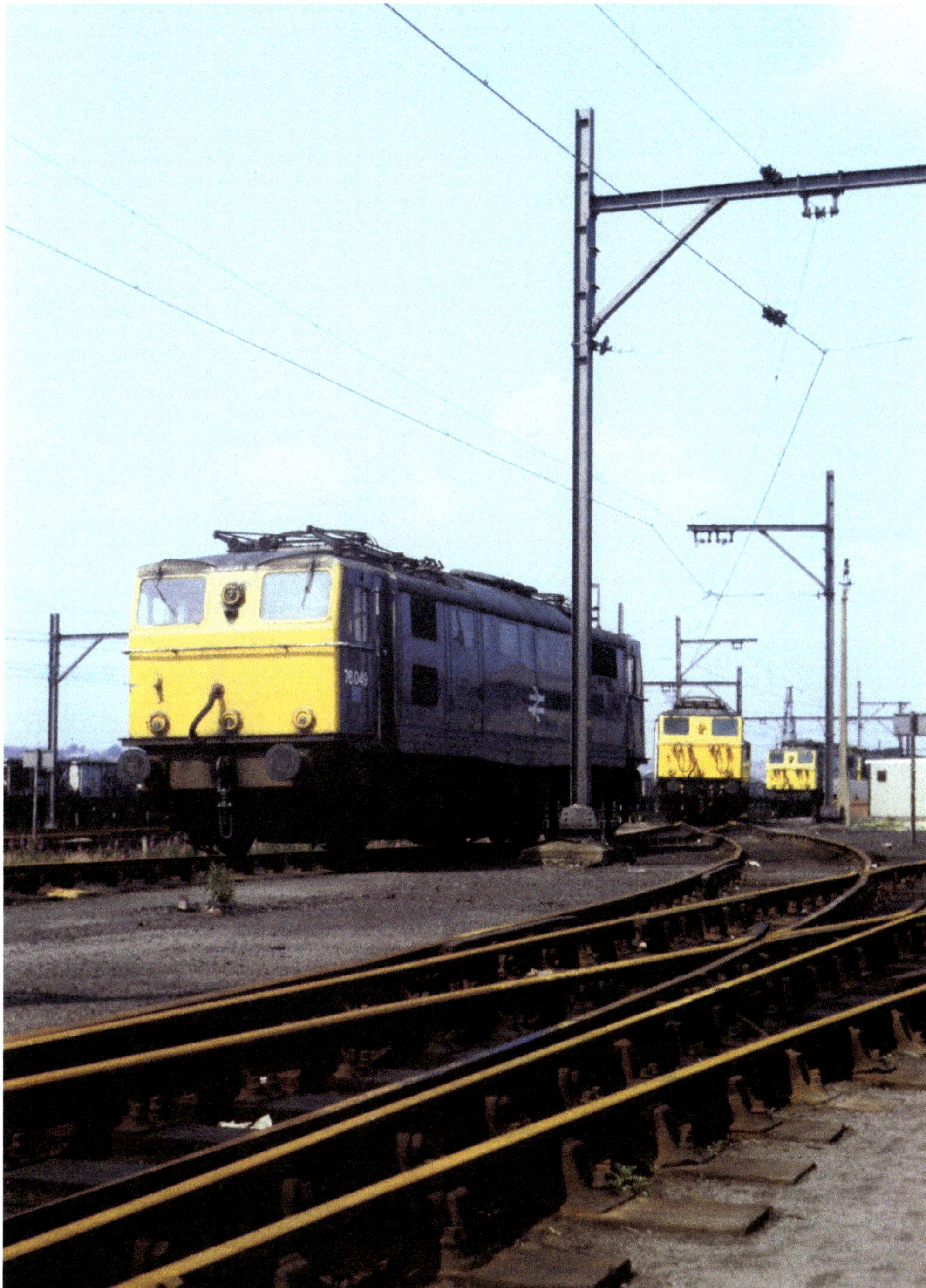

Basking in the sunshine at Wath, 1980

A beautiful summer's day at Wath sees the usual collection of Class 76s awaiting their next duty outside the depot. Nearest the camera is vacuum-braked No. 76049, formerly named *Jason*, with a number of dual-braked examples beyond. The date was 27 July.

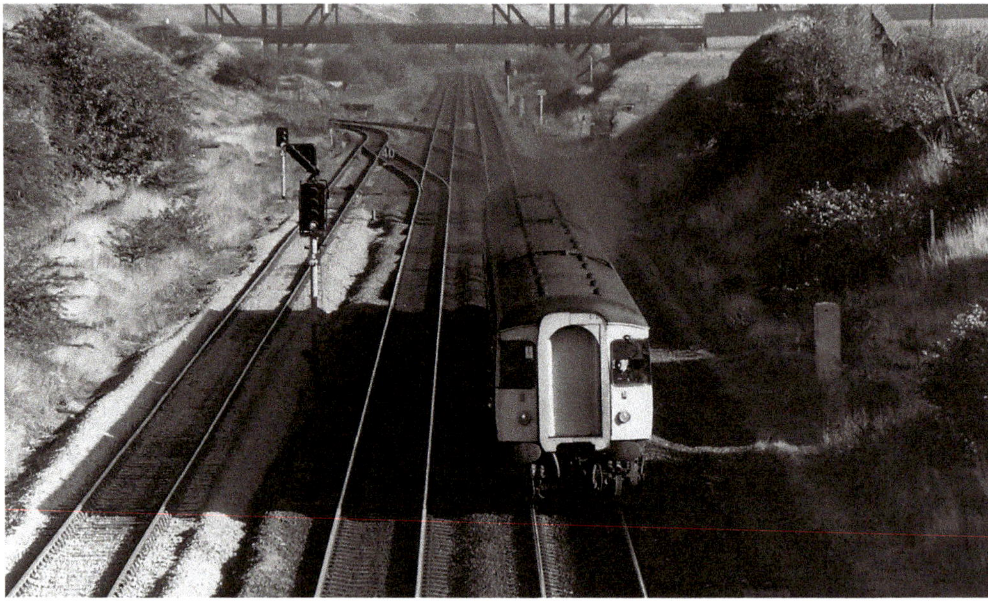

Before Meadowhall was built, 1983

A location which in October 1983 was known as Wincobank Station Junction, but which most people would now identify as 'Meadowhall'. A Trans-Pennine unit speeds towards Sheffield having just passed the site of the present-day Interchange and shopping centre. The ladder junction was relatively new at this time.

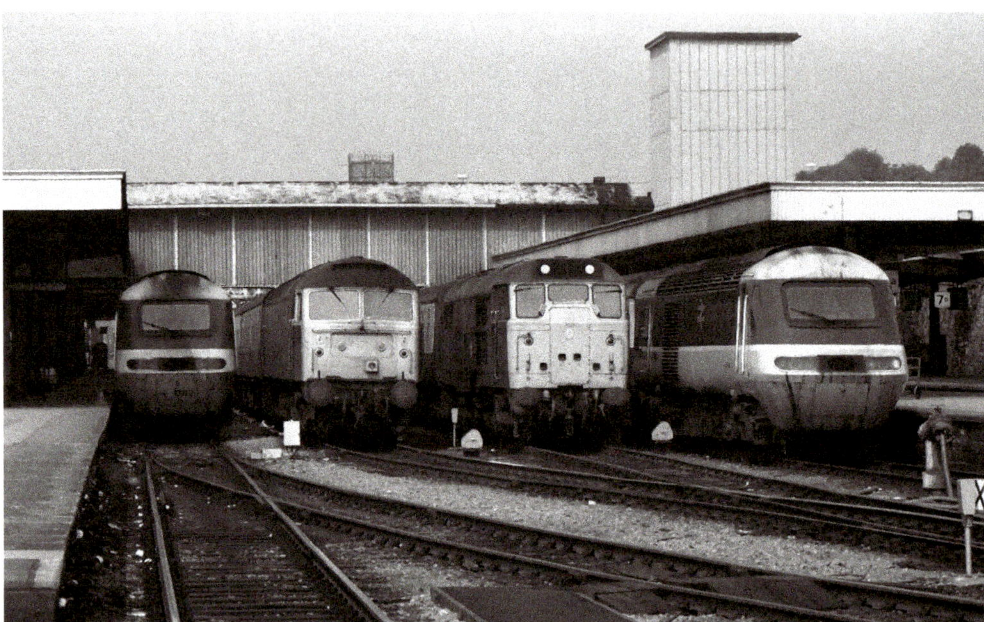

Steel city power, 1984 style

Sheffield station is seen here on a sunny Saturday in August 1984 with all the roads occupied between platforms 5 and 6. Two HSTs on cross-country services bookend locomotive-hauled stock stabled between seasonal turns.

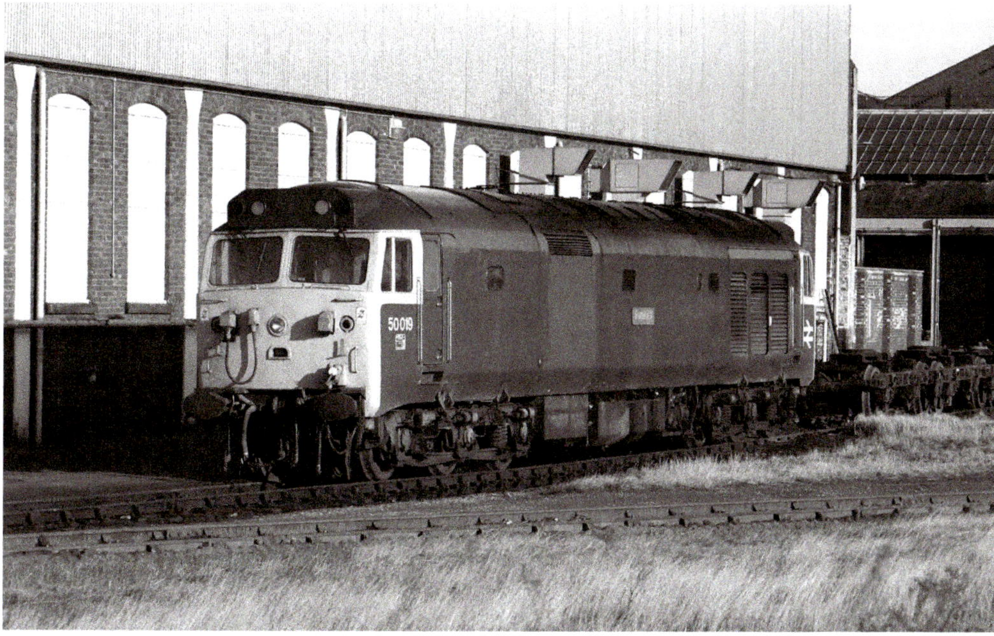

Western Region machine returns for attention

One of the WR's fleet of Class 50s, No. 50019 *Ramillies* is seen here at Doncaster Works in January 1984. The entire Class 50 cohort passed through 'the Plant' as part of a refurbishment programme in the 1970s and early 1980s, and they continued to appear for routine overhaul thereafter. This example was later preserved.

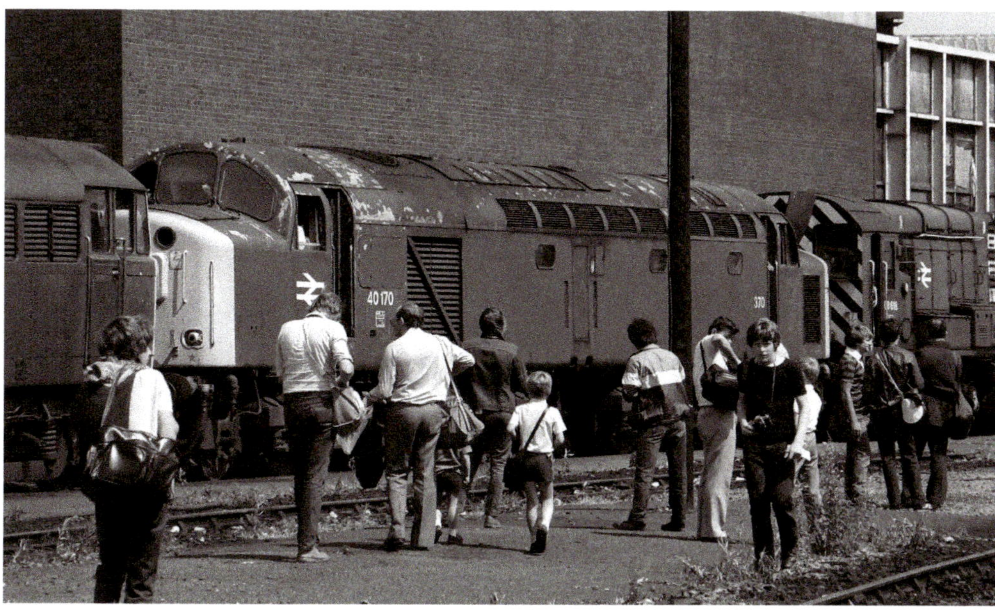

A giant withdrawn

Class 40 withdrawals began in earnest in the mid-1980s, and in 1984 many examples could be found languishing in BR works yards awaiting cutting up. Here at Doncaster, No. 40170 waits in line with a Class 31 and Class 08 for company.

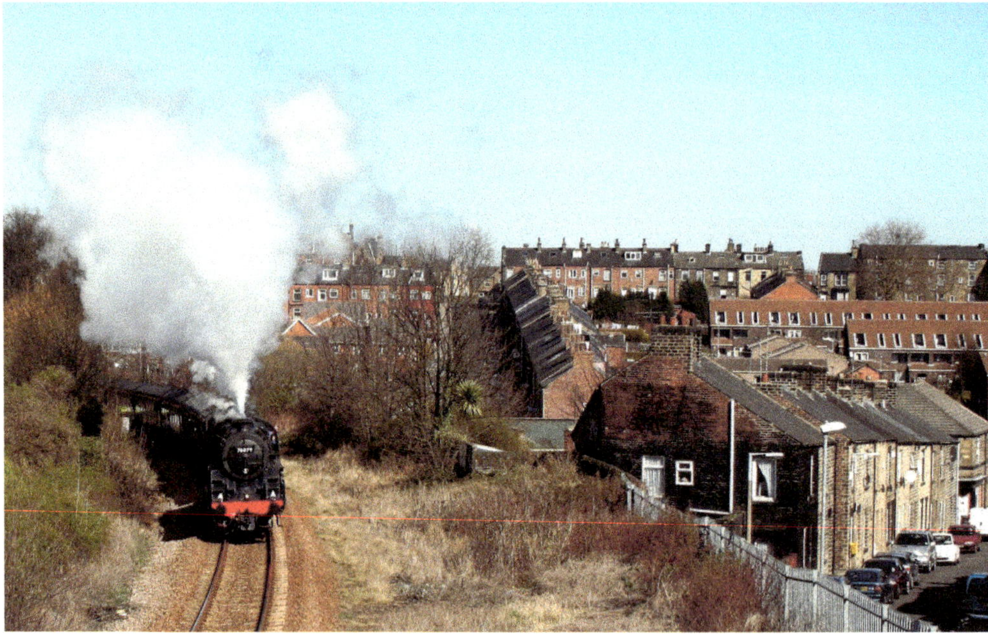

Summer Lane echoes to the sound of steam

A double-headed steam special pounds up the gradient out of Barnsley and is seen here passing the site of the former Great Central station at Summer Lane. Class 4MT No. 76079 leads Class 5MT No. 45407 on the 'Tin Bath' tour of March 2009, making the first appearance of steam on this line for fifty years.

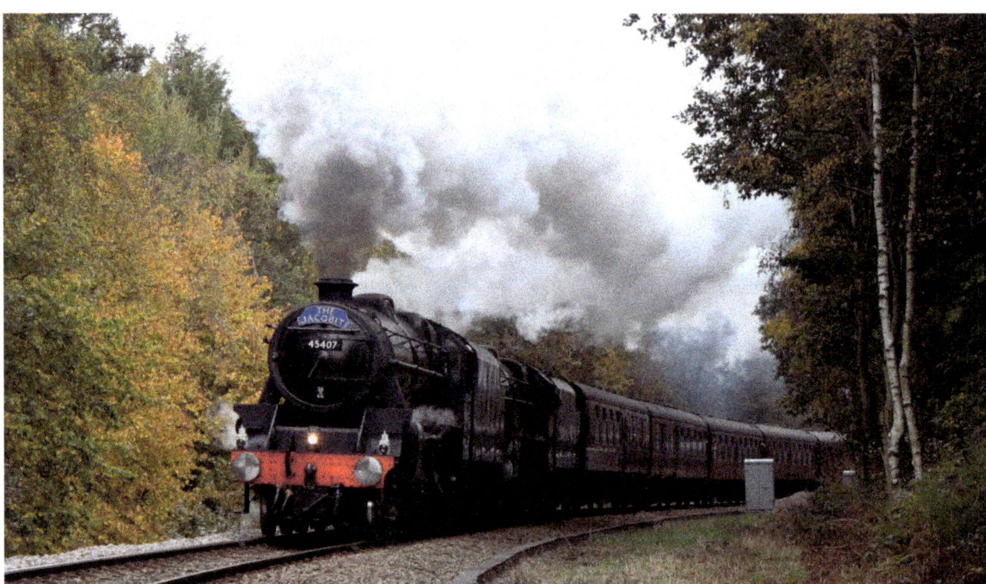

Double-headed steam through Silkstone Fall

Steam returned to the Barnsley–Penistone line in 2009 with the 'Tin Bath' railtours. One such trip ran in October of that year and featured a pair of Black 5s, which put on a splendid show on the steeply graded route. Here No. 45407 leads as the train passes through the woods at Silkstone.

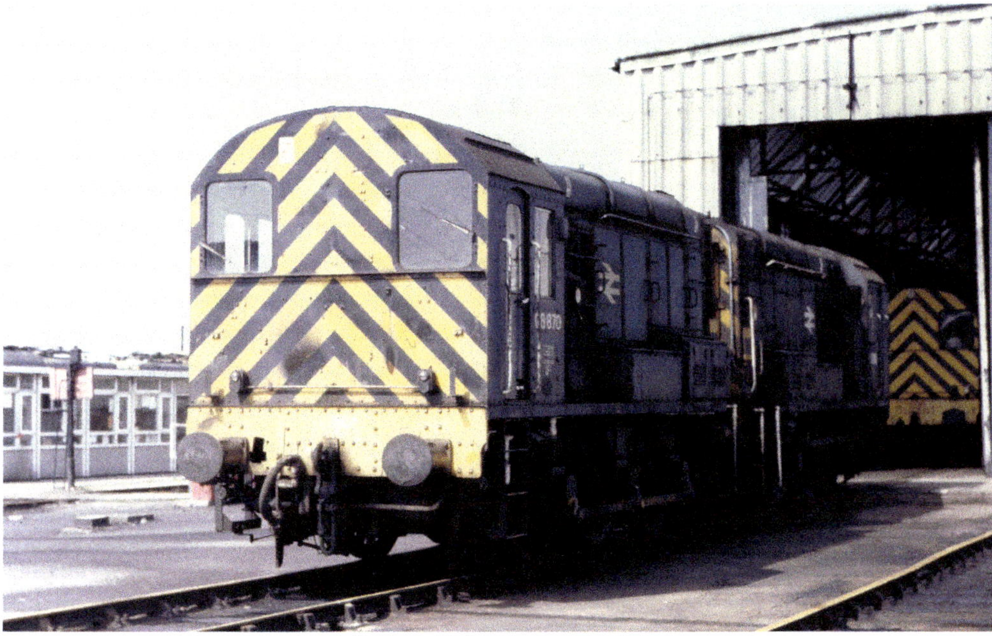

A trio of Class 08s at Wath

A visit to Wath shed usually revealed several of the depot's allocation of Class 08 shunters, and here on a sunny July afternoon in 1980, three are seen at the eastern end of the building. A pair would often be used in nose-to-nose configuration for operating local trip workings, as here with Nos 08870 and 08050. (Vaughan Hellam)

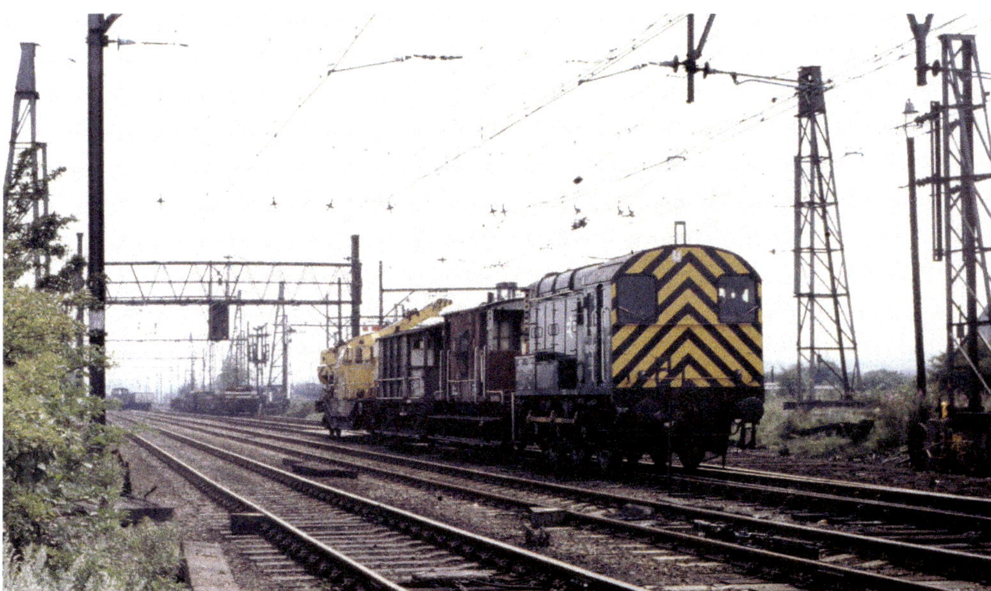

Engineer's trip at Elsecar Junction

The level crossing at Elsecar Junction marked the western extremity of Wath Yard and was the point at which the branch to Elsecar and Cortonwood collieries diverged from the Aldam Junction line. Here one of Wath's allocation of Class 08s, No. 08434, is seen in charge of an engineer's train in August 1980. (Vaughan Hellam)

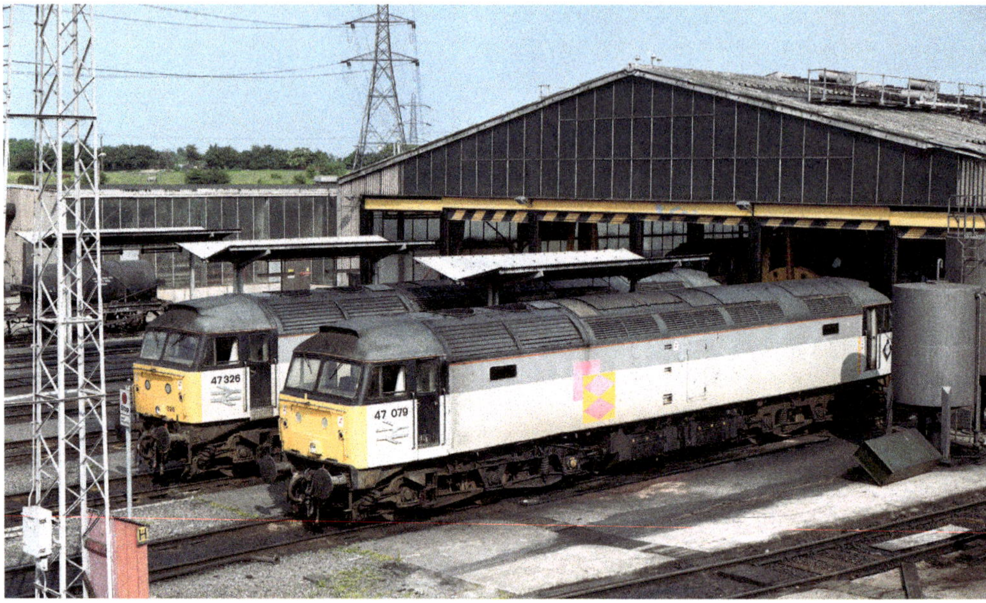

Railfreight sector Class 47s at Tinsley

These two Class 47s were stabled at the westerly end of Tinsley depot on 8 June 1993. No. 47079 was once a Western Region machine and was formerly named *George Jackson Churchward*, but had lost this identity by the time of the Railfreight era. At the time of this photograph it was a Tinsley machine.

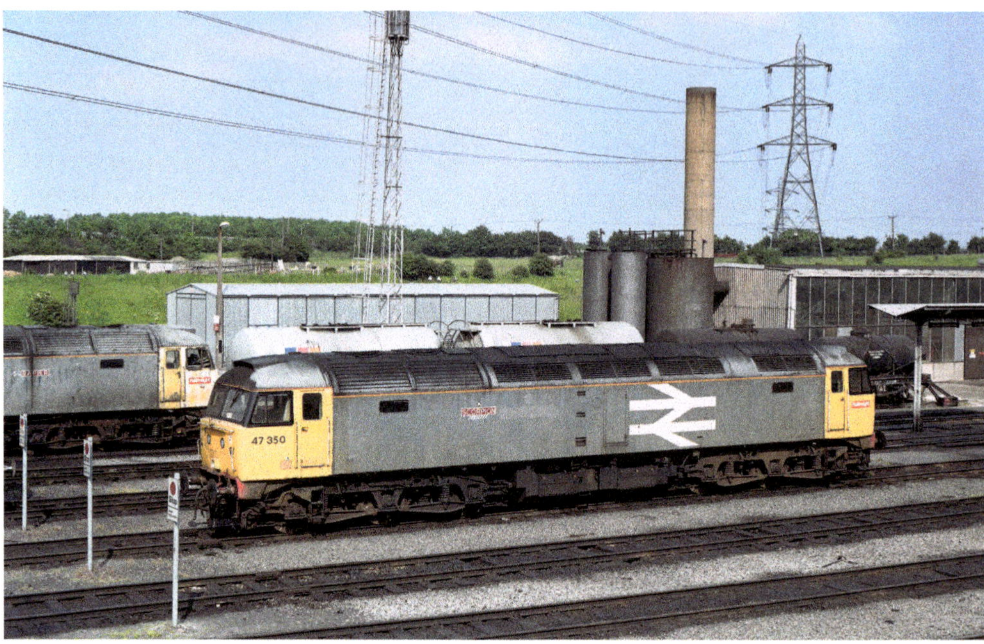

Transformation awaits No. 47350

Class 47/3 No. 47350 *Scorpion* shares the depot yard at Tinsley with its withdrawn classmate No. 47220 on 8 June 1993. No. 47350 was one of its Class selected for rebuilding as a Class 57 in 1999. It became No. 57005 following rebuilding at Brush in Loughborough. No. 47220 was however scrapped in 1994.

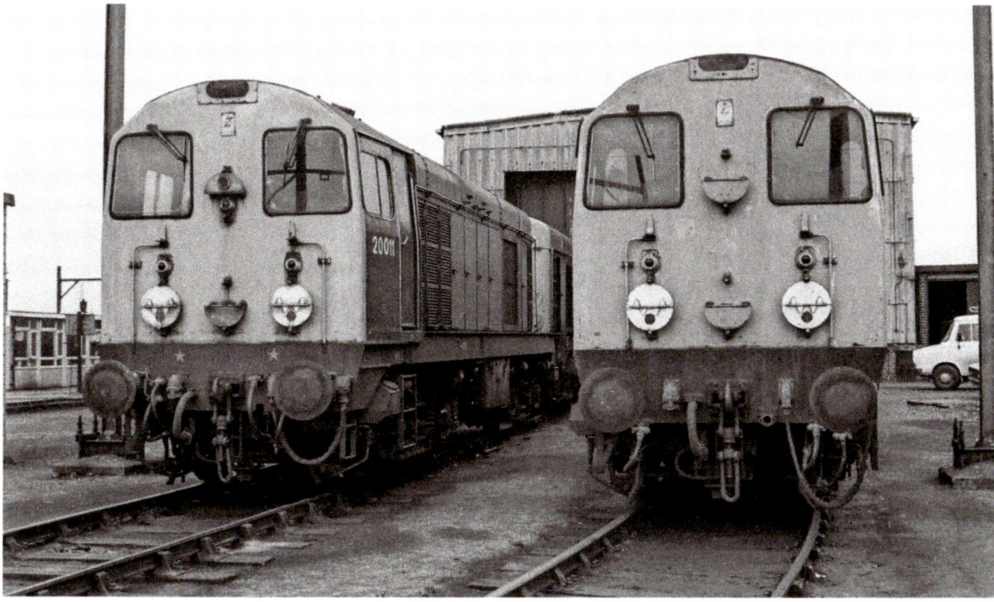

Type 1 workhorses take a rest at Wath

Pairs of Tinsley-based Class 20s were often out-stationed at Wath depot, finding themselves employed on a wide variety of trip workings that saw them visit the Cudworth, Dovecliffe and Dodworth lines among other destinations. Here a quartet of Type 1s takes a break outside the shed in November 1981.

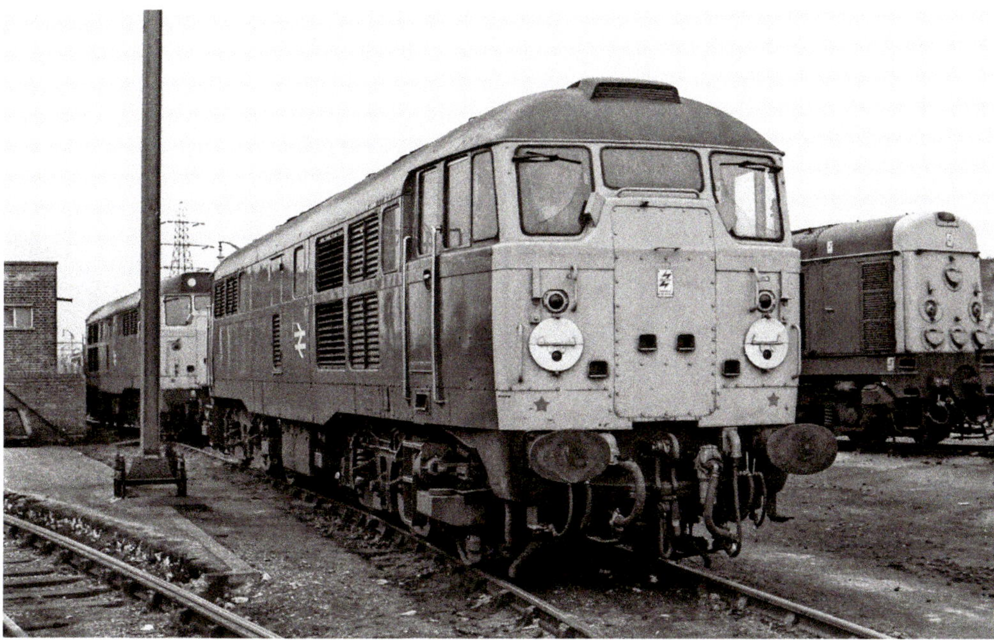

Motive power variety at Wath depot

Tinsley-based Class 31 No. 31102 was a familiar face in the Barnsley area in the early 1980s, and here it is taking a rest between duties at Wath in November 1981. Another 31 and a pair of Class 20s share the yard at the westerly end of the depot. At weekends there would typically be around twenty locos on shed at Wath.

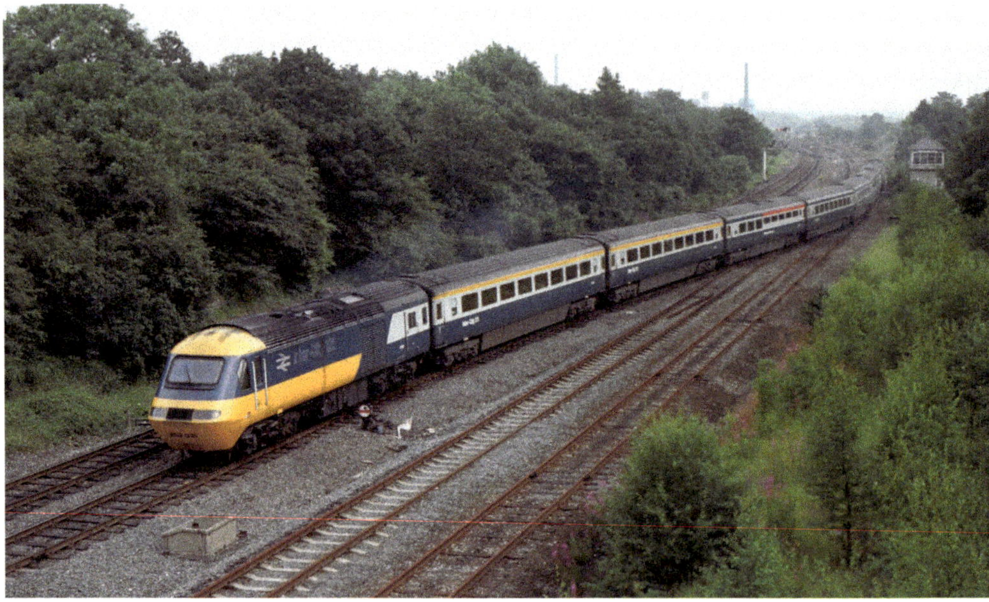

A Western Region HST set passes Royston Junction

A northbound HST set snakes its way across the junction at Royston to gain access to the Down goods line in the summer of 1982. The manoeuvre enabled the train to avoid subsidence-affected trackwork, which caused many speed restrictions in this area at the time. Tree growth has transformed the view here in the last thirty years.

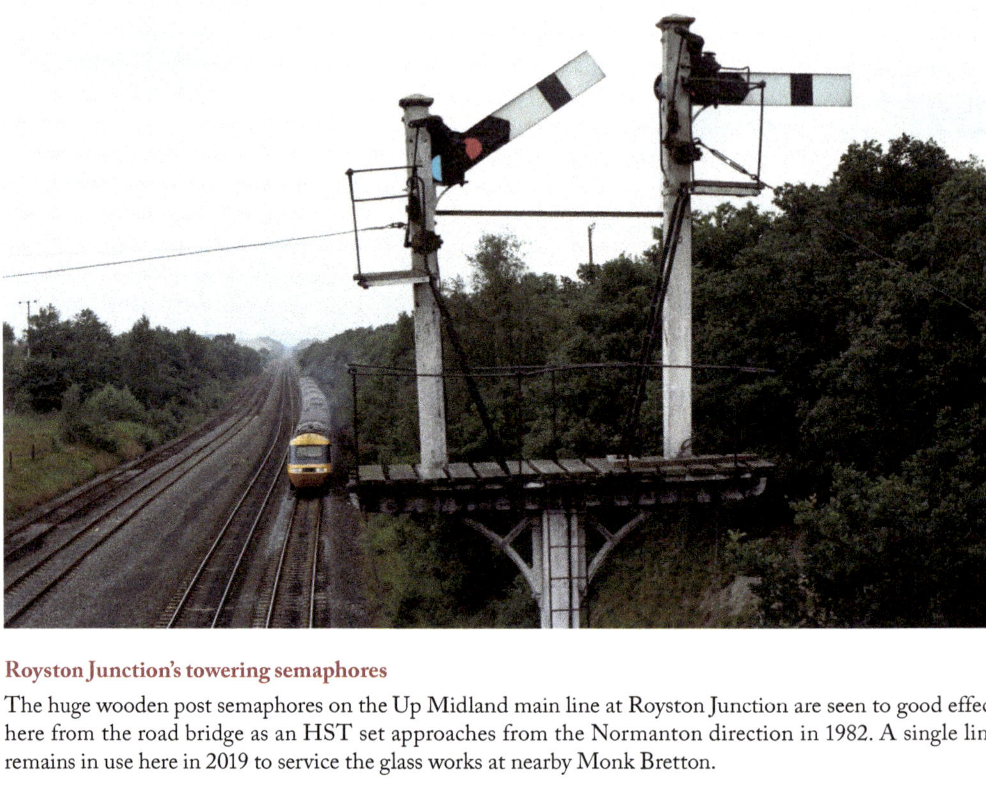

Royston Junction's towering semaphores

The huge wooden post semaphores on the Up Midland main line at Royston Junction are seen to good effect here from the road bridge as an HST set approaches from the Normanton direction in 1982. A single line remains in use here in 2019 to service the glass works at nearby Monk Bretton.

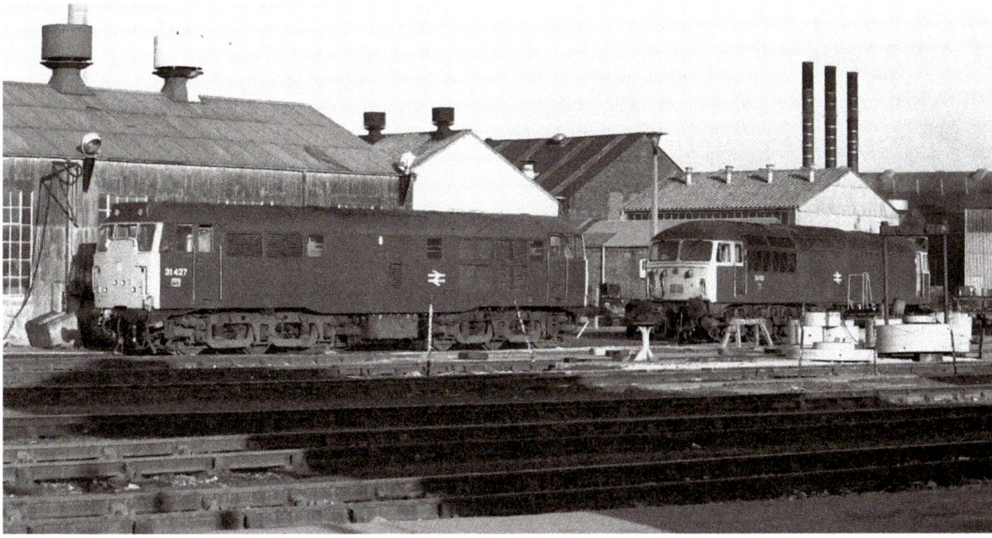

Everyday work for Doncaster's Plant

A bright January day in 1984 sees recently-outshopped Class 31 No. 31427 in the company of Romanian-built Type 5 No. 56010 in the yard at Doncaster works. This was a busy period for 'the Plant', with the usual maintenance schedule for various Classes of locomotive as well as Class 31/4 conversions and the Class 58 new-build programme.

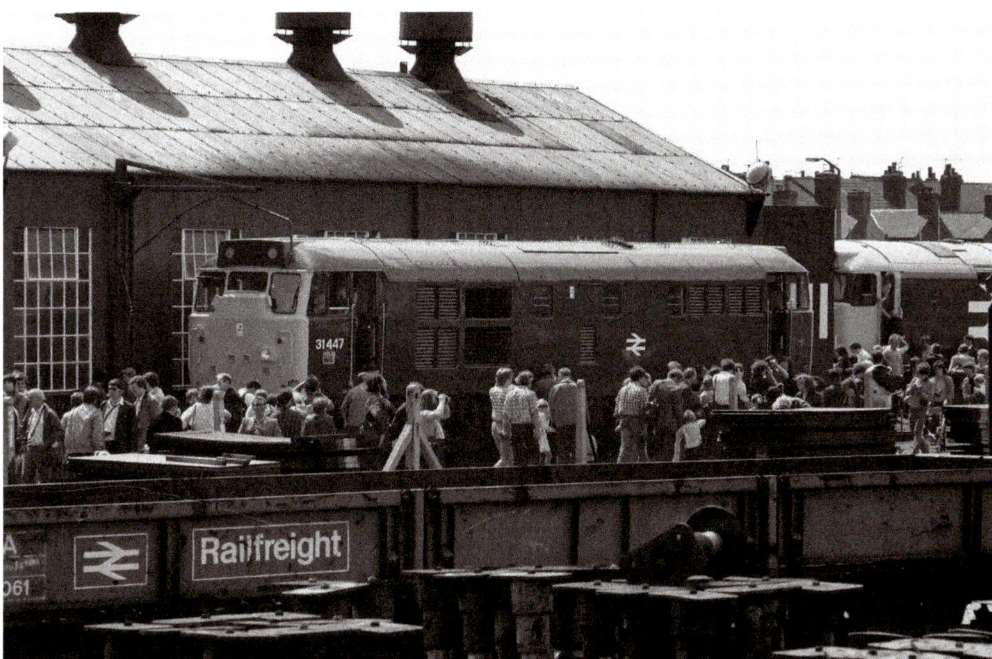

Type 2 attraction at Doncaster Works

Doncaster enjoyed beautiful sunshine for its 1984 Works Open Day, which took place on 28 July. Here a newly refurbished Class 31 No. 31447, renumbered from No. 31295, stands in the works yard among the crowds of visitors. Later renumbered again to No. 31547, the loco was withdrawn in 1998 after thirty-seven years' service.

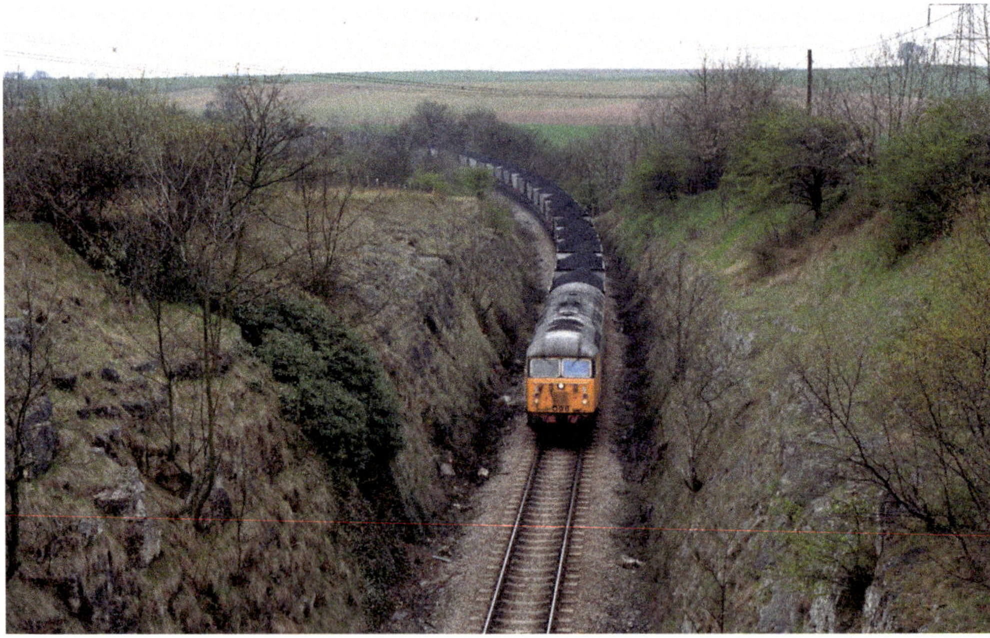

Coal traffic on the South Yorkshire Joint Line

Built from the outset primarily to carry freight, the SY Joint Line ran through the heart of the 'concealed coalfield' to the south of Doncaster. Here a Class 56 approaches Maltby in April 1987 with an MGR train from the nearby colliery, bound for one of the Aire valley power stations.

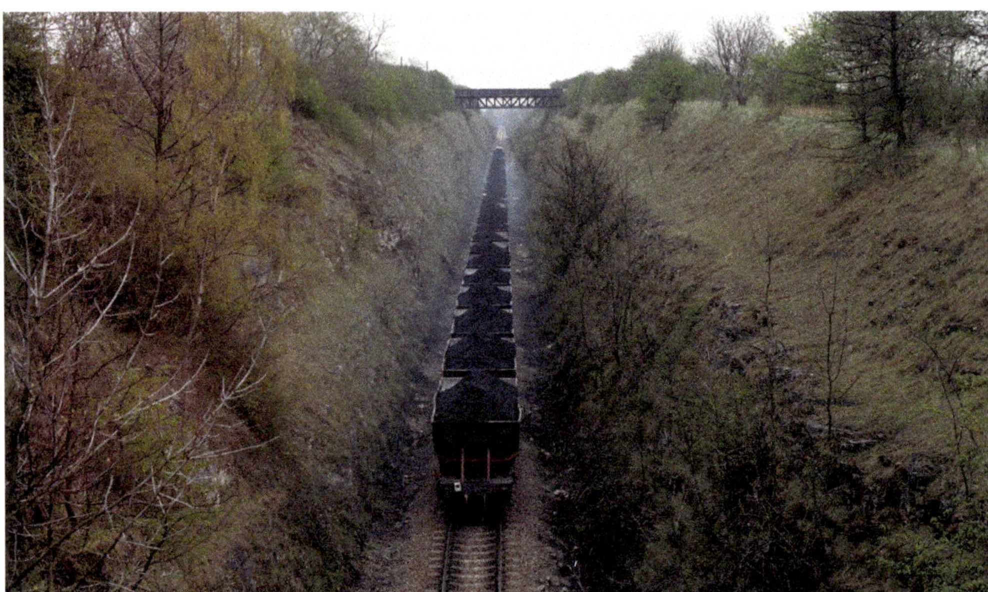

Challenging topography of the SY Joint Line

This tremendous limestone cutting at Maltby gives some idea of the monumental work required by the railway builders when pushing their lines through the landscape in parts of the county. Class 56 No. 56098 traverses the impressive alignment with a loaded MGR service in April 1987.

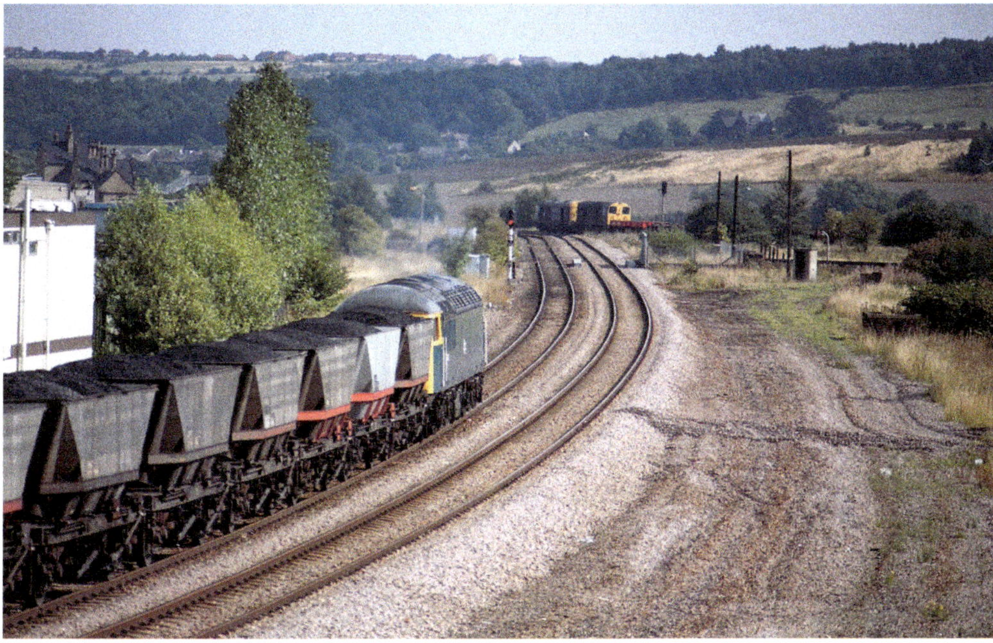

A landscape transformed forever

A fascinating view of a long-lost freight line, as Class 56 No. 56072 slows for a red signal while working an MGR service from Wath along the former Great Central line at Mexborough in September 1986. In the distance a pair of Class 20s passes Mexborough East Junction, heading towards Doncaster. The alignment of the Wath line here is now occupied by industrial development. (Vaughan Hellam)

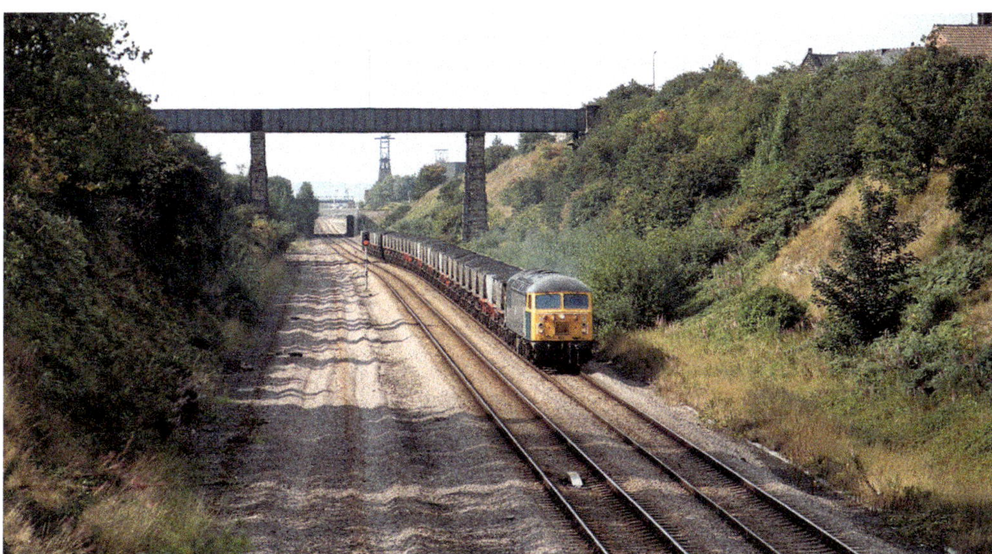

Last days of a coal-carrying network, 1986

There is clear evidence of the once four-track layout here on the former Great Central line at Mexborough, looking towards Wath as a Class 56 approaches with an eastbound MGR service. The train has just passed beneath the Midland main line at Wath Road Junction. (Vaughan Hellam)

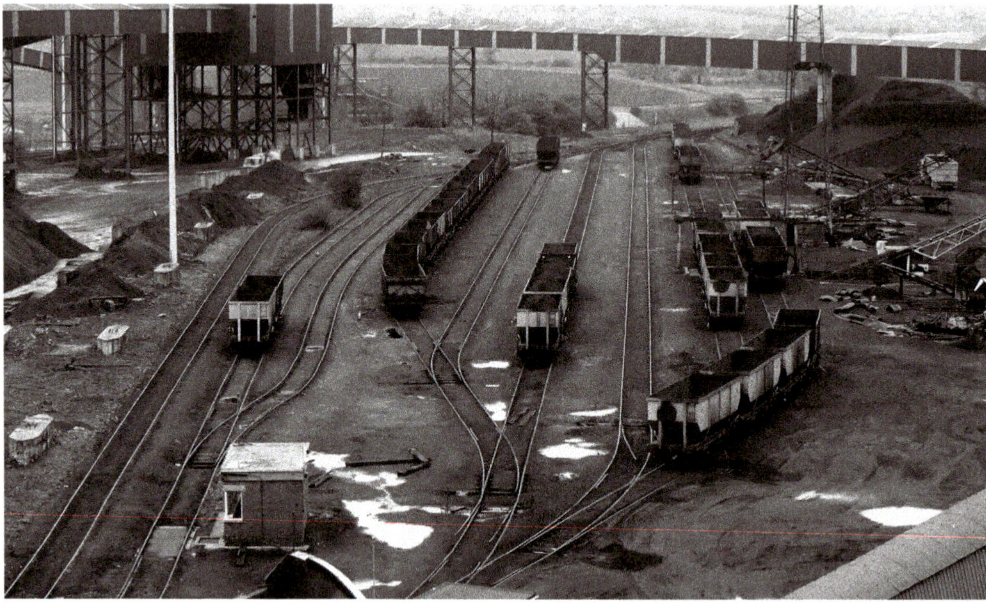

Rarely seen bird's eye view of Grimethorpe Coalite plant, 1991

The huge Coalite processing plant at Grimethorpe closed in 1994, three years after this photograph was taken from the top of the coal bunkers. The sidings contain several internal user wagons for shuttling coal to the coking furnaces. The nearby colliery, which supplied the plant for many years, closed in 1993.

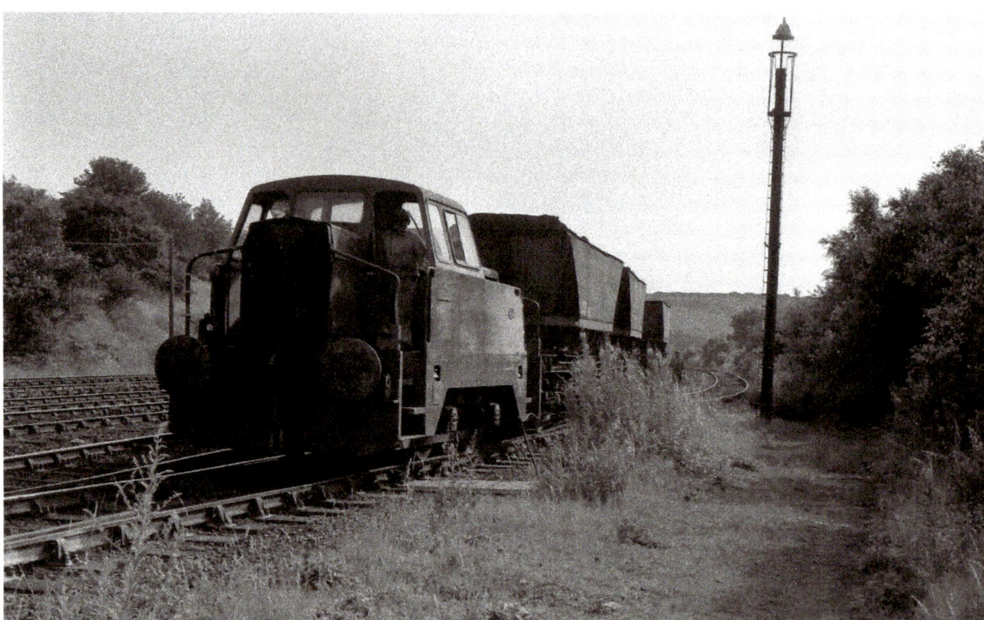

Humble duty for an NCB shunter

The yard at Barrow colliery, near Barnsley, is seen here in the summer of 1983, with one of the pit's diesel shunters busy marshalling a rake of full MGR hoppers next to a characteristic lamp standard. A Class 56 locomotive from Wath will collect the train for onward transit to one of the region's power stations. (Vaughan Hellam)

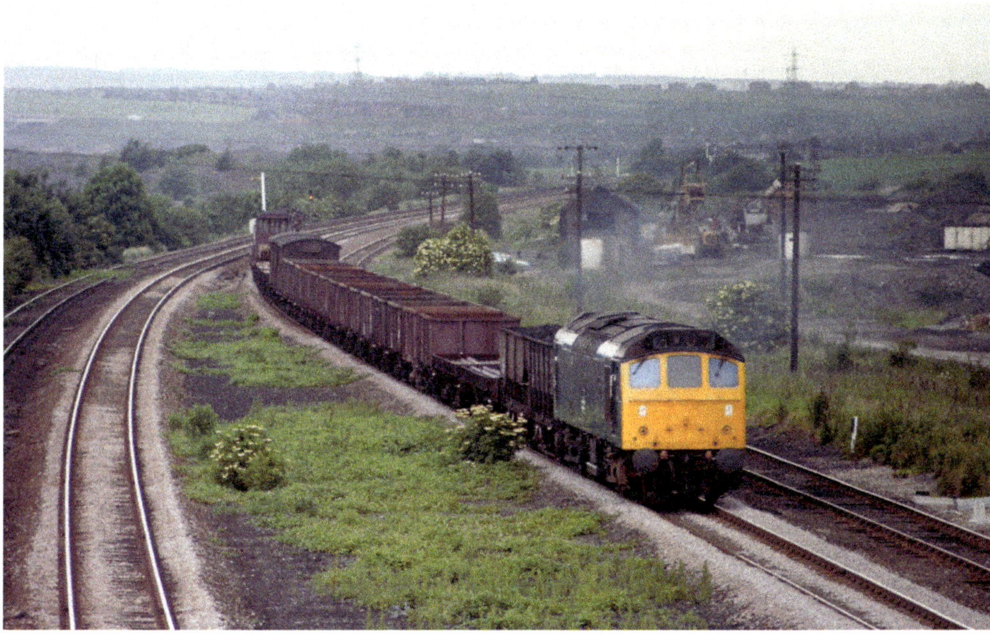

Sulzer Type 2 powers south on the Old Road

The Rotherham Masborough to Tapton Junction line, known as the 'Old Road', has always been a busy freight route enabling trains to avoid Sheffield. Here in the summer of 1980, Class 25 No. 25137 heads south at the site of Woodhouse Mill station, south of Treeton Junction.

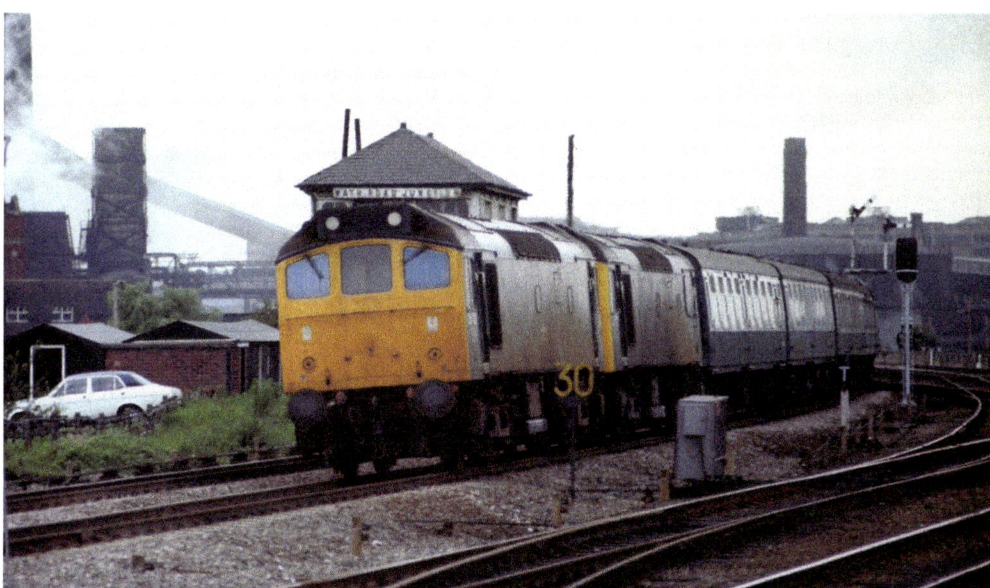

Through the heart of South Yorkshire industry

The Midland main line north of Sheffield cut straight through the middle of the huge Manvers coking plant, seen in the background of this shot at Wath Road Junction with a pair of Class 25s on a southbound passenger service in June 1980. The plant, associated collieries, yards and the main line itself are all long gone.

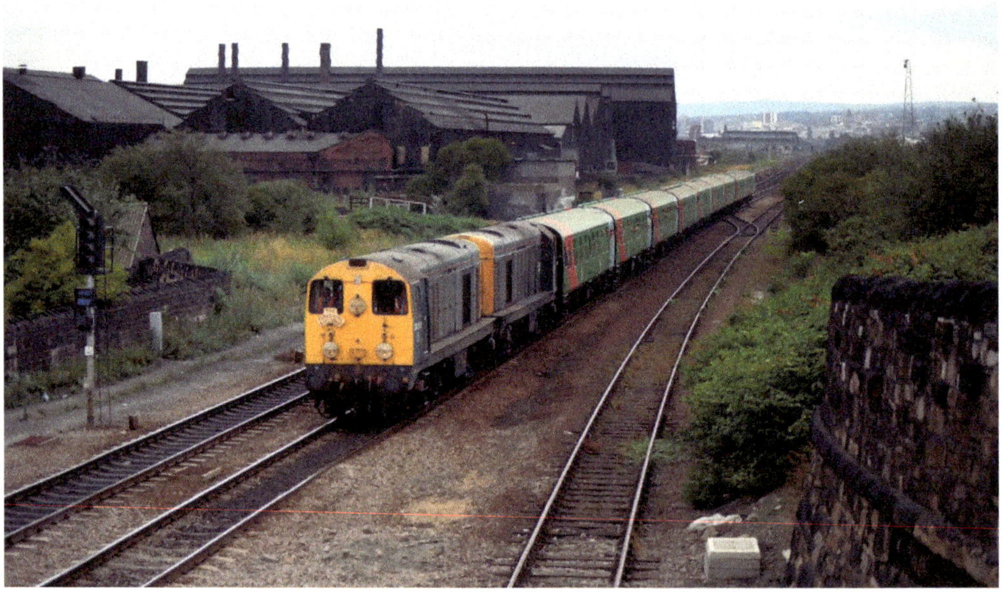

An explorer at Brightside

Class 20s Nos 20031 and 20069 are seen here heading past Sheffield's heavy industry at Brightside with the Birmingham to Birmingham circular 'Yorkshire Explorer' railtour in August 1990. The train will bear left at Wincobank and take the Barnsley line.

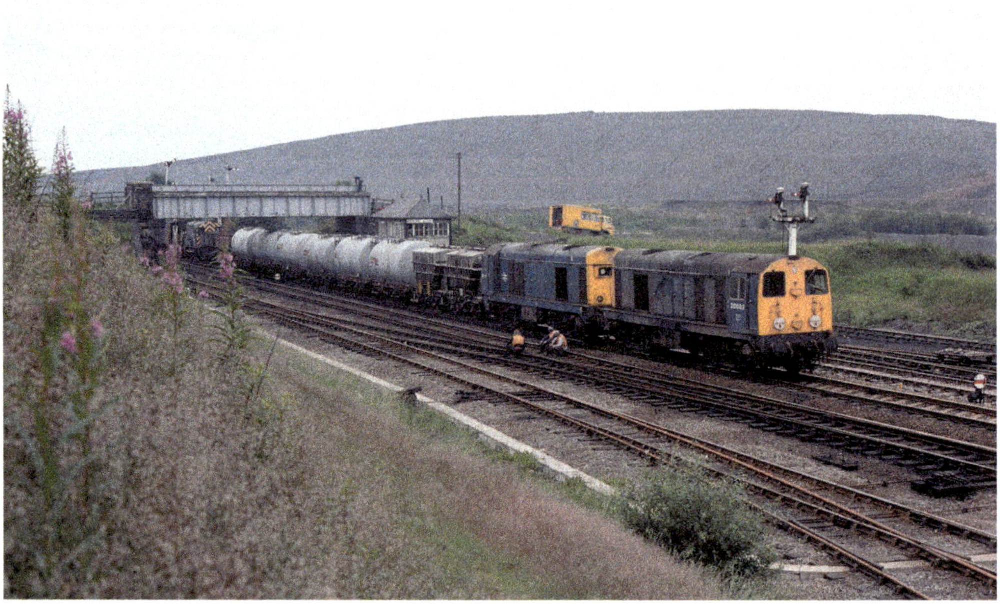

A very mixed freight goes north at Treeton

The assortment of vehicles in this mixed freight even includes a Class 08 shunter. Class 20s Nos 20082 and 20147 trundle past Treeton South Junction on a northbound working which will take the Tinsley line at nearby Treeton Junction. The semaphore signals here would soon disappear as the Sheffield area modernisation plan reached this section of line.

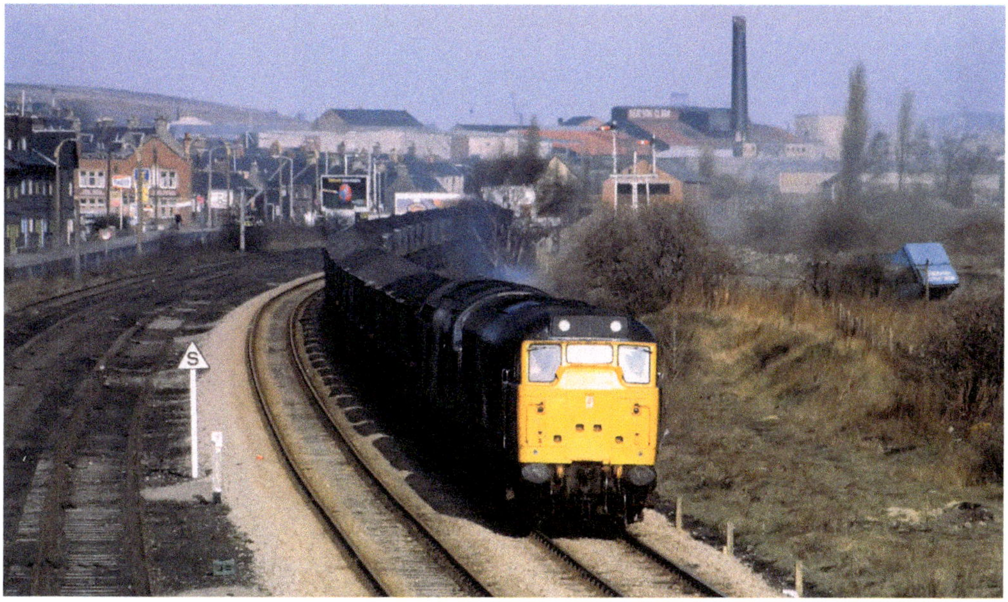

A long-vanished landscape

A double-headed MGR working from Dodworth Colliery to Wath yard powers through Stairfoot on the outskirts of Barnsley in the spring of 1983. Once a busy hub for rail activity, Stairfoot now has no railway infrastructure whatsoever. The Beatson Clark glass factory, at that time still rail-served, is visible on the horizon.

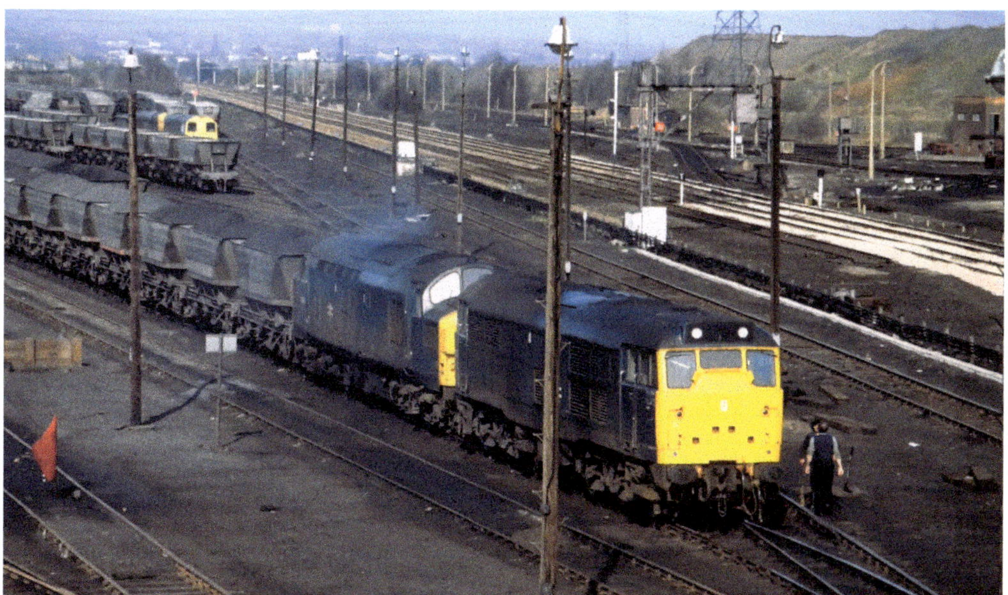

Wath Yard after the wires have gone

Ancient yard lamps have survived at Wath in this image from April 1983, but the once-electrified lines beyond have lost their gantries and wires, constructed a mere thirty years earlier, in the wake of the Woodhead route closure. There is still some coal traffic in evidence however, with Nos 31143 and 36067 in charge of a service from Dodworth.

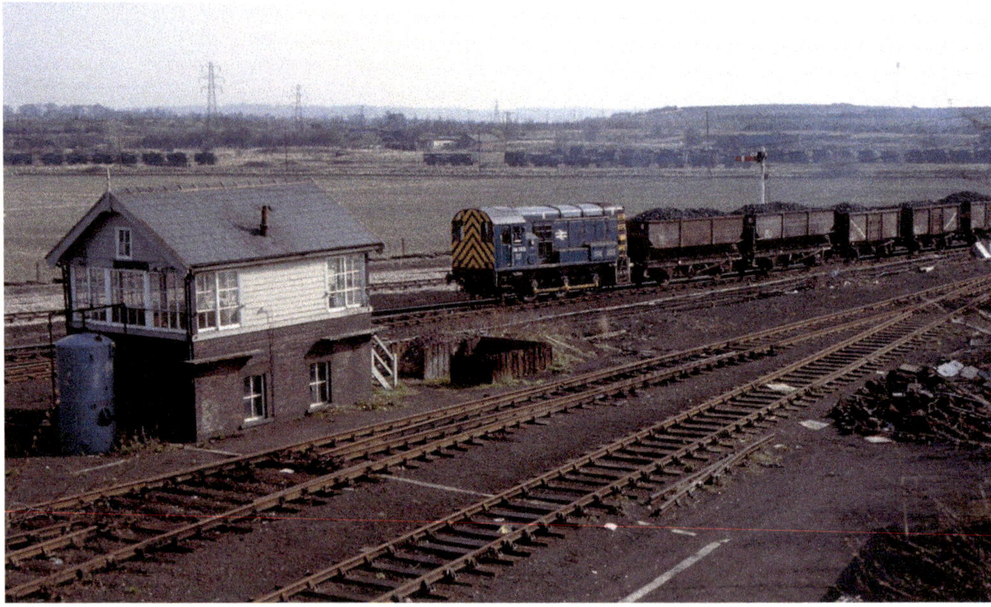

Local trip activity at Wath

A Class 08 shunter brings a trip working from Manvers Main into the yard at Wath in April 1983. The box in the foreground, Moor Road, controlled the eastern end of the marshalling yard here, but by this time it was closed and would soon be gone. The tank next to the box served to supply compressed air for the pneumatic lever frame, a feature of several boxes in this area.

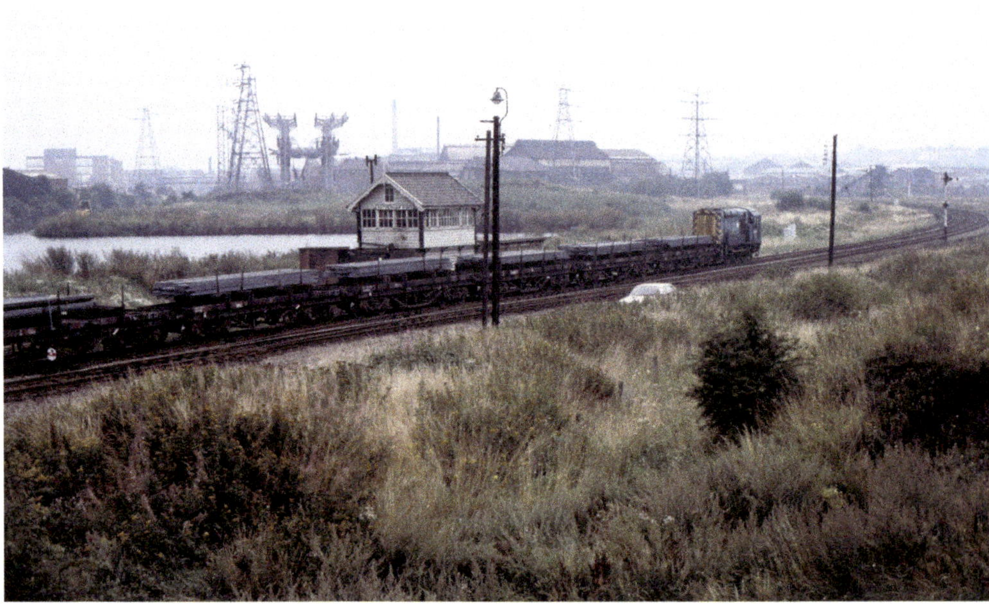

South Yorkshire steel takes its time

Class 08 No. 08244 passes Rotherham Road signalbox at a stately 15 mph and heads for Tinsley Yard with a train of steel bogie wagons from Aldwarke on a dull 24 August 1984. This former GCR stretch of line now carries passenger services following the reopening of Rotherham's Central station.

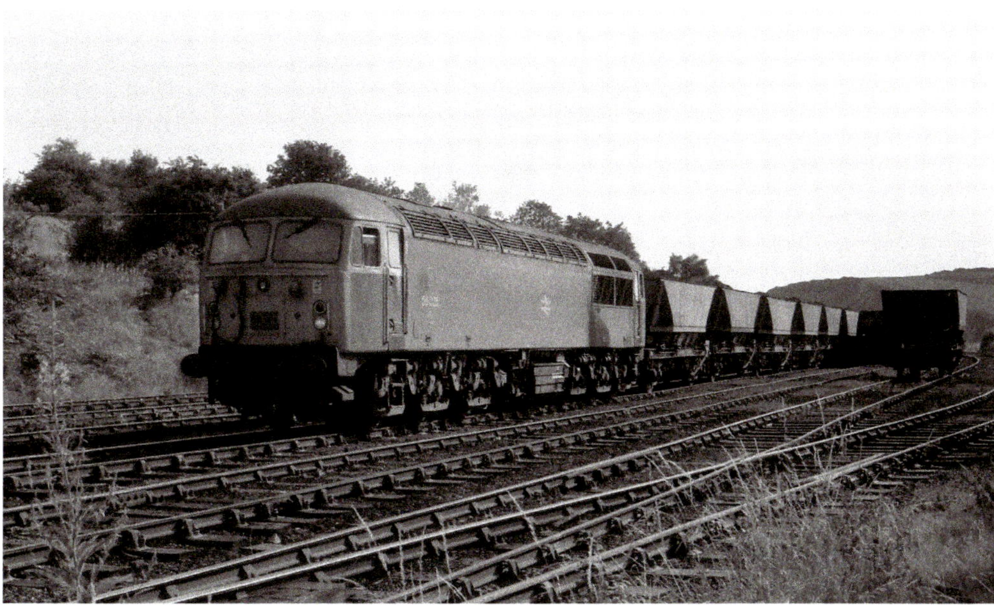

The era of coal draws to a close

Class 56 No. 56025 has arrived from Wath Yard and is marshalling a loaded MGR train in the yard at Barrow Colliery, near Hoyland in Barnsley. The date is July 1983 and soon this pit, like so many before it in the area, will draw its last ton of coal. (Vaughan Hellam)

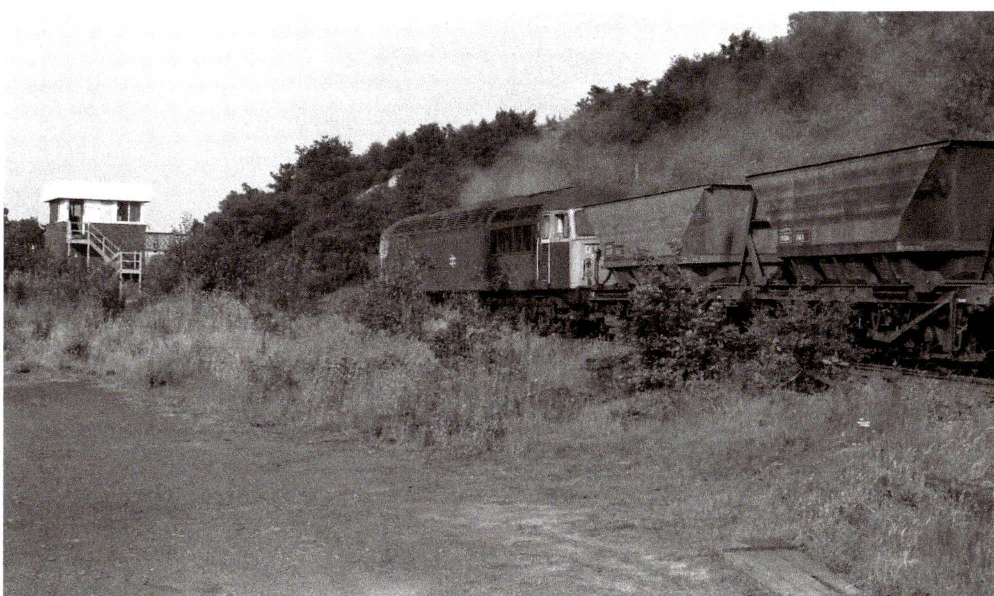

No. 56025 approaches Dovecliffe box

This image shows Tinsley's Class 56 No. 56025, pulling away from the yard at Barrow colliery and approaching the signalbox at Dovecliffe with a loaded MGR working, which will travel, initially, to Wath Yard before going on to one of the region's power stations. Photographs of diesel workings on this former Great Central line are rare. (Vaughan Hellam)

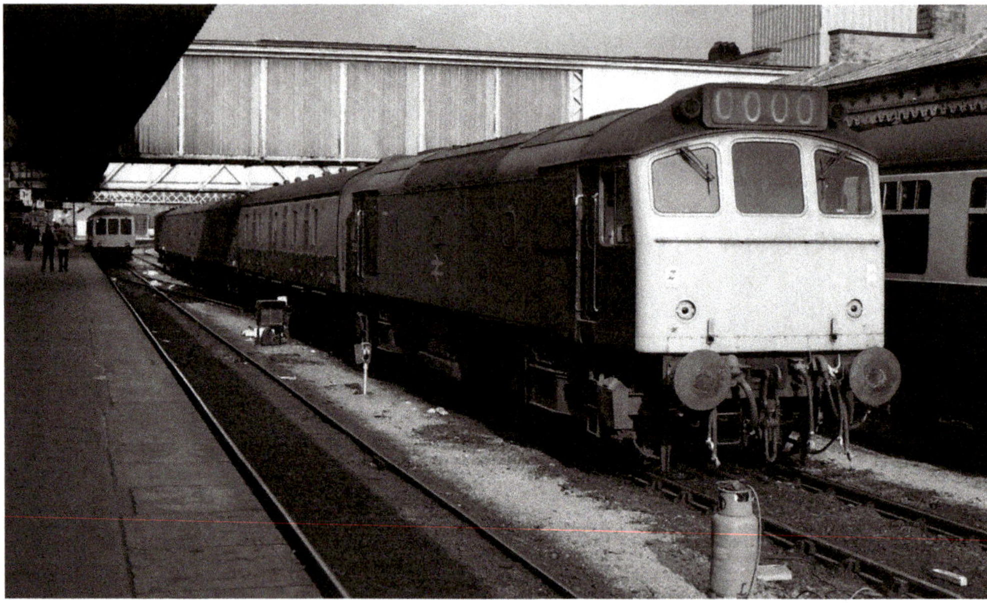

Parcels variety at Sheffield, 1983

Parcels traffic at Sheffield did not often produce Class 25 motive power, but here in October 1983, No. 25287 adds to the traction variety at the head of a short westbound working. The headcode panel on this locomotive has escaped the usual conversion to 'domino' style. (Vaughan Hellam)

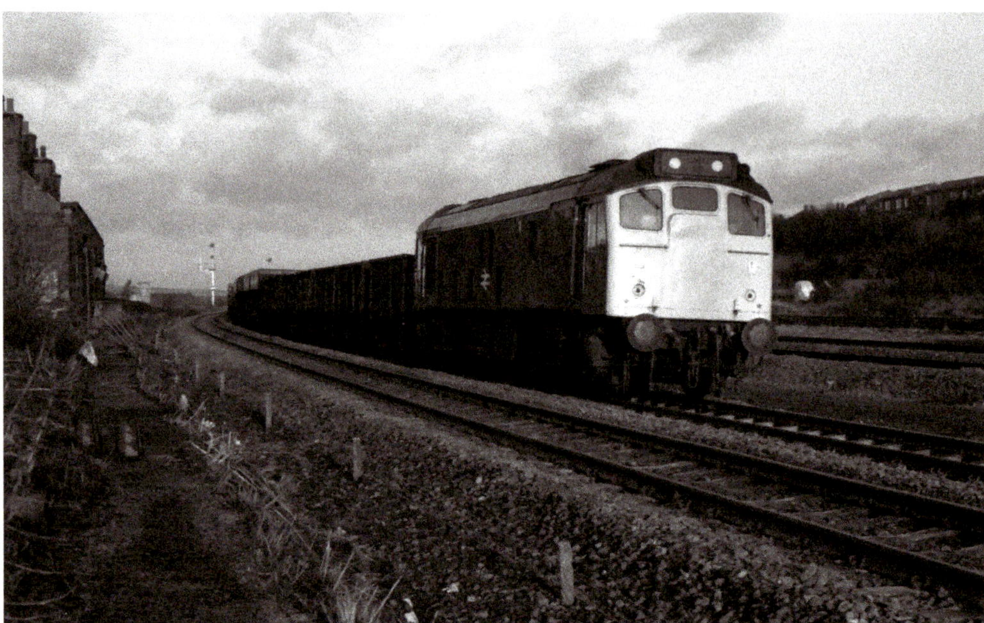

Type 2 on the Midland main line

Bright winter sunshine illuminates Sulzer Type 2 No. 25218 as it speeds south with a mixed freight past the site of the former Midland station at Cudworth in January 1983. The remains of the station building on the Down platform can be seen on the left. (Vaughan Hellam)

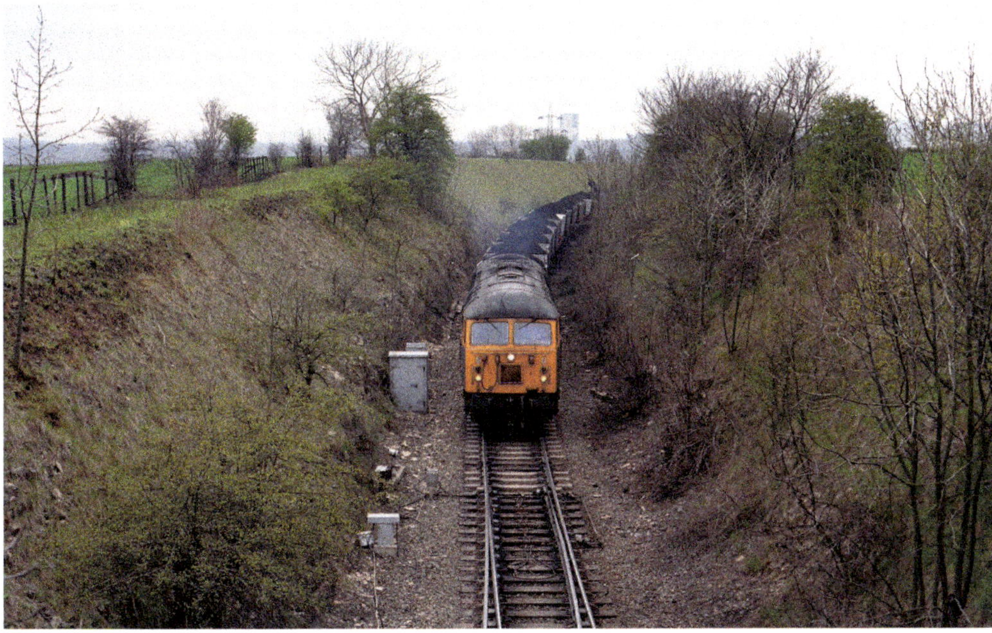

Coal on the move at Firbeck

Another load of power station coal heads towards the Aire Valley from the colliery at Maltby in this image from April 1987. Class 56 No. 56067 approaches Firbeck West Junction, where the line to the colliery at Harworth diverged from the Doncaster route on what is known as the South Yorkshire Joint Line.

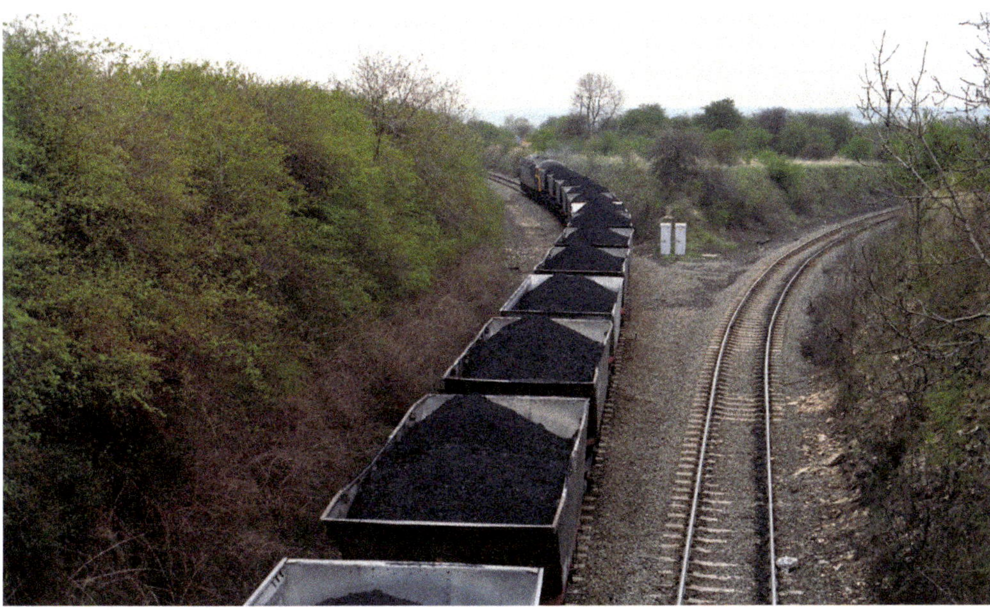

Taking the Doncaster line at Firbeck West Junction

A simple divergence between two single lines is all that remained of Firbeck West Junction in April 1987, with the Worksop to Doncaster route taking the left-hand fork and the now-closed branch to Harworth colliery going right. A Class 56 heads north with a loaded MGR service.

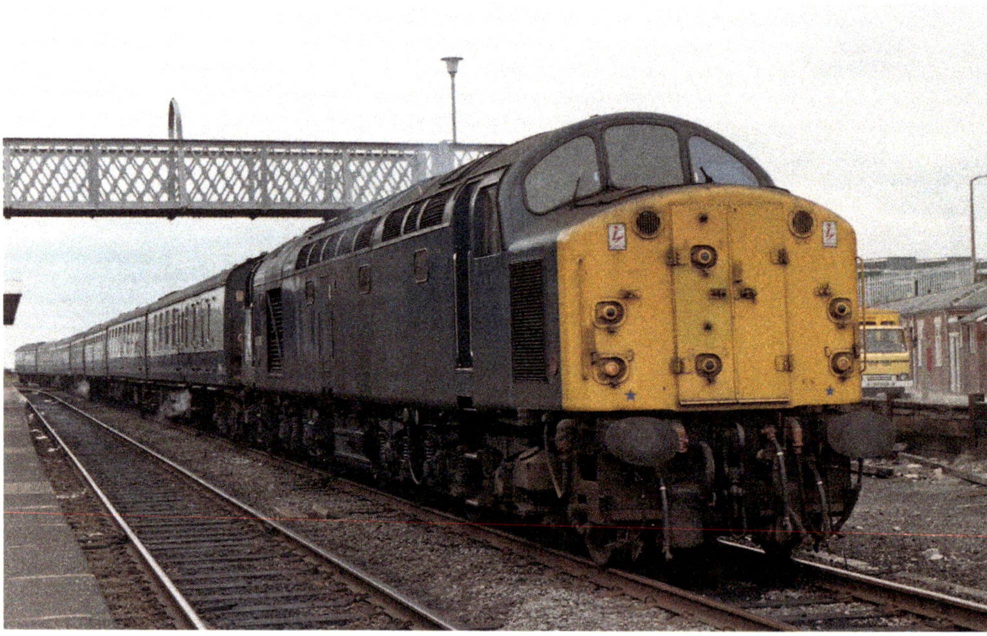

Steam-heated stock on a cool July morning

On 11 July 1981, Class 40 No. 40085 stands at Barnsley with a seven-coach summer Saturday service formed of rather elderly-looking Mk I stock. Wisps of steam from the carriage heating system can be seen escaping at various points along the train as it awaits departure for Sheffield. (Vaughan Hellam)

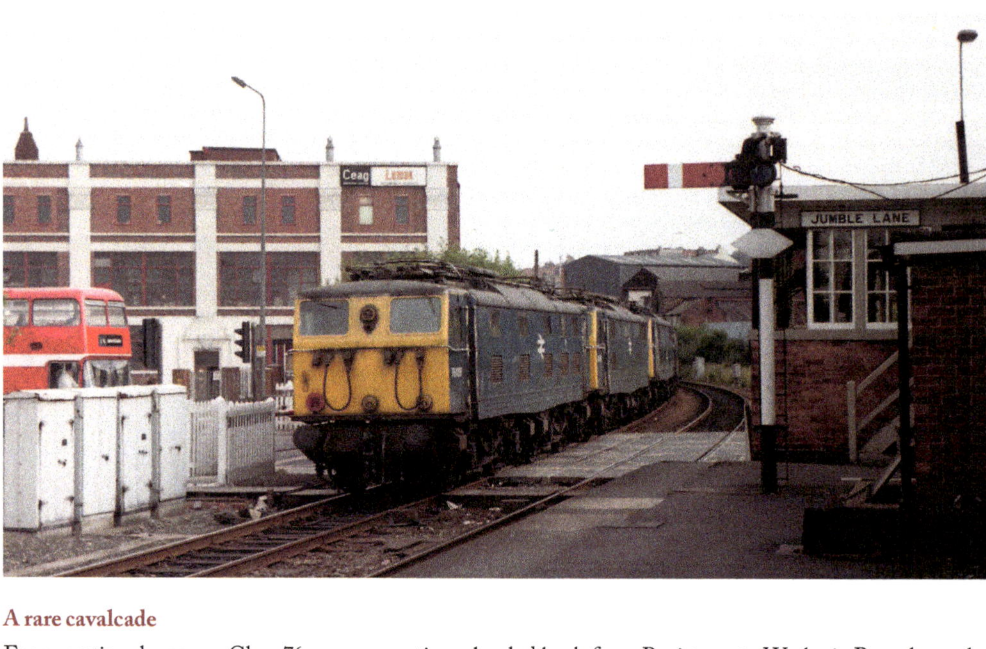

A rare cavalcade

For operational reasons, Class 76s were sometimes hauled back from Penistone to Wath via Barnsley rather than travelling under their own power via the Worsborough line, but the occasions were few and far between. Here a quartet of EM1s passes Jumble Lane level crossing in July 1981, just days before the closure of the Woodhead route. A Class 37 was providing the motive power. (Vaughan Hellam)

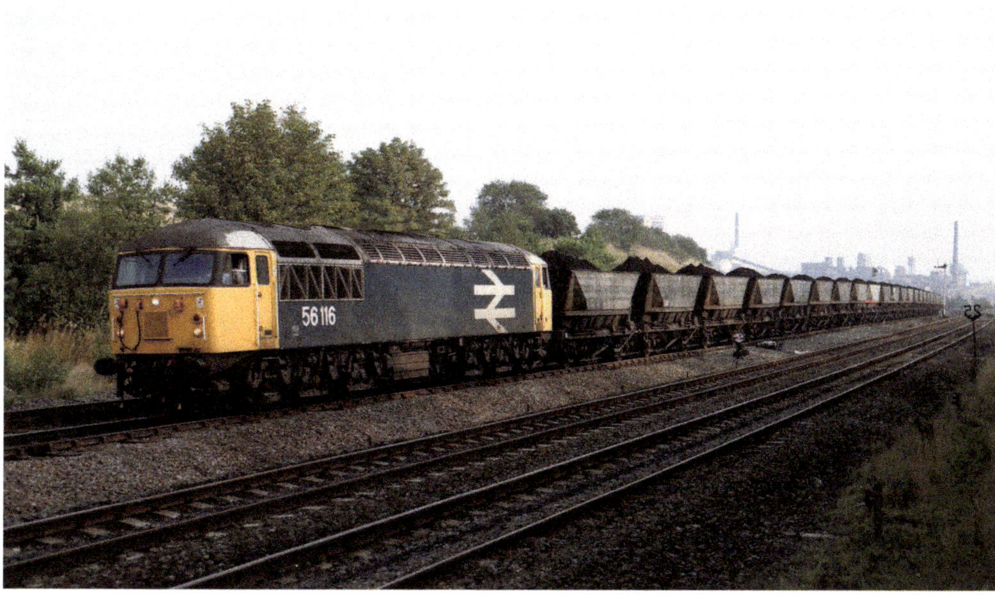

56116 powers past Royston

A loaded MGR service is seen here going north on the approach to Royston Junction on the former Midland main line in September 1983. In the distance can be seen the chimneys and infrastructure of the Monckton coking plant. The coal and coke industries of this region were in their twilight years at this time. (Vaughan Hellam)

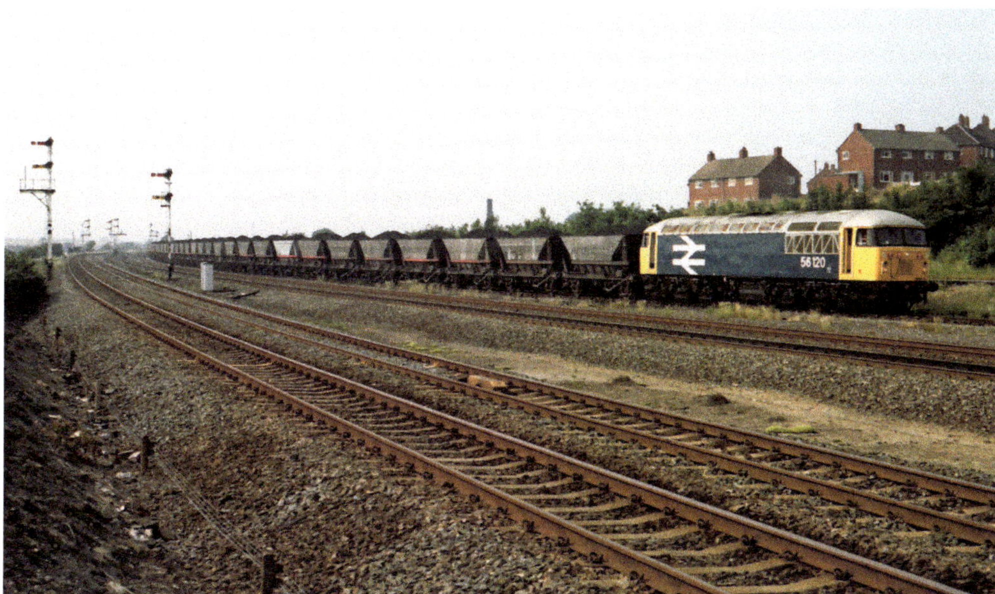

Immaculate Type 5 at Cudworth

This splendid panorama shows the view looking north at the site of the former Midland station at Cudworth on 11 July 1983. Nearly new Class 56 No. 56120 moves along one of the goods loops with a loaded MGR service. Cudworth South Junction is just to the rear of the train. The semaphore signals had just a couple of years left by this stage. (Vaughan Hellam)

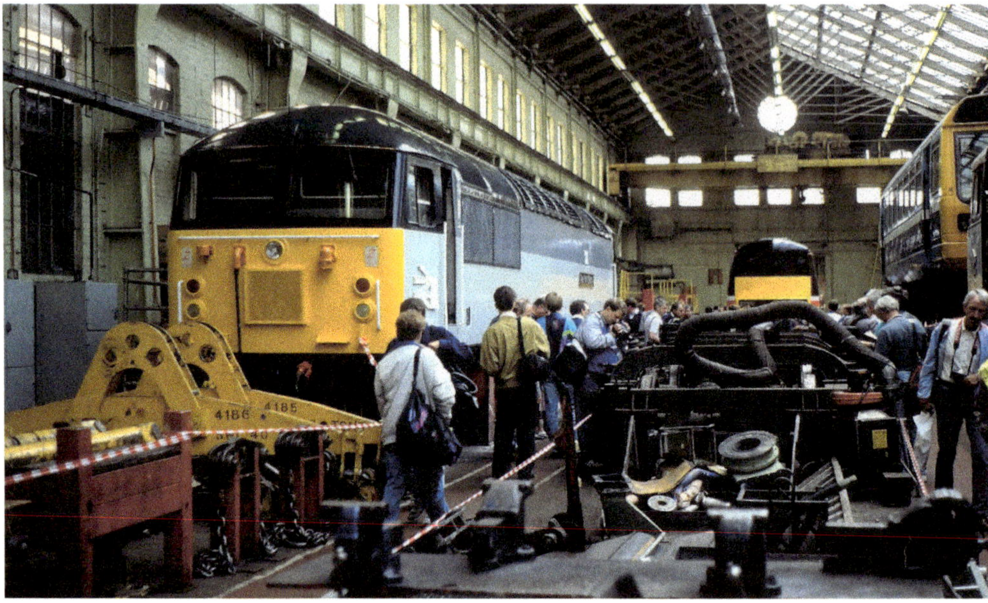

Doncaster hosts a Crewe-built Type 5

Now carrying two-tone grey livery and the name *Drax Power Station*, Crewe-built Class 56 No. 56123 returns to Doncaster for maintenance in the summer of 1992. In the background is one of the East Coast Class 91 electrics, and up on the jacks on the right, a 'Pacer' unit is receiving attention.

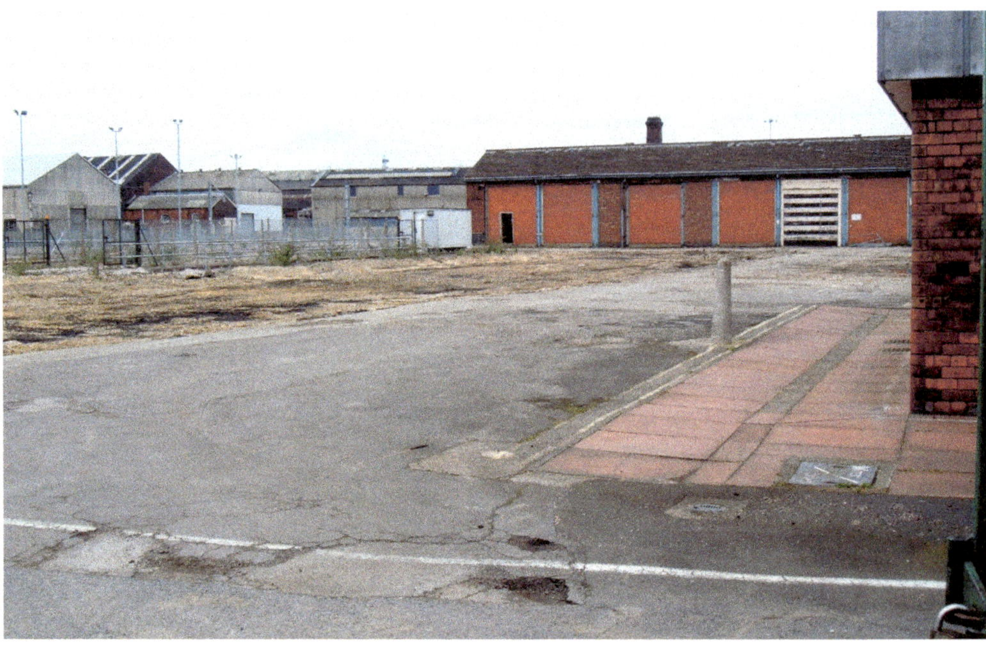

Where pristine machines once stood

This is the paint shop yard at Doncaster Works, seen after closure in April 2006. The doors of the paintshop itself have been bricked up and the tracks lifted as the era of the major works inherited from the age of steam comes to a close.

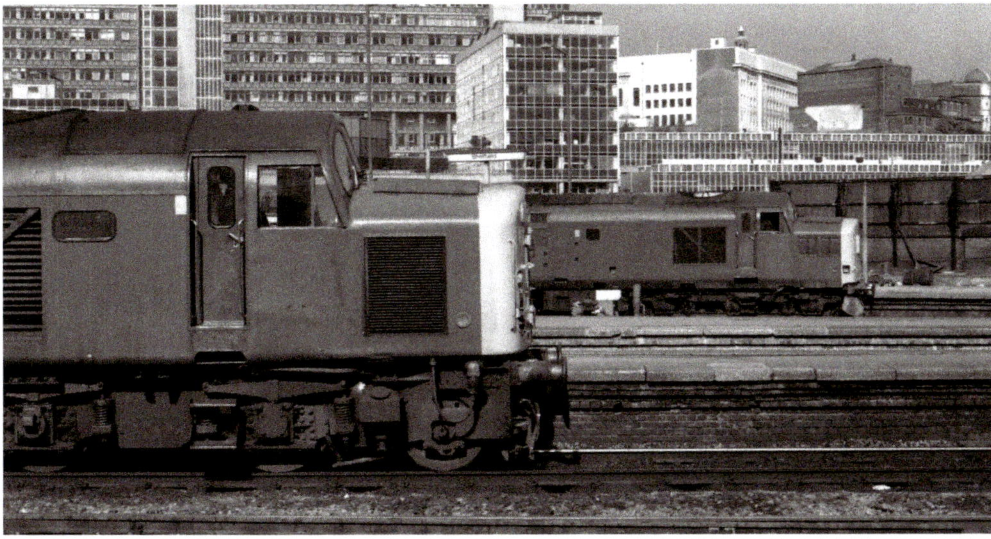

Summer Saturday profiles at Sheffield, July 1983

Locomotive-hauled services to the coast were part and parcel of summer Saturdays until the mid-1980s, and at Sheffield there was always plenty of variety in terms of destination and motive power. Here two familiar English Electric profiles are seen in the form of Nos 40034 and 37228 with Yarmouth and Blackpool services, respectively. (Vaughan Hellam)

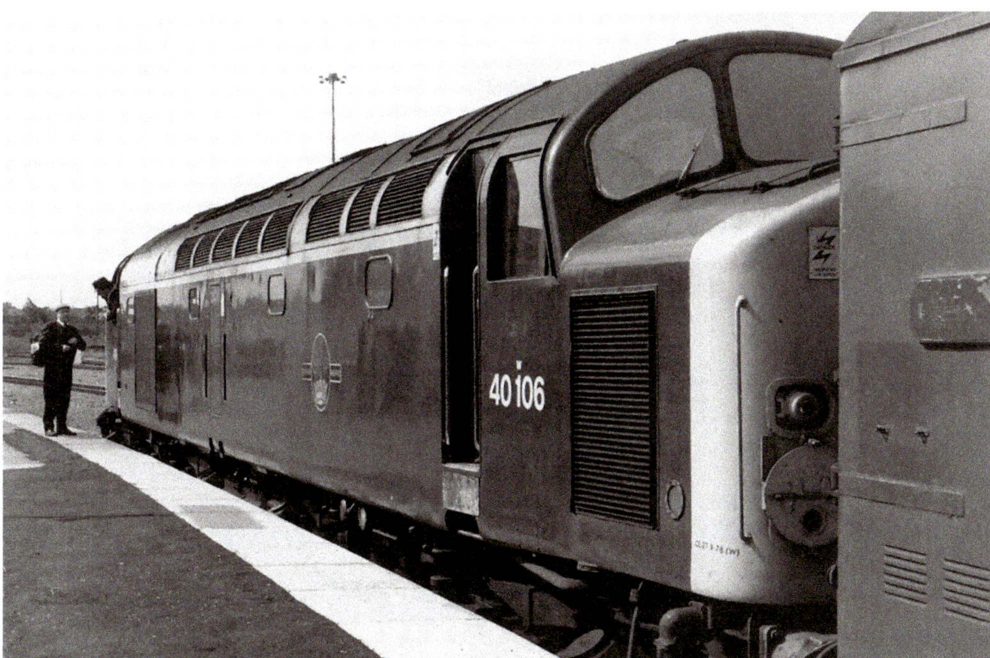

A quick word before departure

Doncaster station in May 1982, and celebrity Class 40 No. 40106, with reapplied green livery, waits for the right-away with the Red Bank parcels service. Parcels and newspaper traffic was not to last much longer on the railway network.

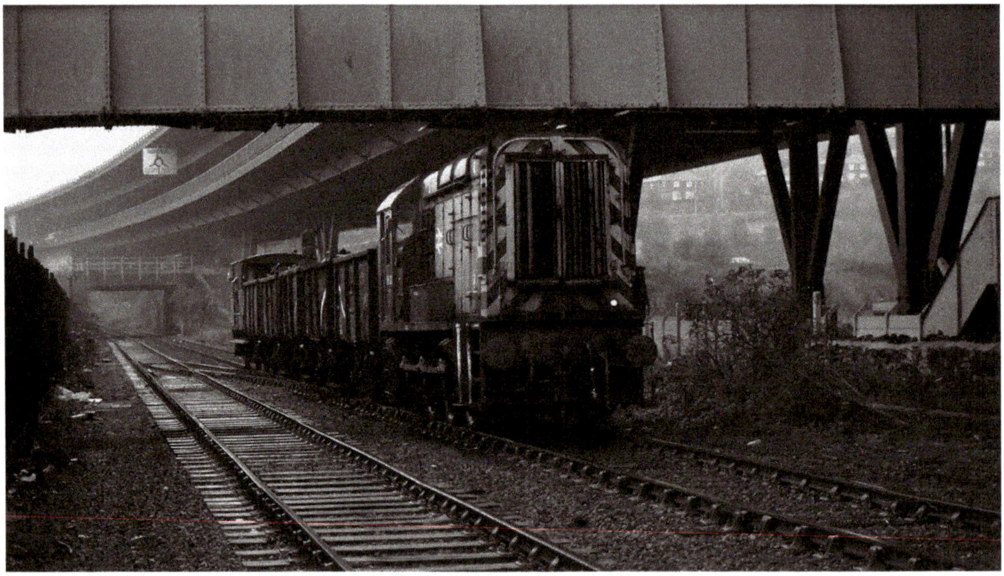

An industrial backwater

A little-seen stretch of track on the outskirts of Sheffield ran beneath the huge M1 viaduct at Tinsley to access scrapyards at Meadowhall and at Smithywood near Chapeltown; remnants of former Great Central lines in the area. Here in November 1984, Class 08 No. 08507 trundles past Tinsley West Junction with a trip working bound for Tinsley Yard.

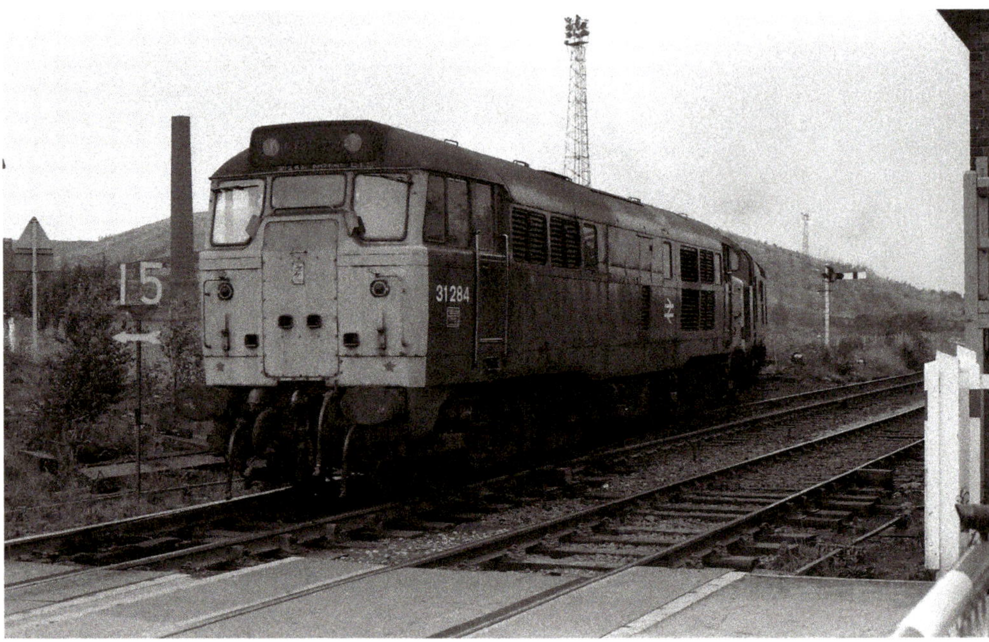

Class 31/37 combination against a colliery backdrop

The landscape here at Dodworth near Barnsley has changed out of all recognition since this picture was taken in July 1983. The line from Barnsley to Penistone survives, and there is still a level crossing here, but all traces of the colliery infrastructure have gone beneath commercial and landscaping development. (Vaughan Hellam)

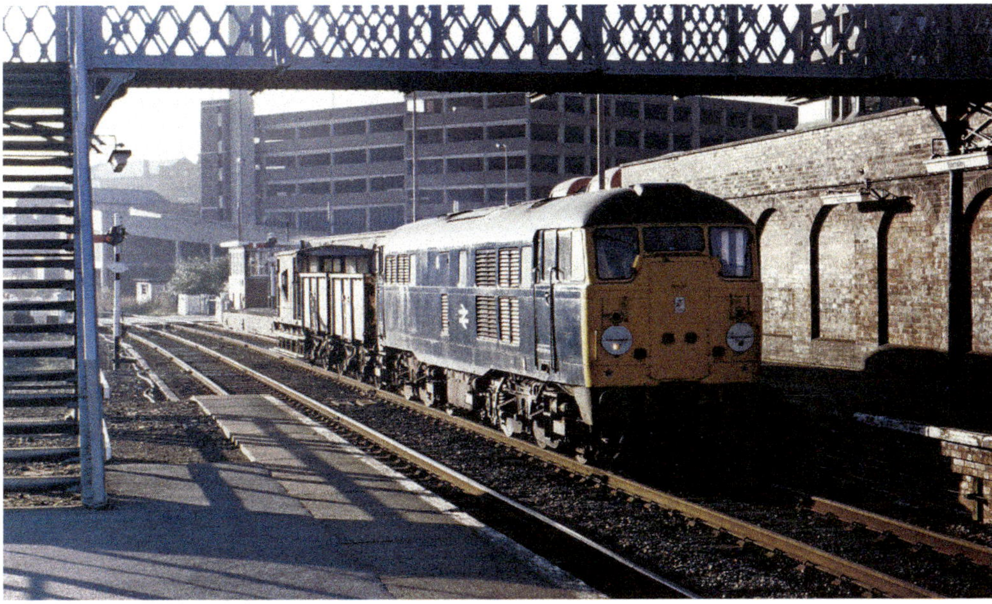

A winter's trip for No. 31102

On a bright and cold 5 November 1981, Tinsley's Class 31 No. 31102 trundles into Barnsley station with a trip working of two 16-tonne mineral wagons and brake van, probably destined for delivery to one or more of the many signal boxes in the vicinity that relied on rail-delivered solid fuel for their stoves. (Vaughan Hellam)

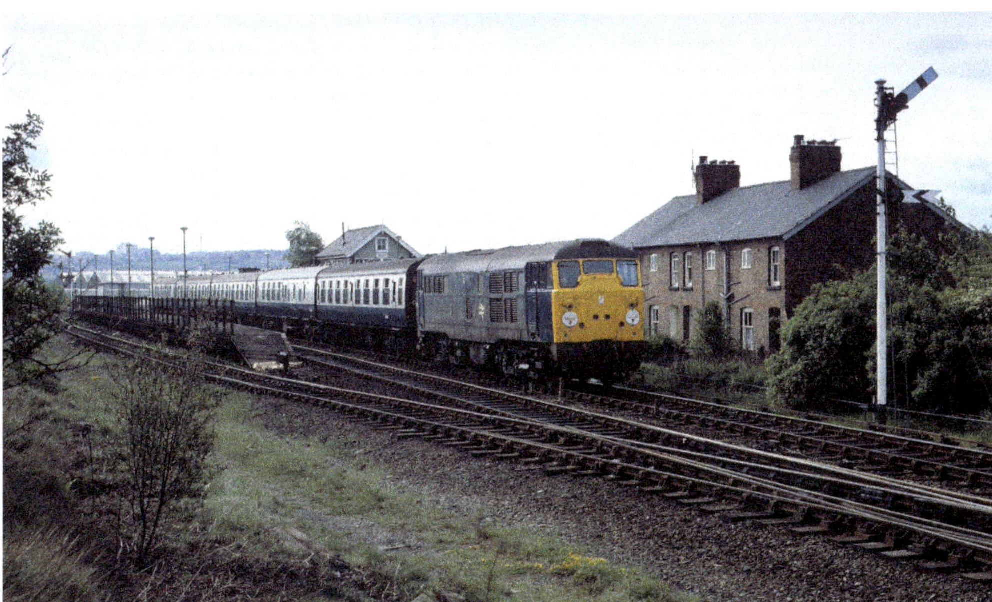

Off to the seaside, 1982 style

Class 31 No. 31102 puts in another appearance here at Darton in May 1982, with a summer Saturday service for Llandudno. The Type 2 will take the train as far as Huddersfield, where it will hand over to a Class 47 with a lengthened consist for the rest of the journey to North Wales.

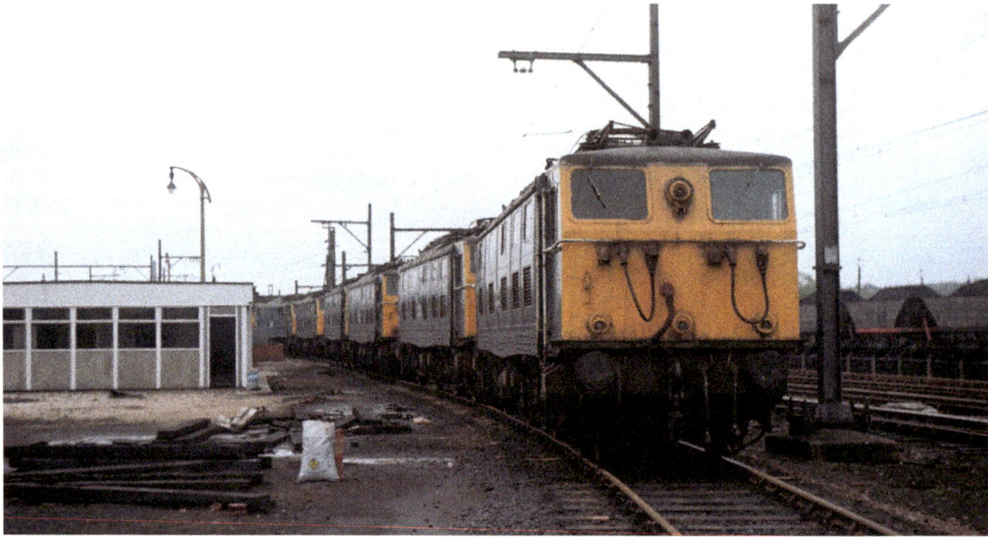

Familiar residents at Wath depot, May 1981

A line of Class 76s awaiting their next duties was a weekend fixture at Wath depot from the 1950s through to the very end of the Woodhead route in July 1981. Here in May of that year, dual-braked example No. 76006 heads up the group. The depot itself survived as a diesel-only location for another eighteen months or so before it too closed.

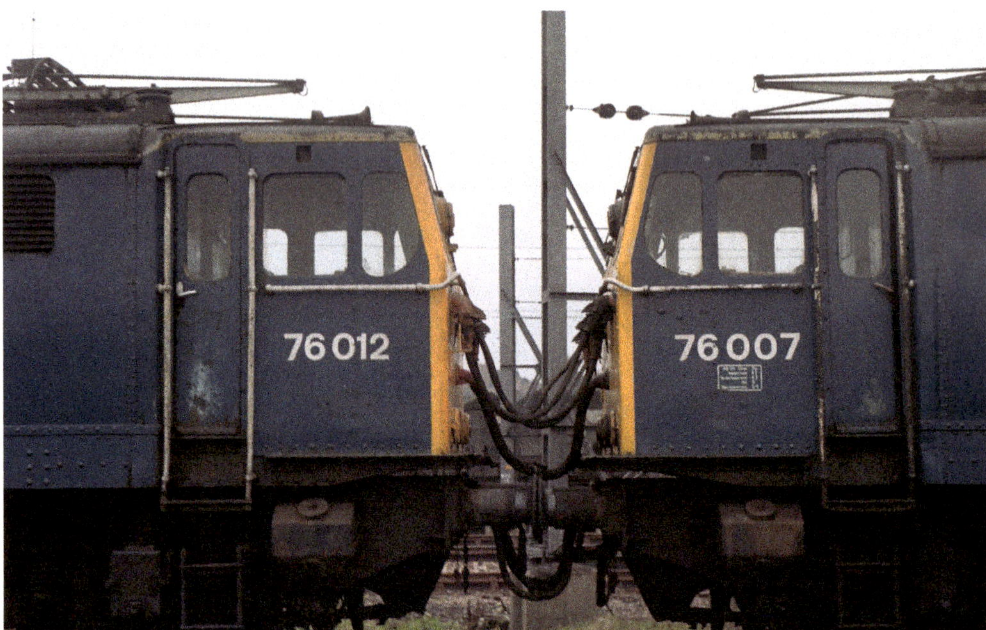

A dedicated pair

Class 76s Nos 76007 and 76012 spent most of their final months in service operating as a pair out of Wath depot, where they are pictured here taking a weekend rest in the spring of 1981. The dual-braked duo would become the very last of their Class to operate over the Wath to Penistone line on the afternoon of Friday 17 July 1981 – a rather sad footnote to the career of these enigmatic locomotives.

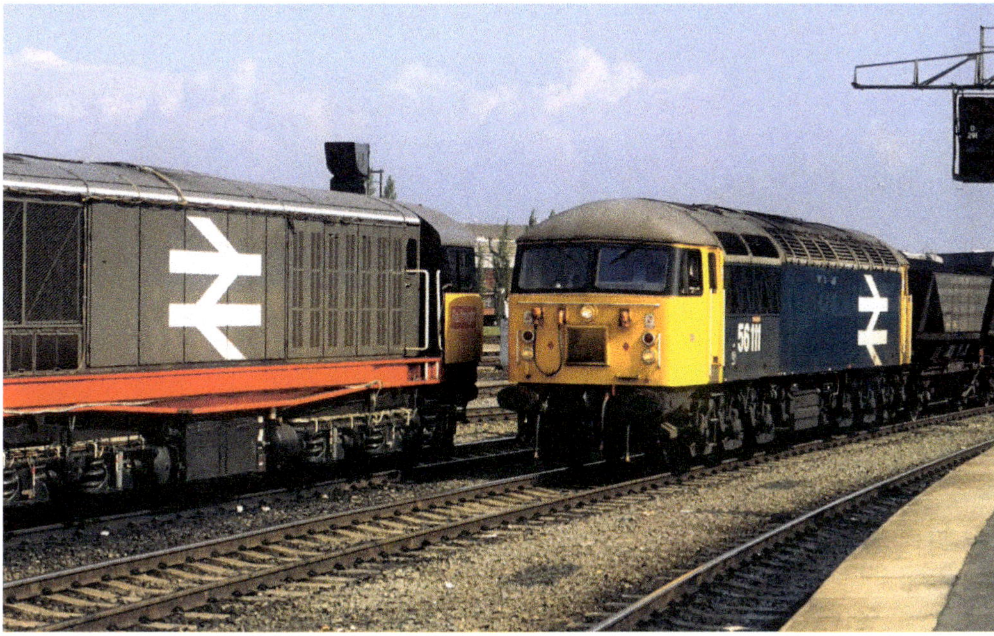

Type 5s pass at Doncaster

A bright June day in 1983 sees large-logo-liveried Class 56 No. 56111 taking the avoiding line around the station at Doncaster with a southbound coal train and passing recently built Class 58 No. 58001 which is waiting with a northbound freight.

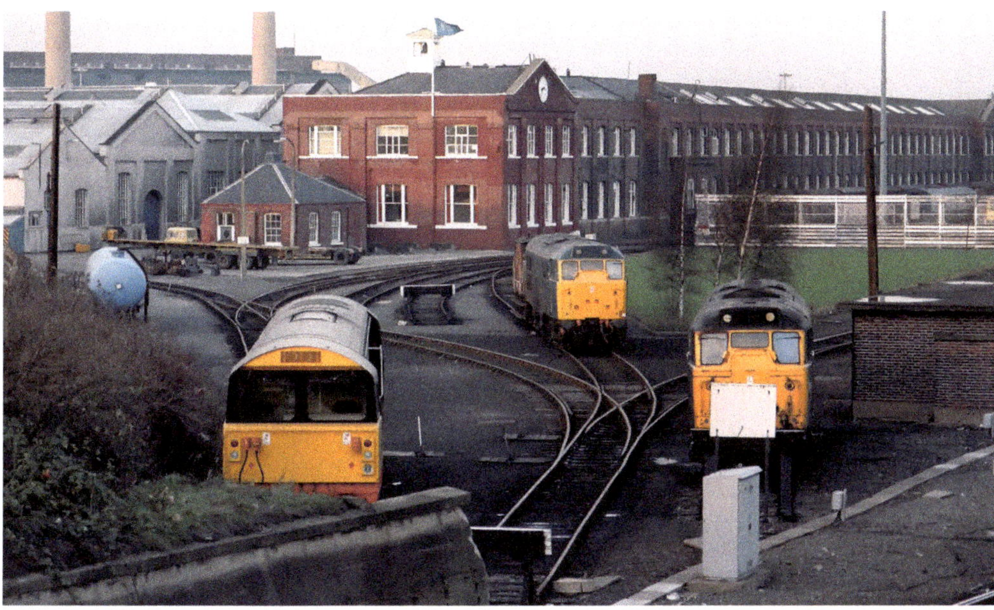

New build and old hands

Doncaster works in December 1984. Newly built Type 5 No. 58020 is about to be released to traffic as Class 31s Nos 31420 and 31457 await attention. No. 31457, in the background, had been outshopped a few weeks earlier and was back at the works to have a fault rectified.

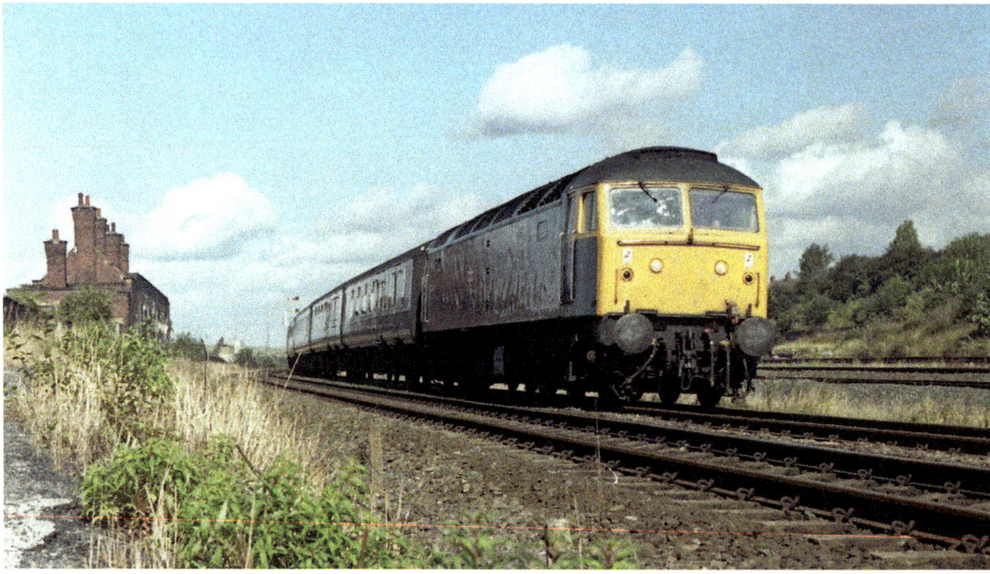

Main line power through Cudworth

The Midland Railway built its first Barnsley station here at Cudworth, some three miles from the town centre, in an effort to maintain minimal gradients on the route north of Sheffield. North East to South West expresses were still routed through here in the early 1980s, though the station had gone in 1968. Here No. 47488 heads south in September 1981. (Vaughan Hellam)

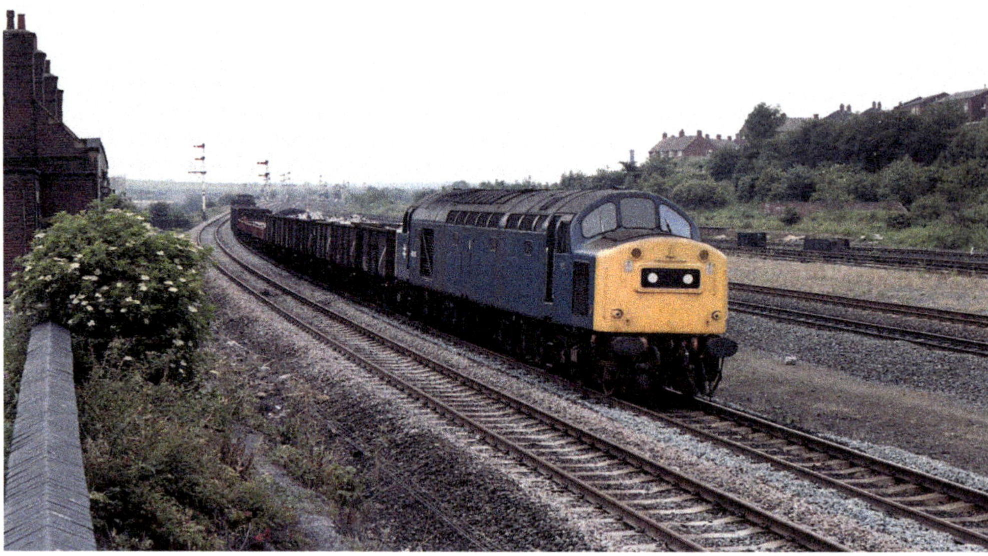

A classic mixed freight under the semaphores

The Midland main line at Cudworth remained un-modernised to the end. Here in the summer of 1982, Class 40 No. 40196 goes south past the remains of the former passenger station. This once substantial junction was very much reduced in status by the end of the 1960s and sadly disappeared completely by the late 1980s. (Vaughan Hellam)

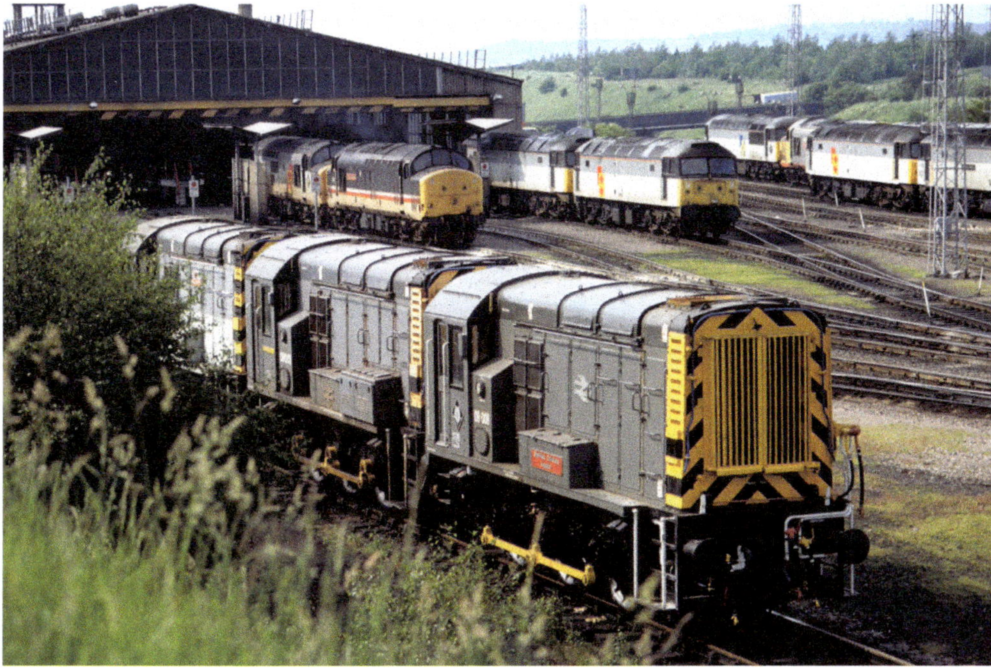

A trio of EE shunters at Tinsley

This nicely turned-out Class 09 was on shed at Tinsley in the summer of 1993. No. 09008, named *Sheffield Children's Hospital*, looks to have had a recent repaint and stands in front of sister No. 09013. Behind is Class 08 No. 08509, a veteran of the Sheffield scene.

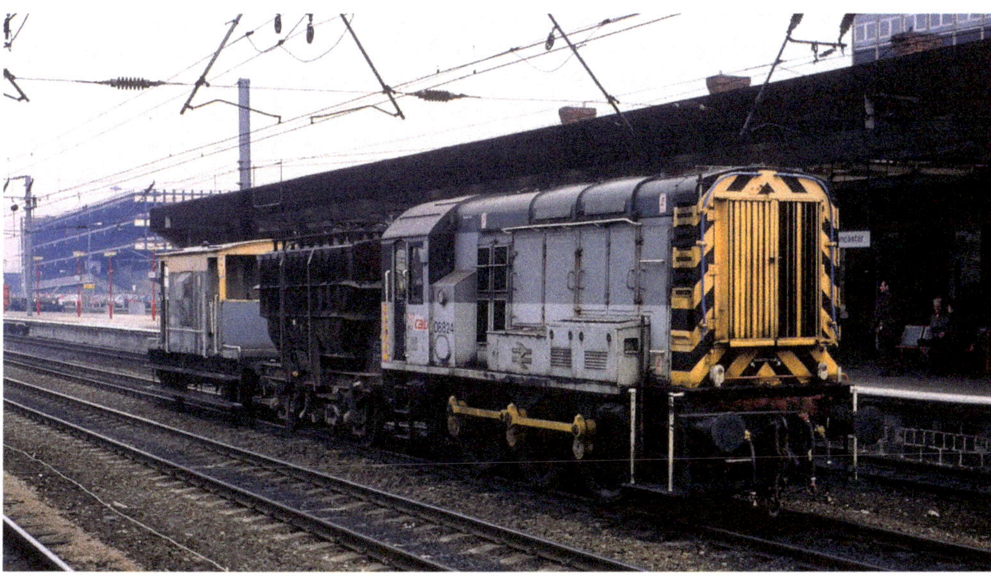

Short-term freight at Doncaster

Hauling a train that is not much longer than itself, Class 08 No. 08824 trundles through Doncaster on the Up fast line with a single wagon and brake van on 14 November 1992. Later used as an internal shunter at Crewe International Electric Depot, No. 08824 was re-liveried into LNWR black and given the number IEMD 01.

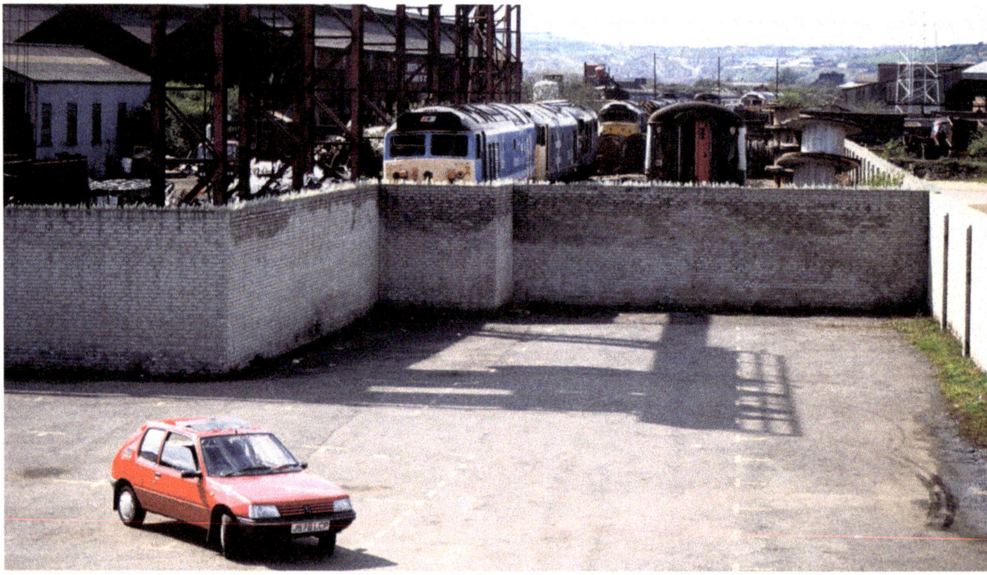

A far cry from Vulcan Foundry

Class 50s Nos 50023 and 50040 find themselves at the end of the road here at Booth's scrapyard in Rotherham. Built by English Electric at Vulcan Foundry in 1967, the Class 50, or D400, fleet was gradually depleted during the 1990s. Many went on to survive in preservation, some subsequently returning to the national network to enjoy a new lease of life.

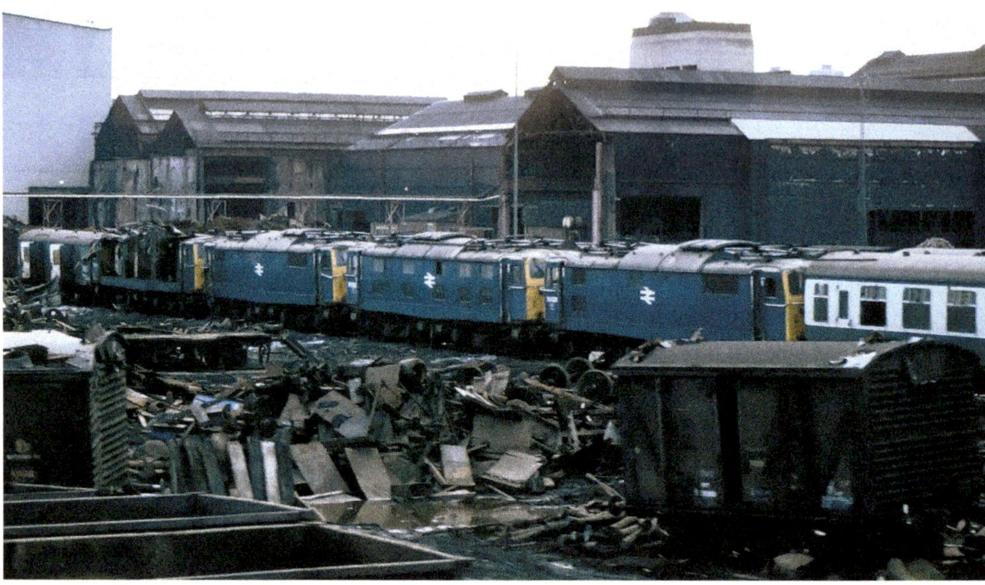

Built in Manchester, scrapped in Sheffield

Four of the 'Woodhead' electrics meet the cutter's torch at Cooper's scrapyard in Attercliffe, in this image from March 1983, around eighteen months after the closure of the trans-Pennine electrification. The requirement to remove asbestos from some of the Class 76 bodyshells delayed the scrapping process, meaning that several withdrawn examples languished in a boarded-up condition at Reddish depot for many years in the late 70s.

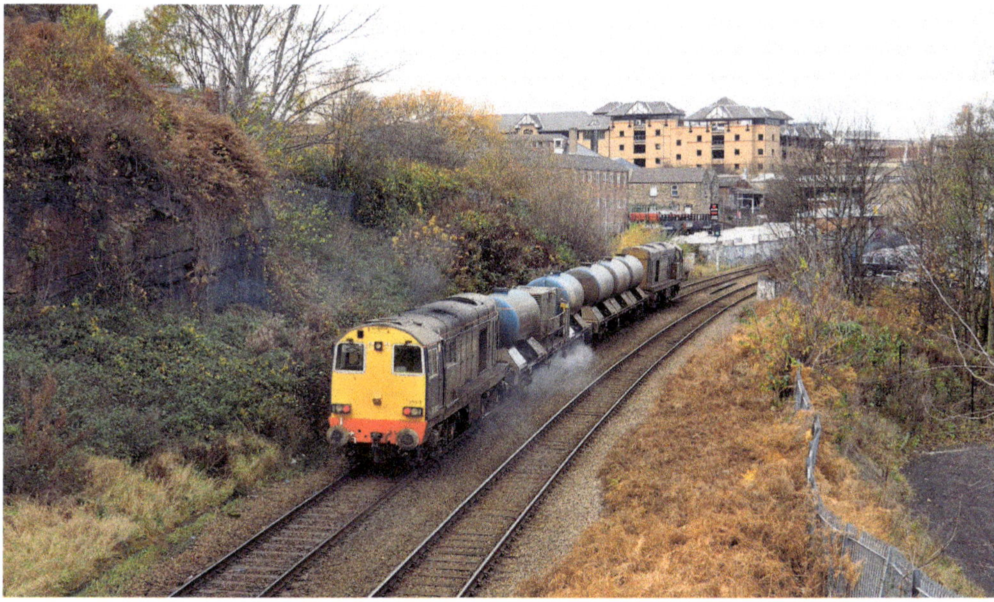

More water jetting activity at Barnsley

Another pair of Class 20s makes its way towards Barnsley with the Rail Head Treatment Train in December 2017. The train is about to pass beneath Harborough Hills Road with the town's Alhambra shopping centre prominent on the horizon.

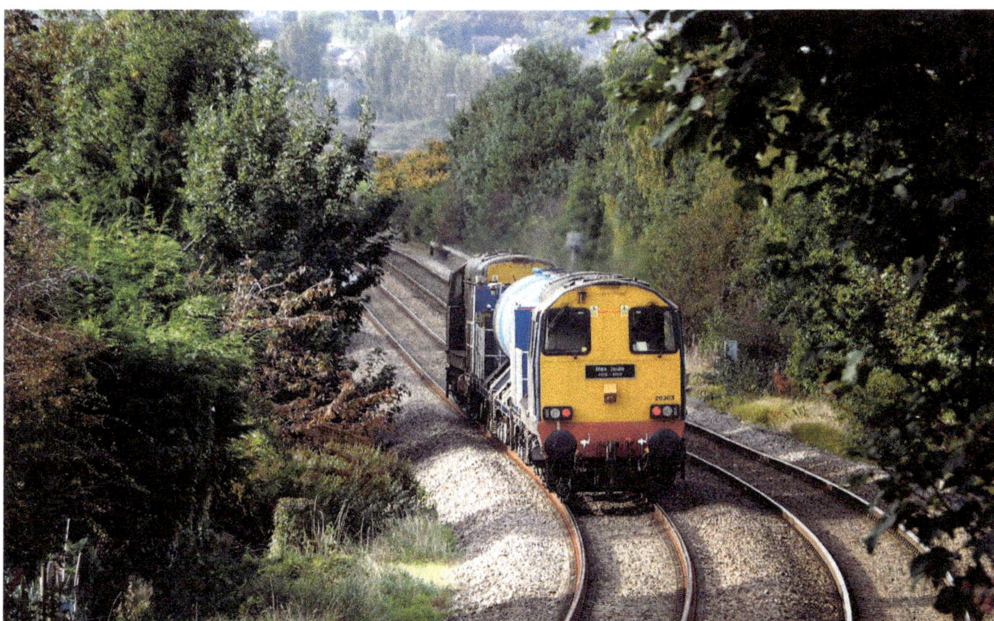

Leaf fall imminent at Willow Bank

Illustrating the risk to traction posed by leaf fall on the lines, a Rail Head Treatment Train passes through a tree-lined Willow Bank, between Barnsley and Darton, in October 2016. Many lines have seen incredible tree growth in the last couple of decades and the RHTTs work hard to keep the rails clear.

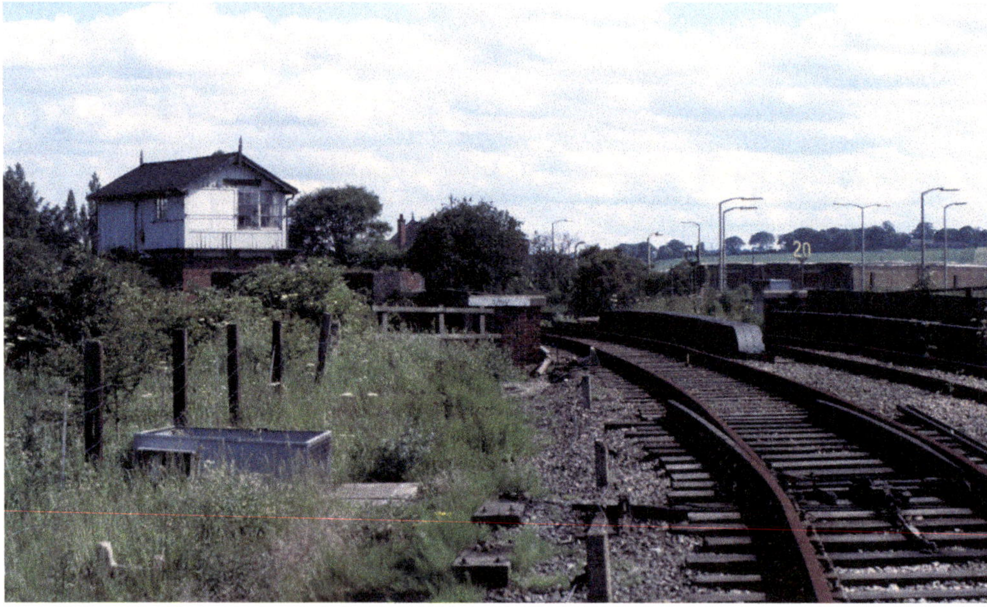

The end of railways at Stairfoot, 1985

For virtually a century, railway lines criss-crossed the landscape in and around Stairfoot to the east of Barnsley, legacy of the Victorian promoters and the numerous railway companies who sought access to coal reserves in the area. By 1985, the rusting former Hull & Barnsley lines and the shell of the GC box at Stairfoot Junction constitute the forlorn remains of a once thriving network.

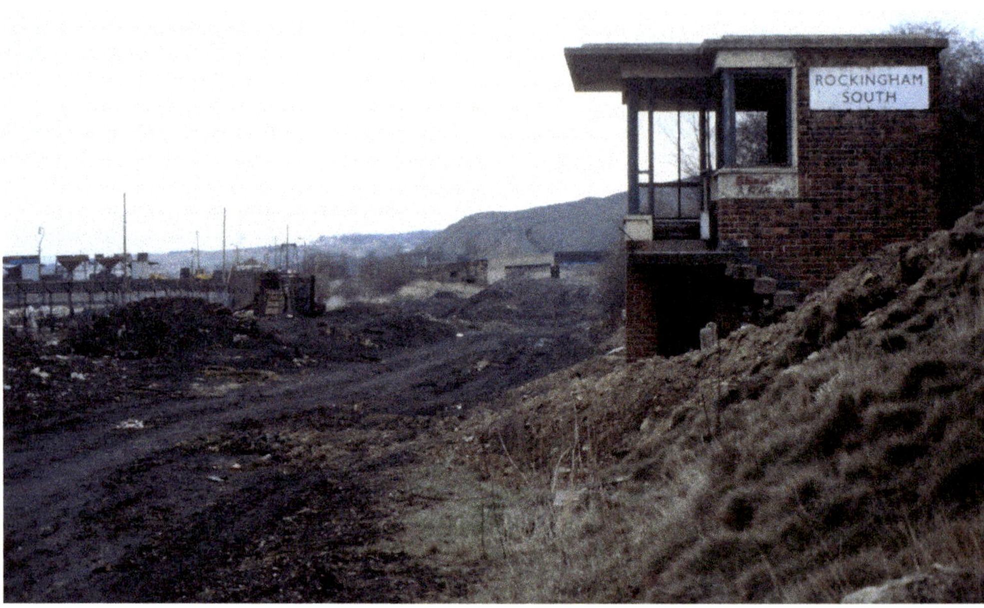

Remains of industry and railway at Rockingham South

Birdwell, to the south of Barnsley, was the location of Rockingham colliery and the site of a former Great Central station on a route which once ran from Wombwell to Sheffield. Here in 1985, the shell of Rockingham South signalbox is about all that remains of the infrastructure in the wake of the closure of the pit.

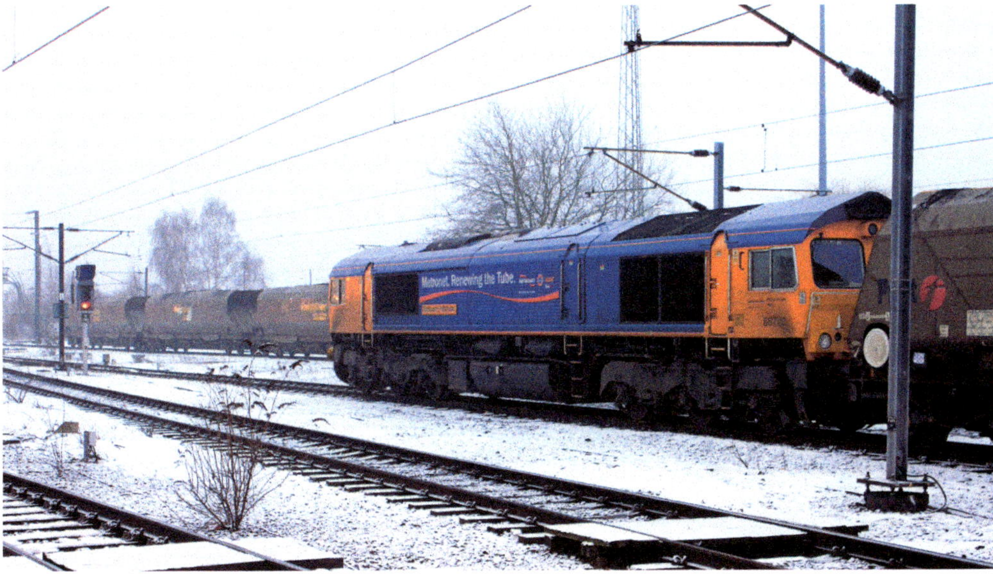

Freezing Doncaster, January 2010

A freezing mist envelops Doncaster station on 14 January 2010. Class 66 No. 66720 waits in one of the loops with a southbound coal train. This locomotive was later the recipient of a multi-coloured vinyl wrap livery designed by six-year-old schoolgirl Emily Goodman, who won a 'design a livery' competition organised by rail operator GBRf.

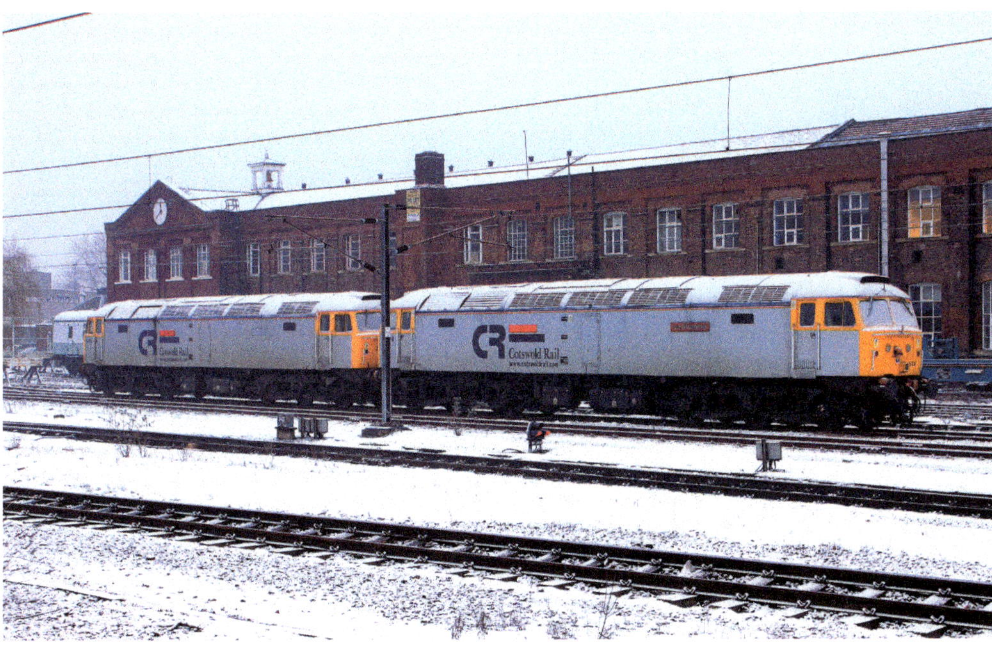

Blending with the mist at Doncaster

Wearing their relatively short-lived Cotswold Rail colours, Class 47s Nos 47813 and 47828, *Joe Strummer*, stand outside the works at Doncaster on what looks like a bitterly cold 14 January 2010. Somewhat aptly, No. 47813 was renamed *Jack Frost* in 2019.

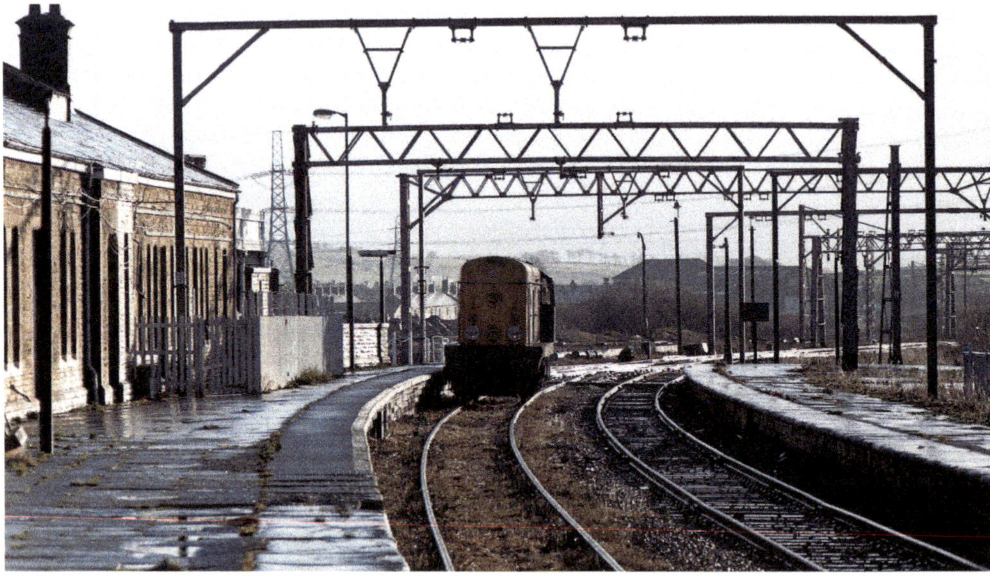

Forlorn remnants of a brave new world

Just thirty years earlier, this was the scene of a pioneering electrified main line between Sheffield and Manchester. By 1987, the skeletal remains of the overhead gantries stand starkly against the Pennine sky as a single Class 20 makes its way to Penistone Goods to assist in salvage work on the former Woodhead line. (Vaughan Hellam)

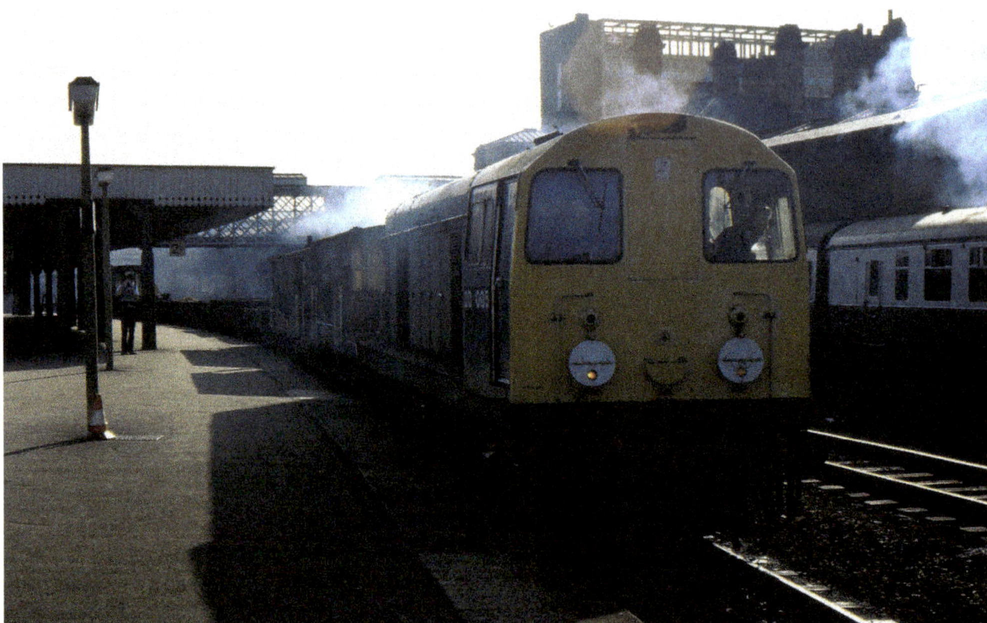

Autumnal atmosphere at Sheffield

A chilly October morning in 1982 sees Tinsley-based Type 1 No. 20005 standing at Sheffield station with an engineer's train. The two leading brake vans are smoking away merrily, their stoves clearly in good working order. It's unlikely that this sort of atmospheric emission would be tolerated today though. (Vaughan Hellam)

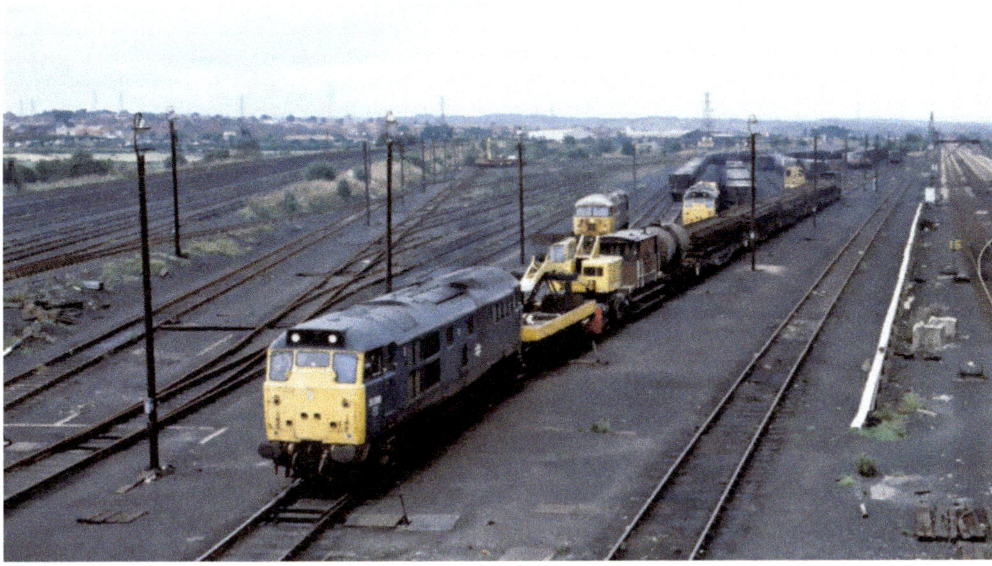

A busy scene at Wath Yard, 1982

It's a deceptively busy picture at Wath Yard in September 1982, as much of the activity seen here is associated with dismantling and salvage of the Woodhead route and the marshalling yard itself, which was very much in its twilight years. Many of the sidings lie empty as No. 31316 stands at the head of a track recovery train.

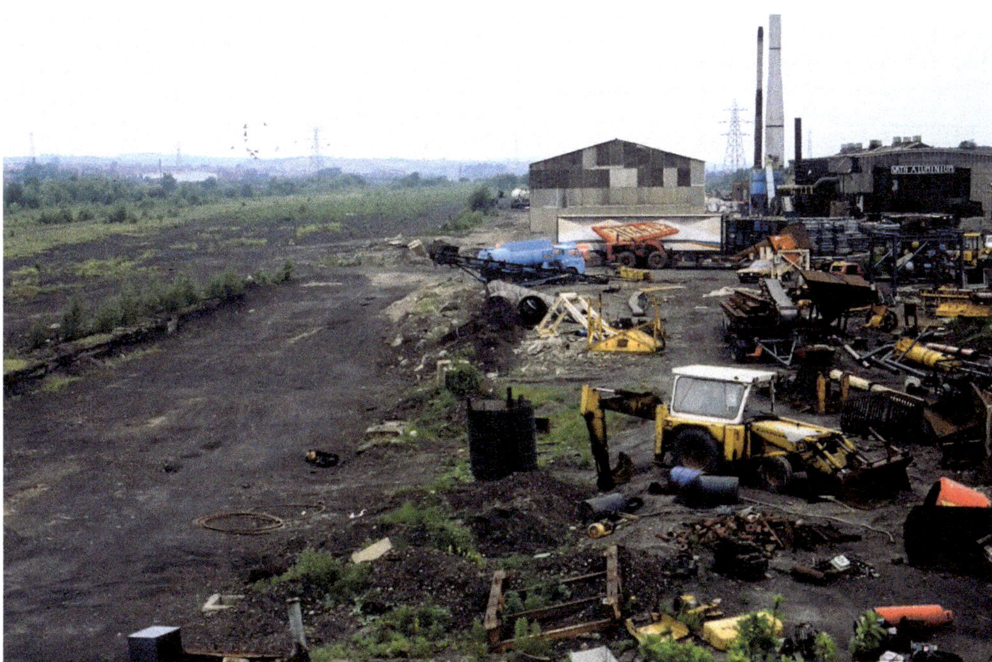

Industry of another sort, Wath 1990

Following its closure as a diesel maintenance depot, the shed at Wath was turned to other uses. Here in 1990 the former marshalling yard presents a desolate picture alongside the aluminium smelting business established on the site of the depot. This is around three years after the last tracks were lifted here.

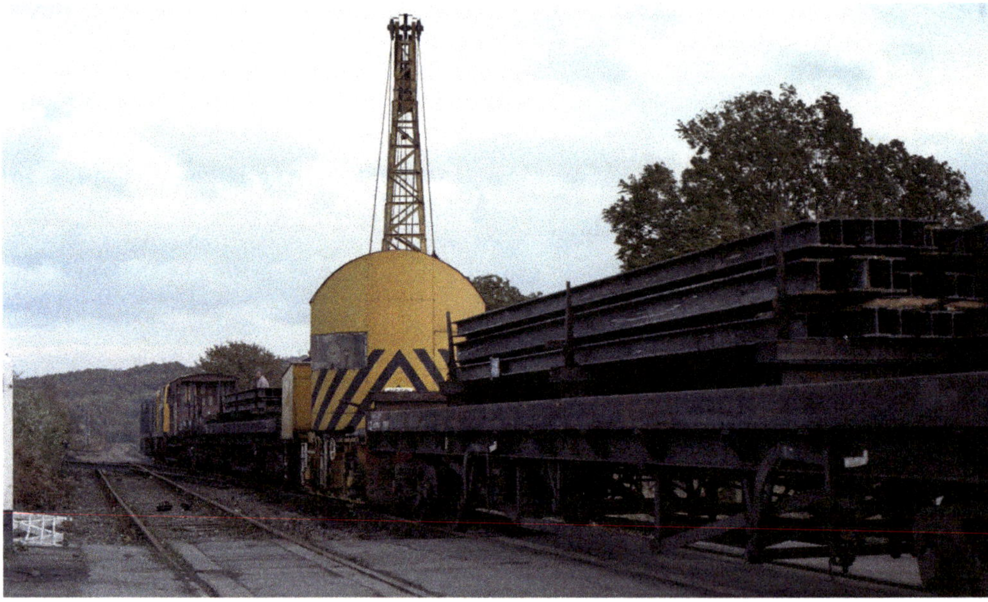

Salvaging the remains of the Wath branch at Worsborough Dale

It did not take long for the salvage crews to move in following the closure of the line from Wombwell Main Junction to West Silkstone Junction in the summer of 1981. Here in November of that year, a crane lifts the severed electrification gantries onto wagons. This is at the site of Worsborough Dale level crossing.

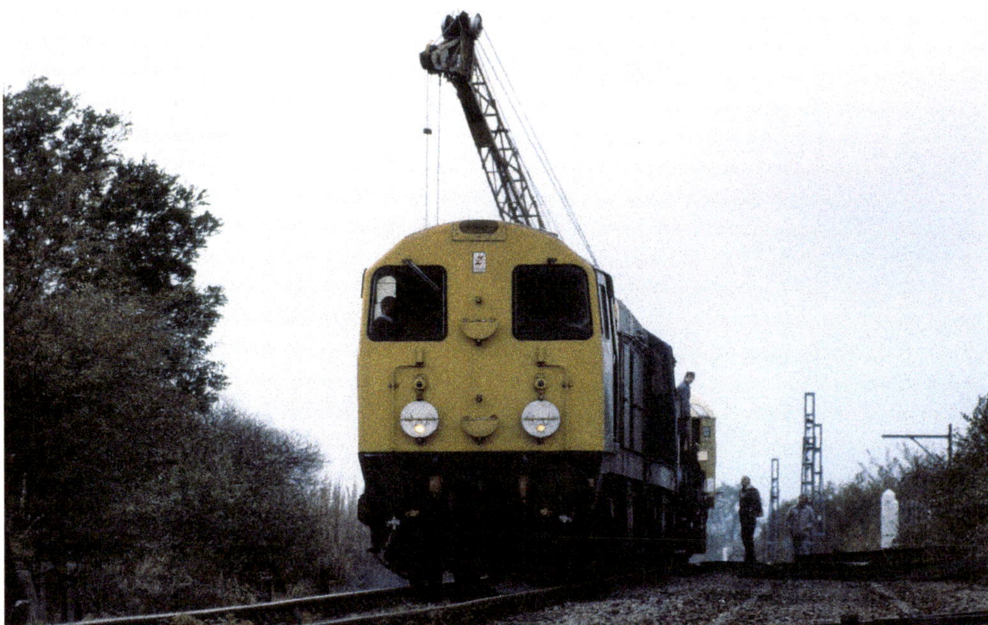

Dismantling the Wath branch at Worsborough Dale

The dismantling of the Penistone to Wath section of the Woodhead line began almost straight away after closure in July 1981. The line was already reduced to a single track by the time of this picture, in November of that year, showing a pair of Class 20s engaged in overhead gantry recovery. (Vaughan Hellam)

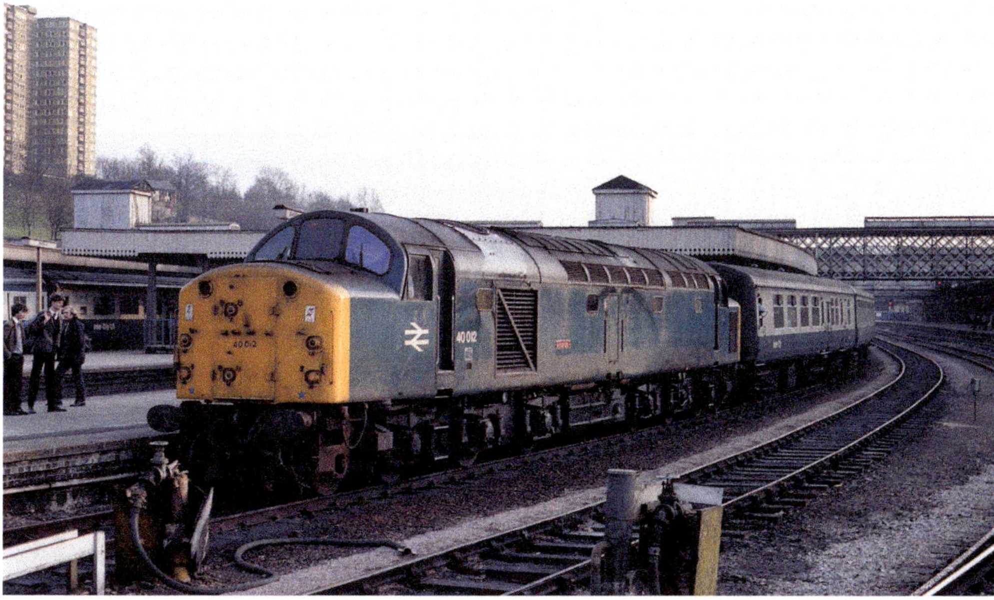

The days of locomotive hauled InterCity trains

The engine is at the front, not under the floor, for the passengers on this Birmingham to Leeds service, seen at Sheffield with Class 40 No. 40012 *Aureol* on 10 March 1983. A rake of Mk II stock provides the spacious accommodation for travellers – and for those who do want to hear the mechanicals, a window can always be opened. (Vaughan Hellam)

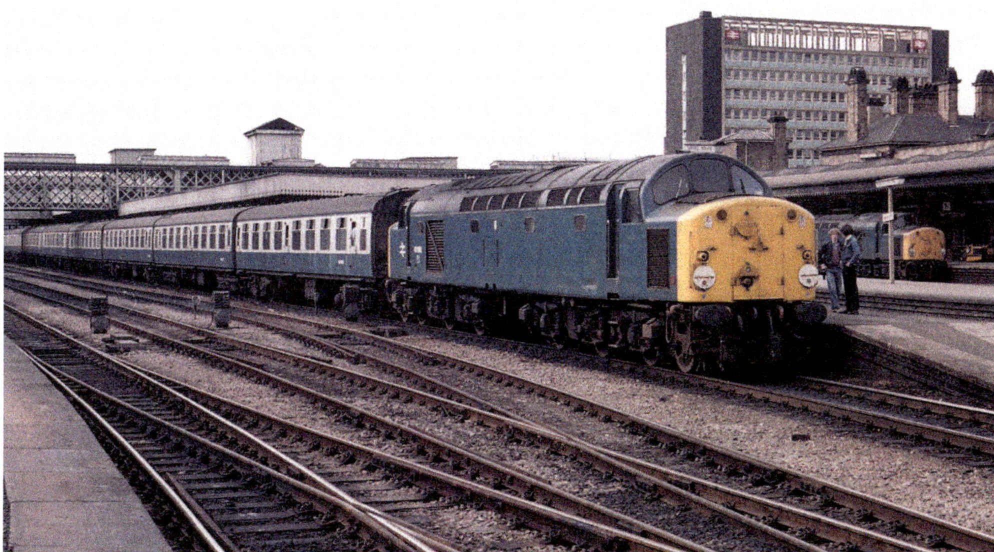

More Class 40 variety at Sheffield

The morning of 3 July 1982 saw several Class 40-hauled services scheduled to call at Sheffield. Here, two of them await departure, with No. 40082 in the foreground on a Manchester to Skegness turn, while No. 40081 is at platform 1 with a service for Blackpool. (Vaughan Hellam)

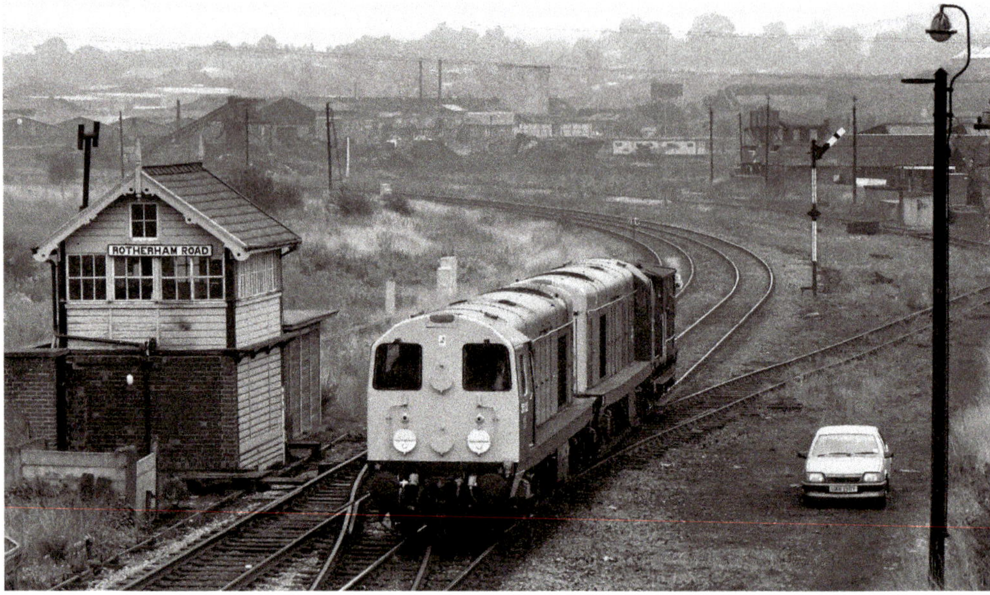

Under semaphores at Rotherham Road

Despite the roll out of modernisation schemes across the region, some lines and freight-only backwaters escaped upgrading for a remarkably long time. Here at Rotherham Road in 1984, a pair of Class 20s trundles north with a brakevan, passing the classic GC manual box, which would survive for another four years.

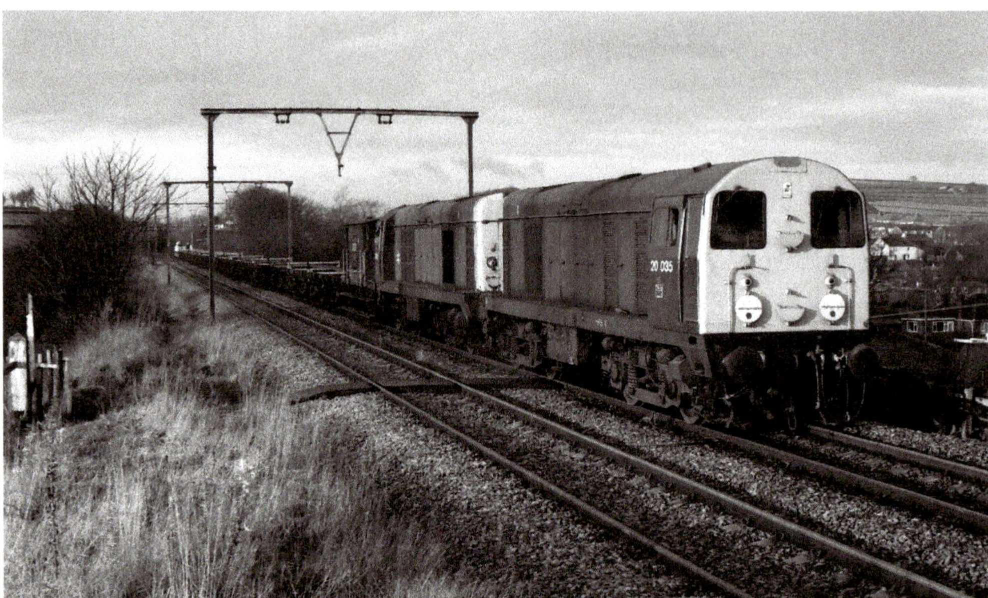

One of the last Woodhead winters

The well-maintained permanent way near Penistone Goods is seen to good effect here, as a pair of Class 20s heads towards Sheffield with a salvage train from Dunford Bridge. It is November 1983, and soon there will be just a single track here, as the relentless process of dismantling continues. Even two years after closure, this does not look like a life-expired railway line. (Vaughan Hellam)

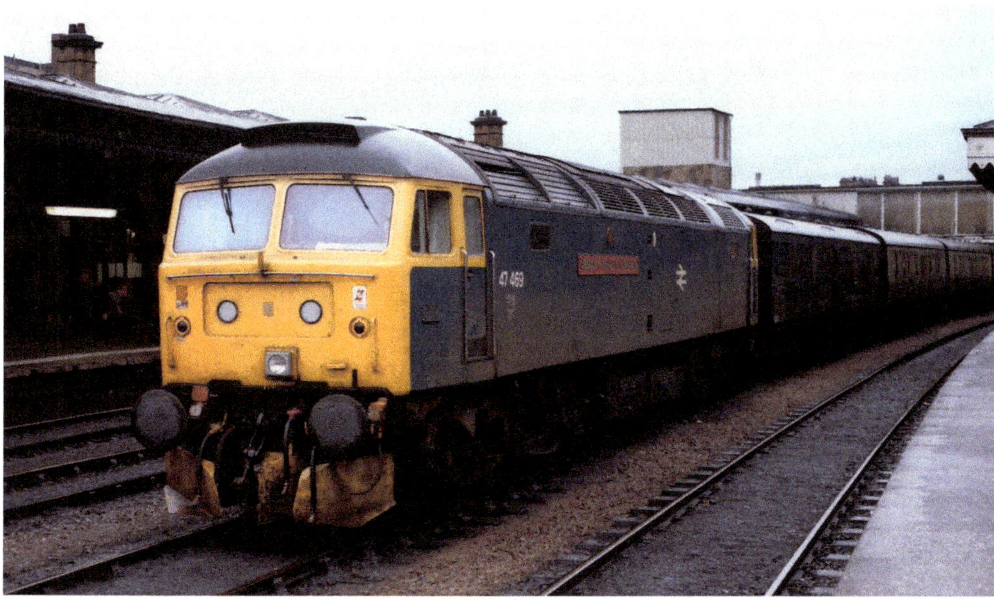

Scottish Brush Type 4 on parcels

Class 47 No. 47469 *Glasgow Chamber of Commerce*, one of a number fitted with small snowploughs, stands at Sheffield in October 1984 with the Cleethorpes–Red Bank empty parcels service, which had hitherto been a regular Class 40 diagram. (Vaughan Hellam)

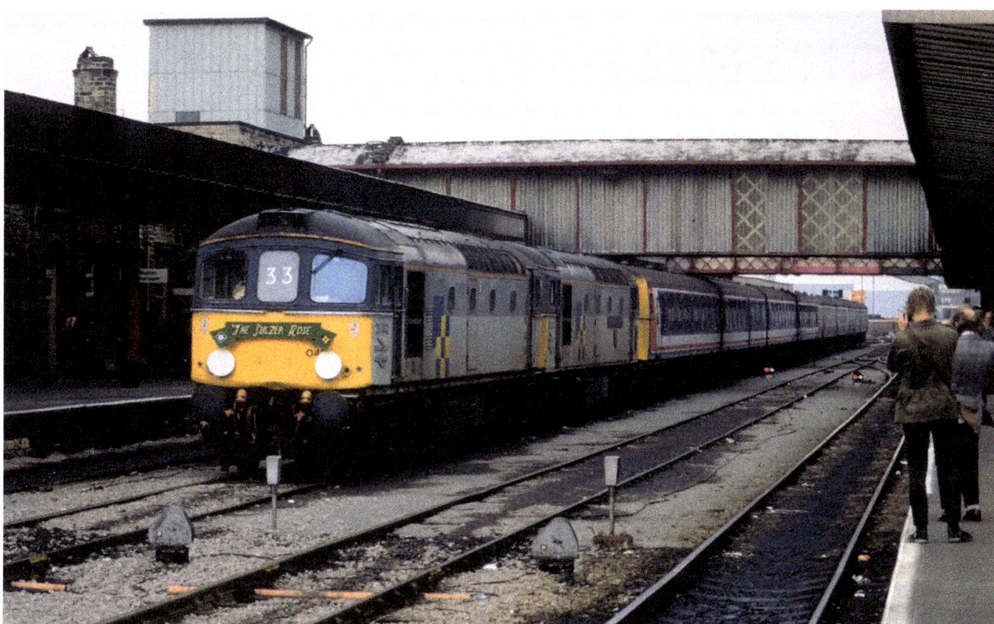

Rare visitors to Sheffield for the Tinsley Open Day, 1990

A pair of Class 33s was rostered for the 'Sulzer Rose' railtour of 29 September 1990. The trip ran from Eastleigh and employed two 4TC EMU sets for the coaching stock. Here Nos 33042 and 33207 stand at Sheffield while tour participants head to Tinsley by DMU shuttle.

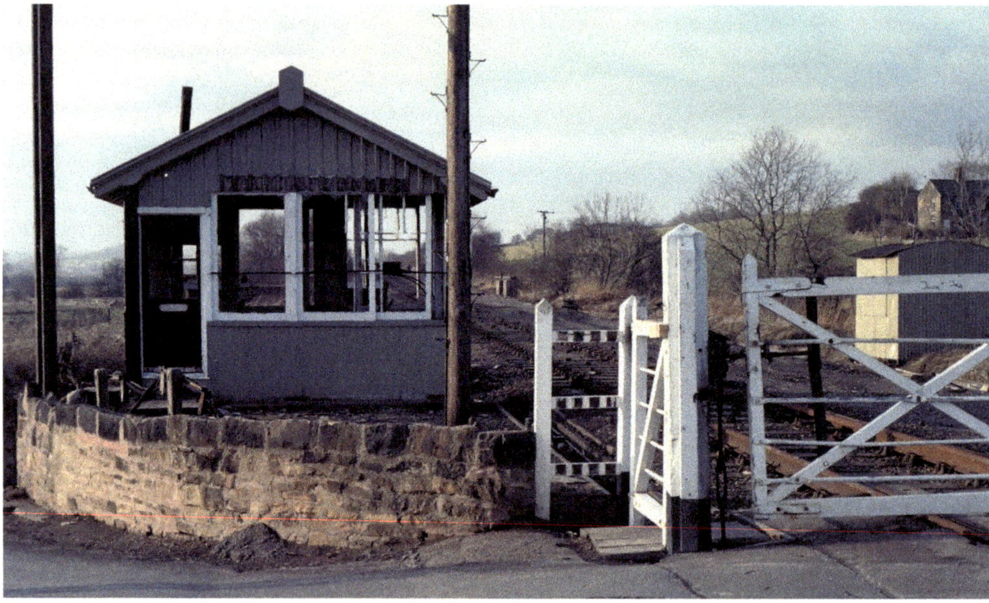

Quiet desolation at Kendall Green

Following the closure of the Wath to Penistone branch, a somewhat piecemeal dismantling process began. Here at Kendall Green, the small gate box was reduced to a shell by January 1982, around six months after closure. One track remains across the road.

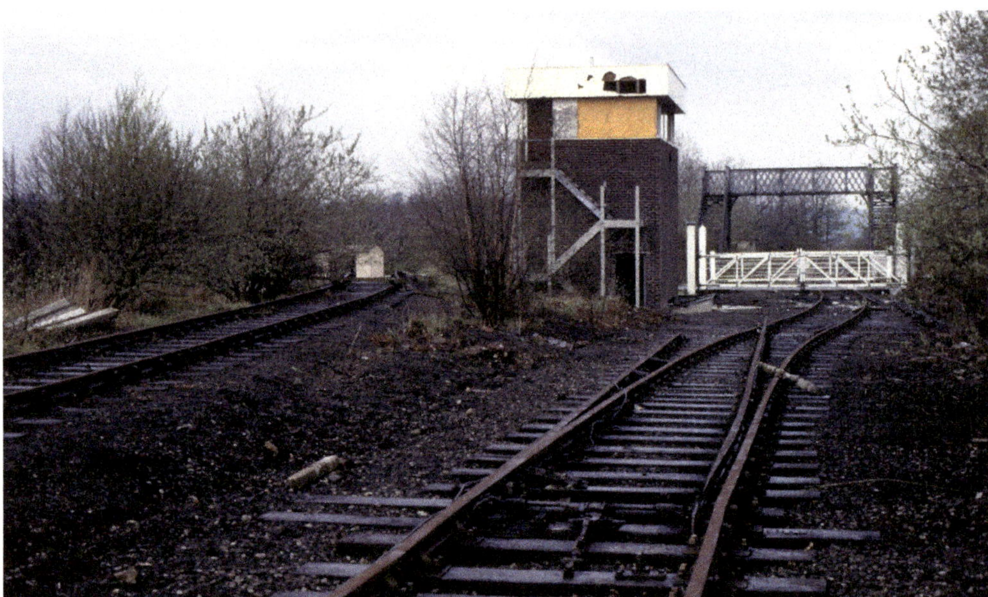

Dovecliffe gently decays

The BR-built signalbox at Dovecliffe, on the former GC route from Wombwell to Sheffield, was only commissioned in 1974 to replace the ancient MS&LR structure there. By 1986 it was sitting derelict following the closure of nearby Barrow, the last remaining colliery on the line. It remained in this state for several years, BR management seemingly having washed its hands of any responsibility for tidy demolition.

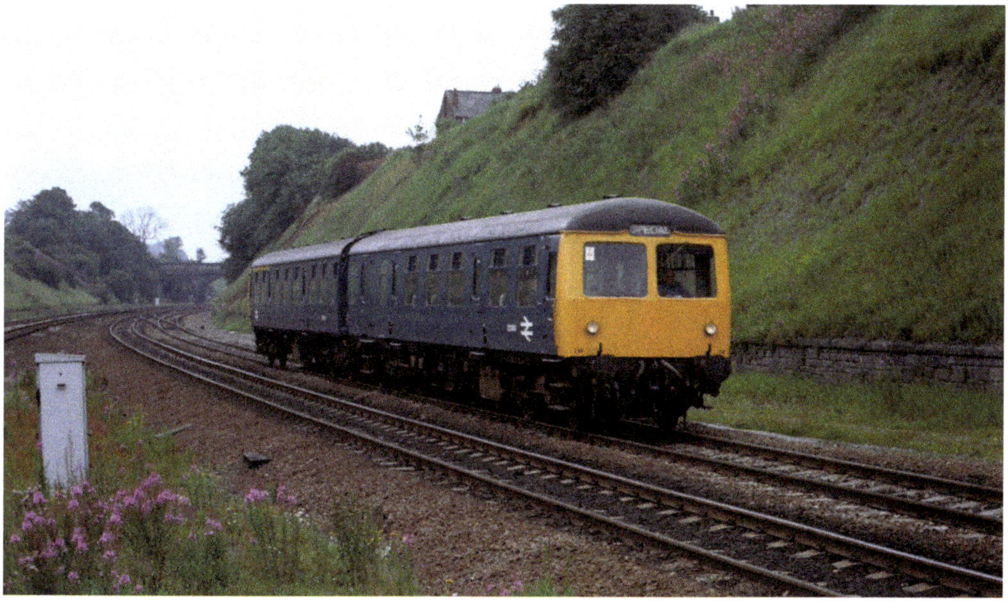

On the approach to Masborough

Looking north from the now-closed Rotherham Masborough station, a Cravens DMU approaches on the Treeton lines in the summer of 1982. The 'special' destination blind is appropriate, as there were no timetabled passenger services on these tracks at the time, so this is a somewhat unusual working.

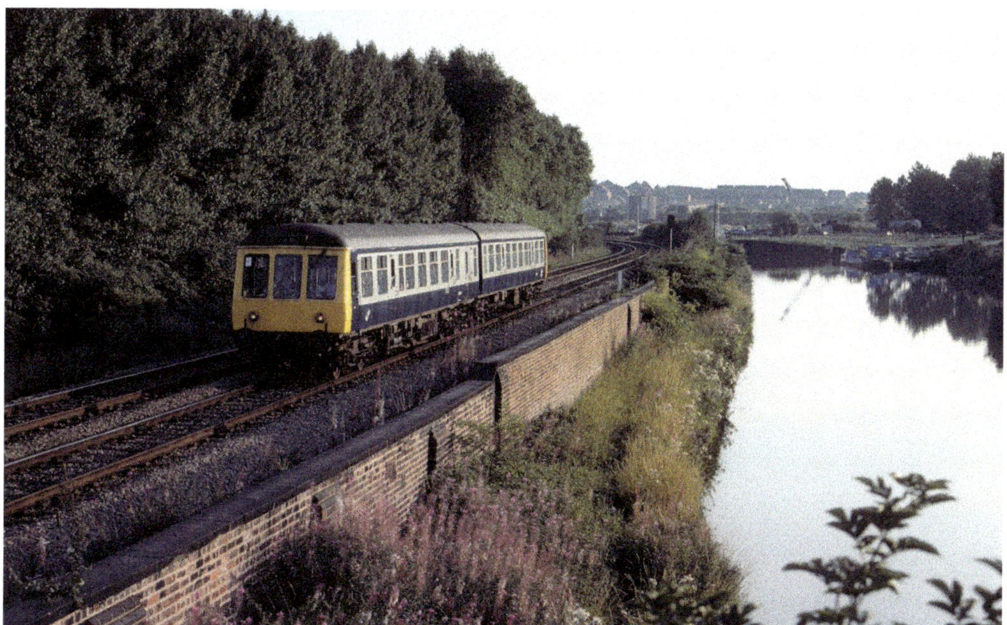

On former Great Central metals

A Sheffield to Doncaster DMU is seen here running alongside the canal between Kilnhurst and Mexborough on 24 August 1984. This was before passenger services north of Sheffield were rerouted to use the reinstated Swinton curve from the Midland main line to Mexborough. Freight services still use the GC lines here.

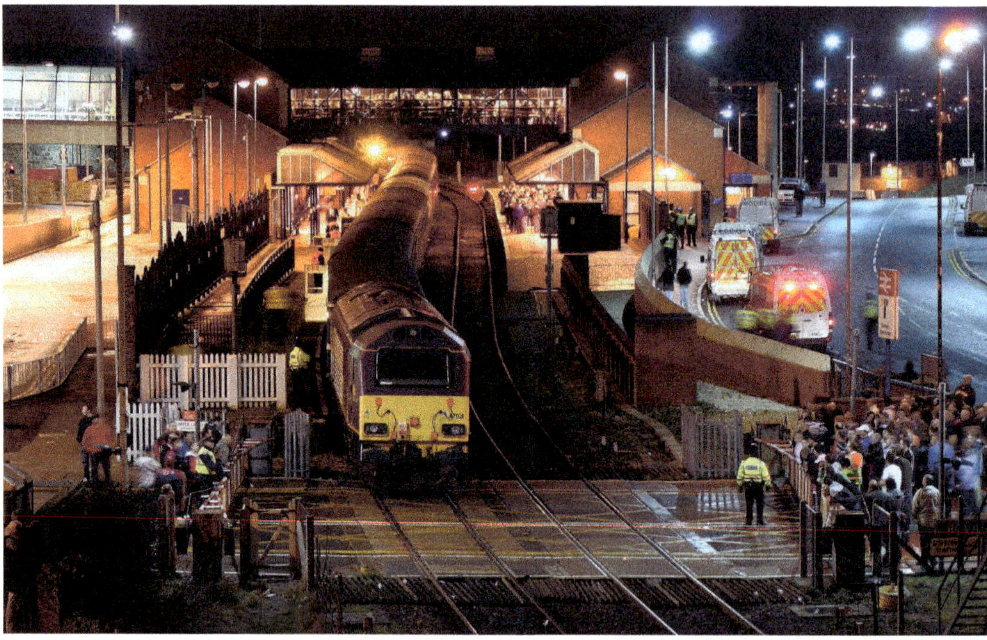

Taking the fans home from Oakwell

Chelsea fans will have to console themselves on the way home after a defeat to Barnsley in the FA Cup in 2008. Class 67s Nos 67021 and 67023 were top-and-tailing the special train, seen here waiting to leave the station on the evening of 8 March. The multi-storey carpark vantage point has since been demolished.

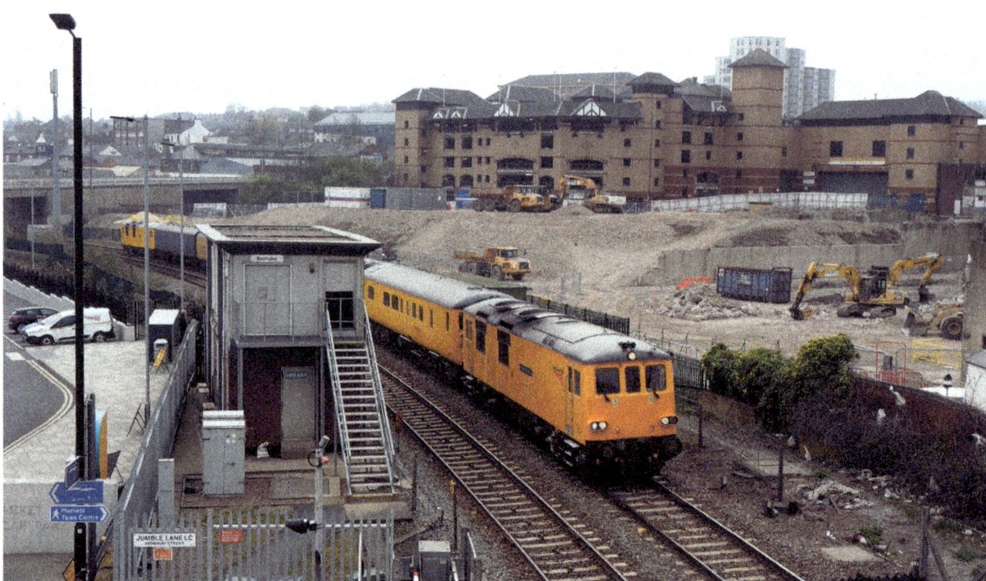

Barnsley's evolving urban landscape

It is all-change for Barnsley's town centre skyline in this view from a new footbridge at the station. Redevelopment work takes place in the background as a Network Rail inspection train from Derby approaches with motive power in the form of top-and-tail Class 73s on 6 April 2019.

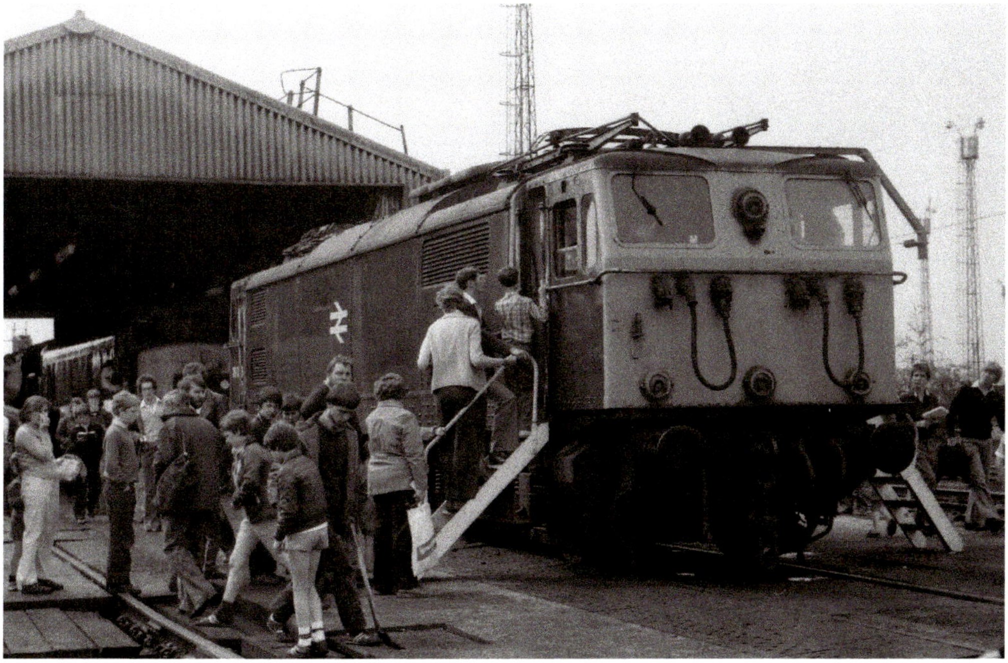

Woodhead visitor at Tinsley Open Day, 1980

This would be the last time that a Class 76 found itself on display at Tinsley depot. On 15 June 1980, No. 76033, one of the air-braked only cohort, is seen outside the running shed in the yard. (Vaughan Hellam)

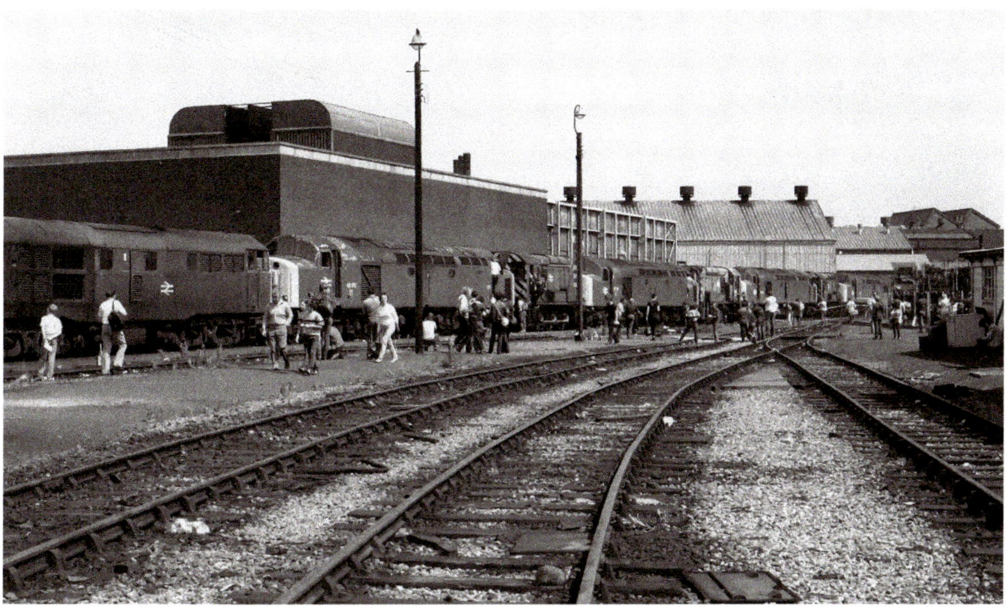

Little and large...Doncaster Works 1984

A trio of Class 08 shunters seems to have found use here as barrier vehicles among a line of withdrawn Class 40s at Doncaster Works in July 1984. The programme of scrapping of the veteran Type 4s was well underway by this stage, with the South Yorkshire works taking its fair share of the condemned machines.

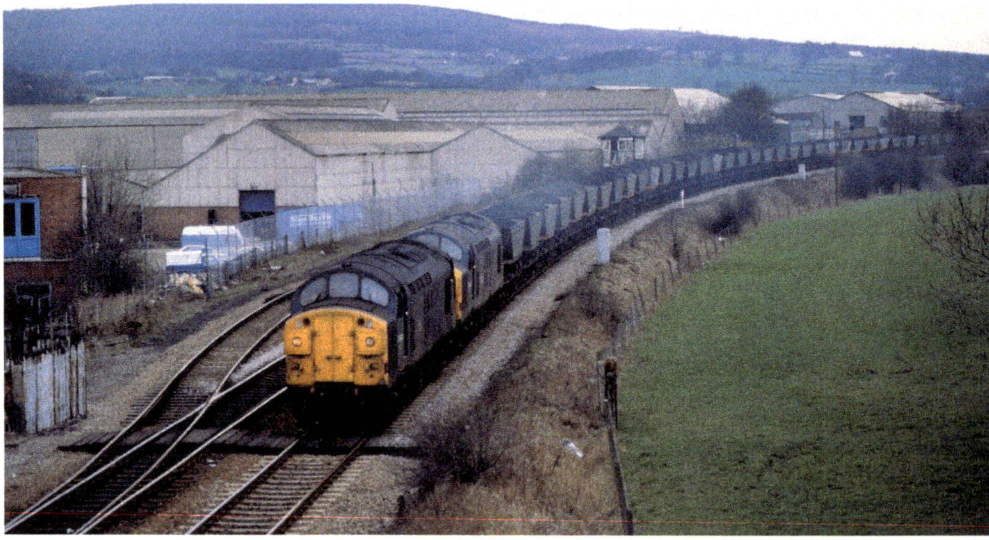

Double-headed power for Dodworth MGR service

Class 37s Nos 37040 and 37048 power past Ecclesfield West in April 1985 with a loaded MGR working from Dodworth. This was a short-lived diagram following the closure of the Barnsley to Wath line via Stairfoot that lasted until the closure of the pit at Dodworth. These Class 37s will run round their train at Brightside and take it via Mexborough to Doncaster for the Aire Valley power stations.

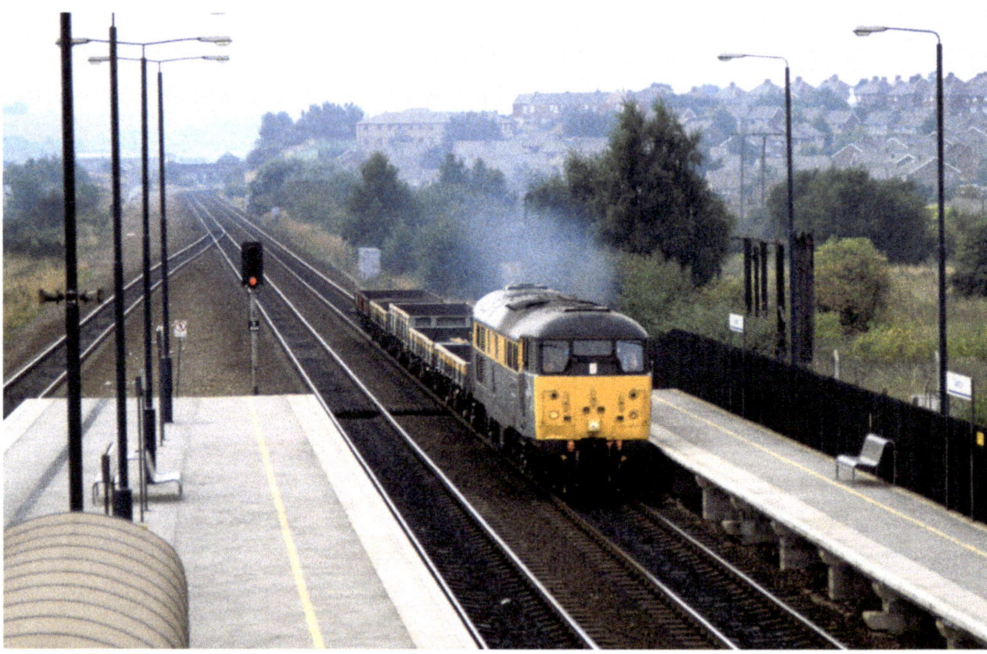

31105 passes rebuilt Swinton station, 1993

There was a former MR station close to this spot in Swinton on the main line north of Sheffield until 1968, then, in 1990, BR built this new station, bringing passenger services back to the South Yorkshire town after a gap of over twenty years. A reinstated connection with the former GC line to nearby Mexborough opened up a range of new timetable options.

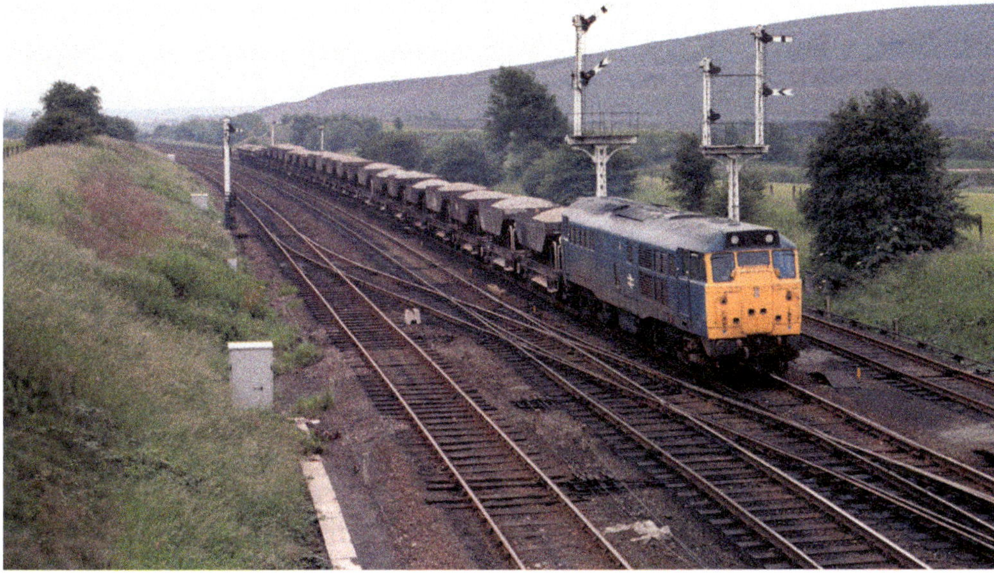

A landscape formed by coal

With the spoil heap of Orgreave colliery behind, Class 31 No. 31240 heads a fully loaded ballast train north towards Rotherham at Treeton South in July 1982. Infrastructure modernisation would soon spell the end for the characterful semaphores and the complex trackwork, including the single slip, at this location.

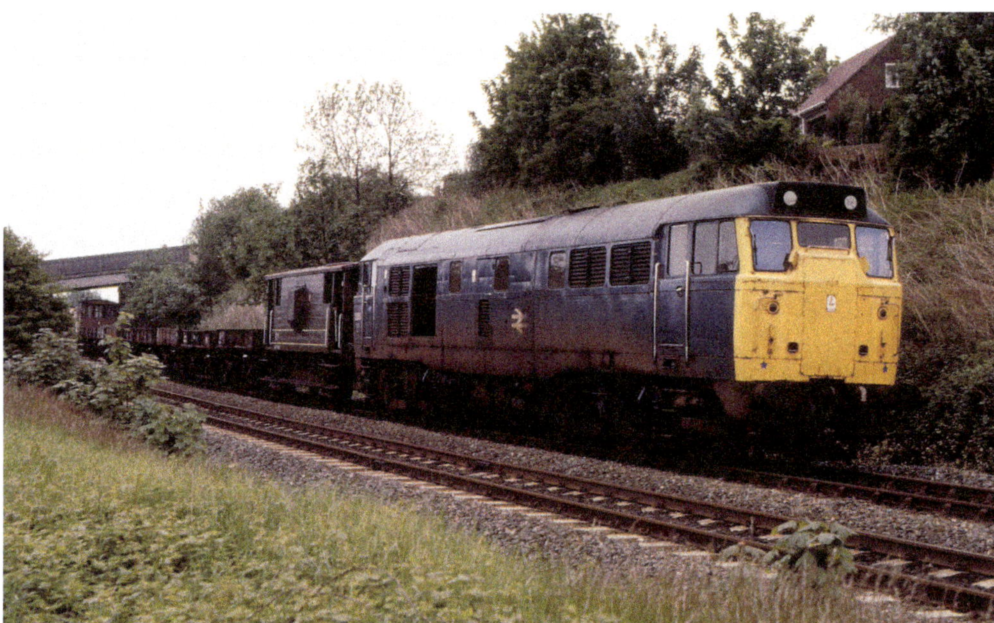

Engineer's occupation at Willow Bank

Another trackside maintenance operation and another Class 31. This time it is No. 31280 in attendance at Willow Bank, between Barnsley and Darton, in the summer of 1983. The short rake of open wagons features a BR standard brake van at the far end and a vintage LMS version behind the loco. (Vaughan Hellam)

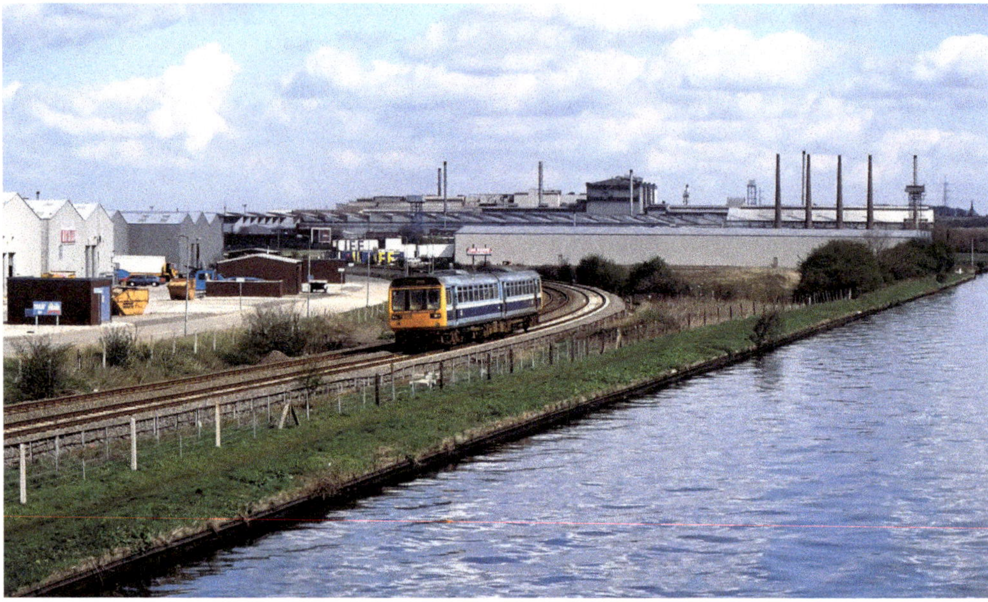

Road, rail and canal merge at Parkgate

The industrial heritage of Rotherham is evident in this 1993 image of a local passenger service heading for Sheffield at Parkgate, on the route via the recently reopened Rotherham Central station. An electrified tram system now runs alongside the railway here.

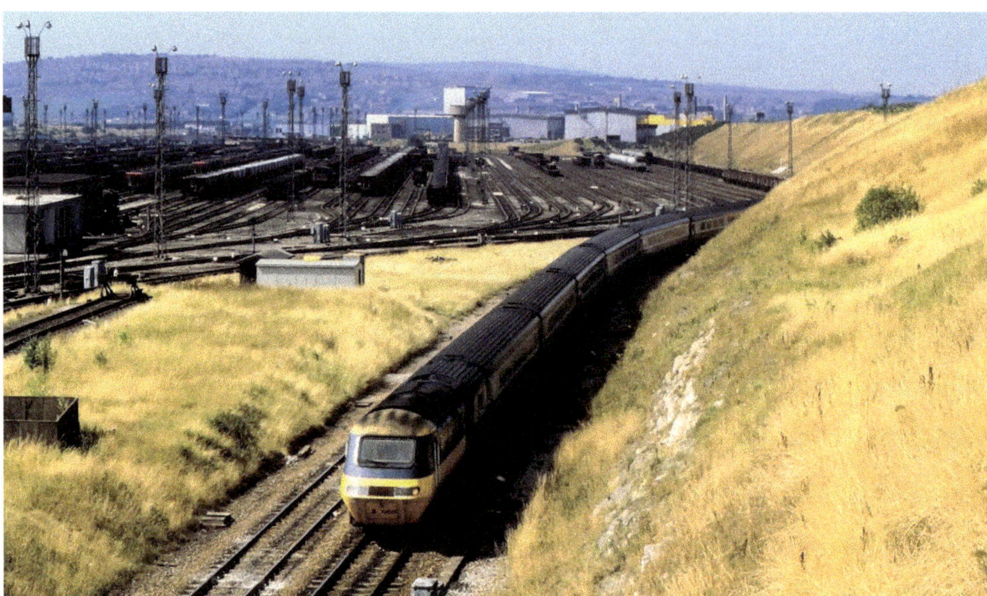

Skirting the yard at Tinsley

The huge fan of sidings at Tinsley Yard, Sheffield, can be seen to good effect in this image from a gloriously sunny 12 August 1984. An HST, diverted from its usual route due to engineering work, skirts the edge of the complex on the approach to Treeton Junction on a southbound service. The yard at Tinsley was opened in 1965 and replaced several smaller yards scattered across the city.

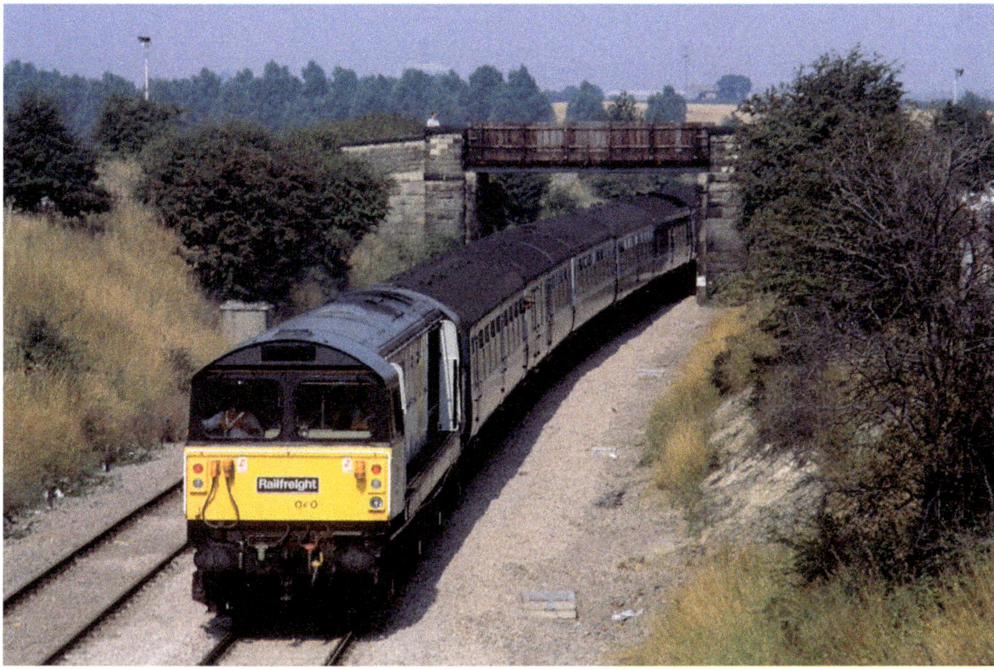

Passenger duty on the SY Joint Line for Railfreight Type 5

Class 58 No. 58040 has just passed the site of Dinnington Station Junction and is heading towards Worksop from Doncaster with an enthusiasts' special in conjunction with Worksop Depot Open Day on 1 September 1991. Class 56 No. 56007 was at the rear.

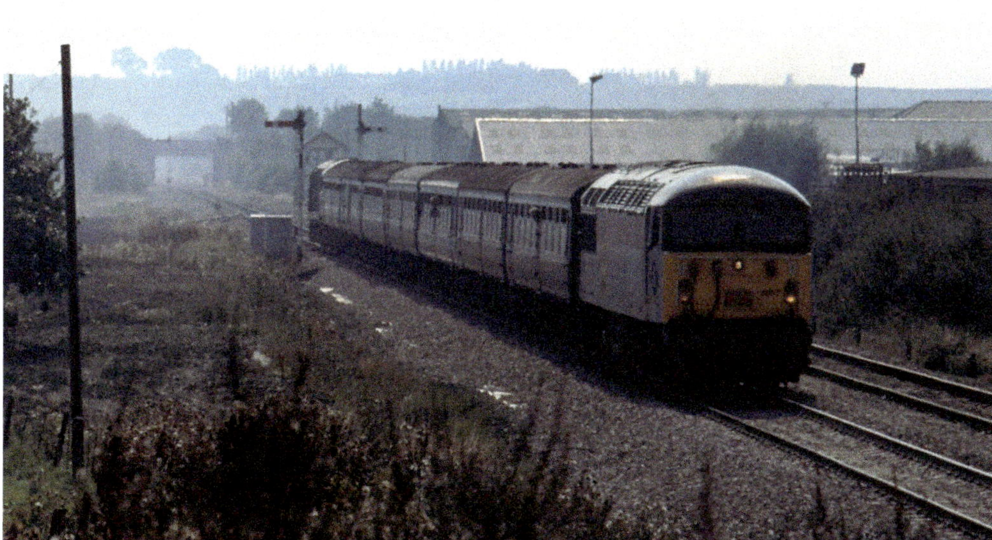

South Yorkshire Joint Line special

Silhouetted in the sun at Dinnington Colliery Junction, Class 56 No. 56007 heads a special passenger service over the SY Joint Line in September 1991. A number of trains ran over the freight-only line on this day in conjunction with an event at Worksop Depot.

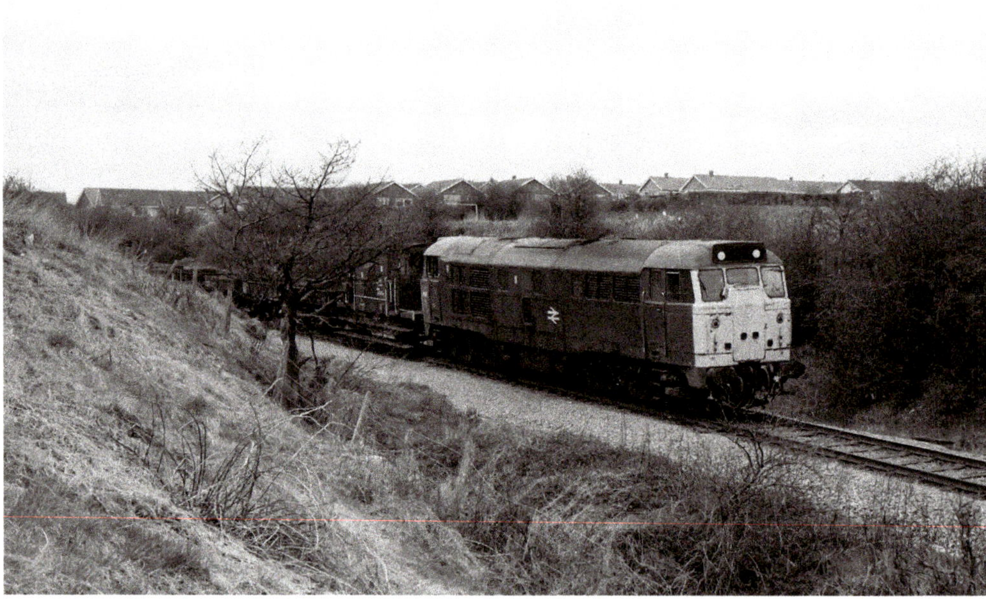

Engineering activity on the Penistone branch

A little-seen stretch of the Barnsley to Penistone branch is host to Tinsley-based Class 31 No. 31147 in this image from April 1983. The train is on the section between Dodworth and Summer Lane at Pogmoor, where the ubiquitous palisade security fencing – and vegetation growth - now renders this view unattainable.

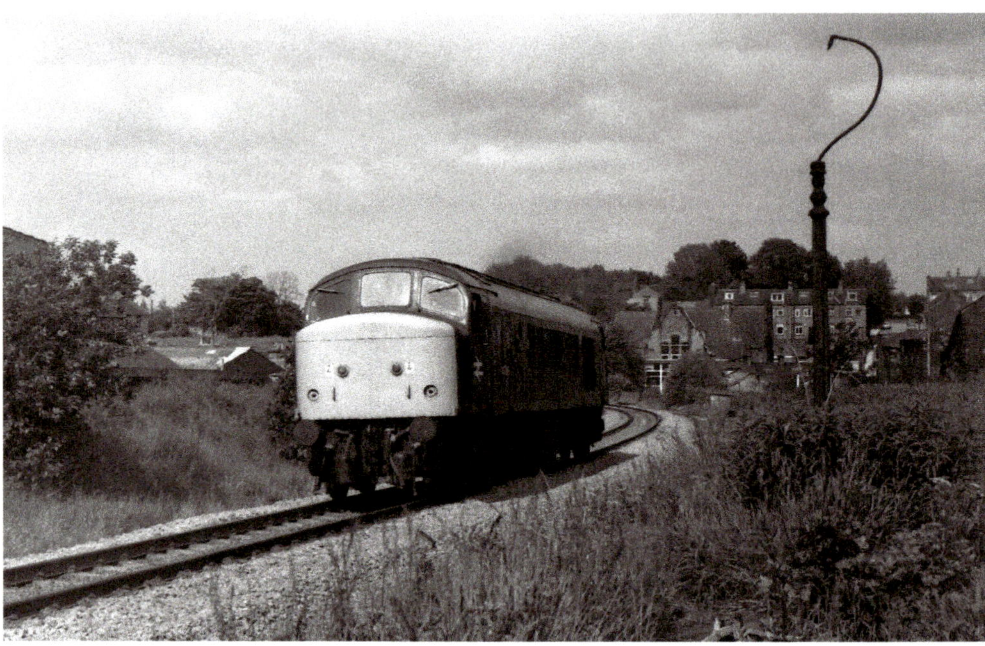

Relics of a bygone age, Summer Lane

Class 45 No. 45006 *Honourable Artillery Company* trundles past long-closed Summer Lane station in Barnsley as it heads towards Dodworth Colliery in June 1981. The station last saw passenger services in 1959. (Vaughan Hellam)

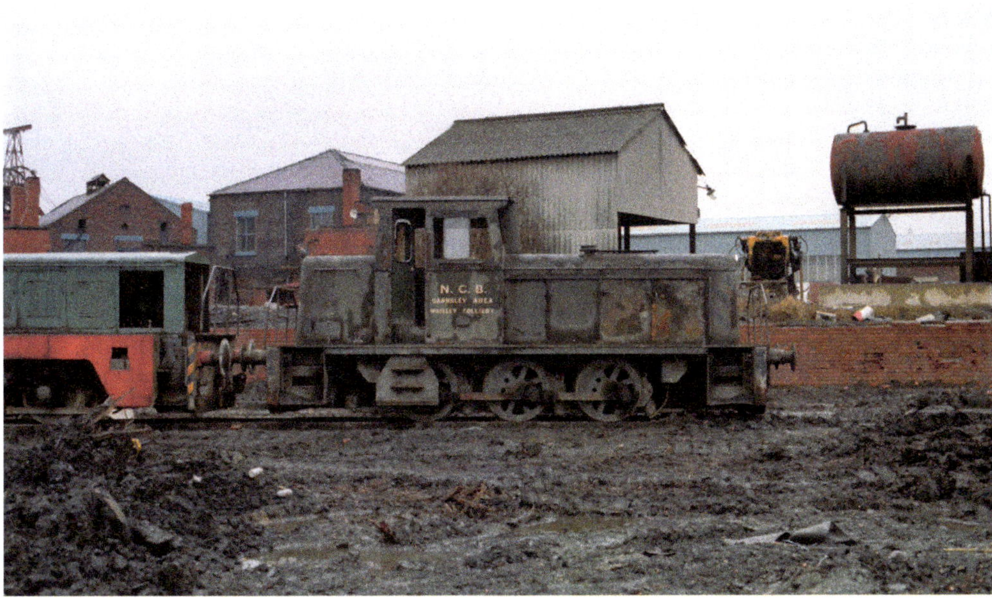

No more shunting duties at North Gawber colliery

The widespread closure of collieries across the region left many industrial shunters redundant, including this one, seen at North Gawber colliery, near Darton, in 1986. This example had previously worked at nearby Woolley.

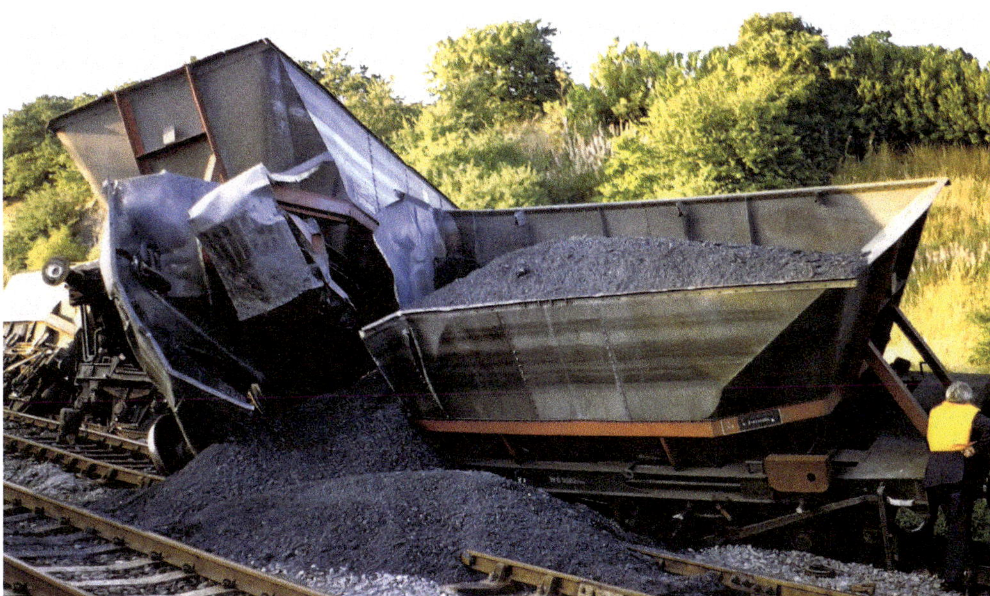

Darton derailment

This image shows the aftermath of a serious derailment at Darton in September 1983. A 'merry-go-round' coal train has left North Gawber colliery but the wagons have become derailed at the exit from the goods loop onto the main line. Thankfully there was nothing passing on the adjacent Barnsley line at the time, but the wreckage was substantial nevertheless.

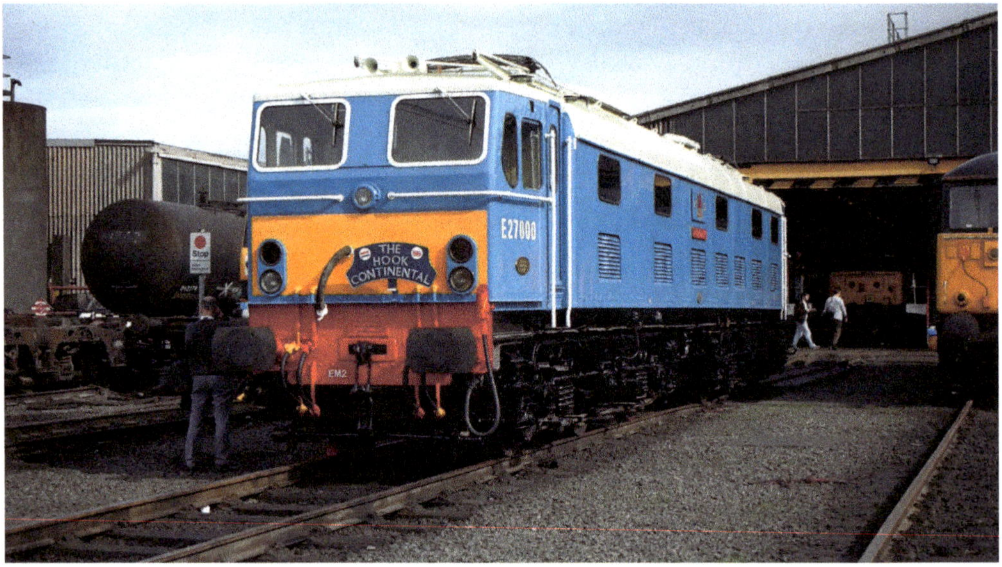

Pioneer EM2 visits Tinsley

Having recently been repainted from Brunswick green into this distinctive electric blue, the first of the Woodhead route EM2 Co-Co locomotives, No. E27000 *Electra* is seen on display at the Tinsley Open Day in 1996. No. 27000 entered traffic in December 1953 and was withdrawn a mere fifteen years later.

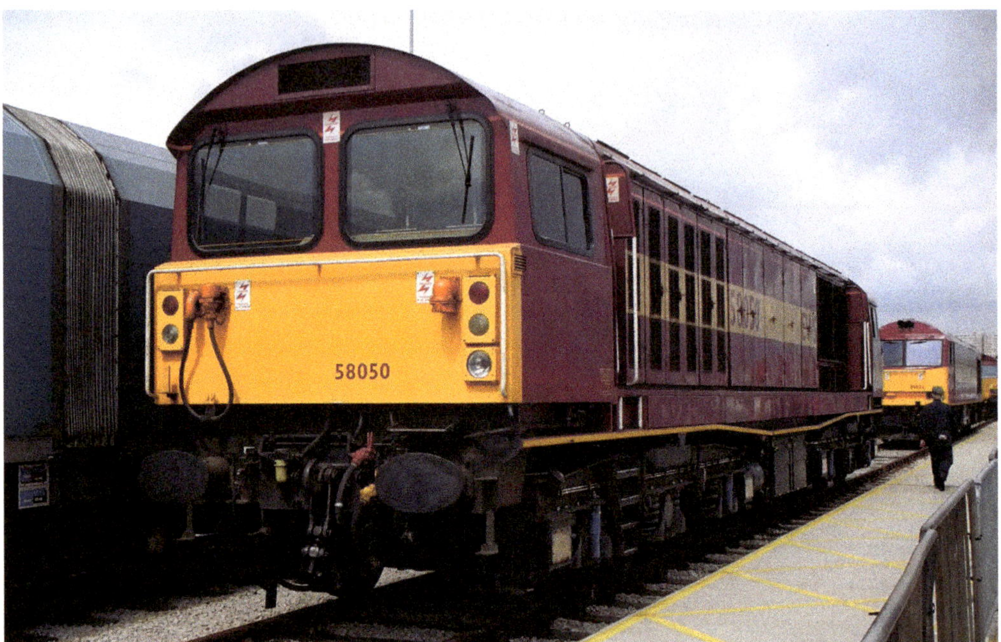

New look for Class 58

An open day at Doncaster's Belmont Yard in 1998 afforded the opportunity to see the last of the Class 58 build, No. 58050, in its new EWS maroon livery. The running number is now on the bodyside rather than cabside as originally built, but the EWS style featured an additional small cab front number.

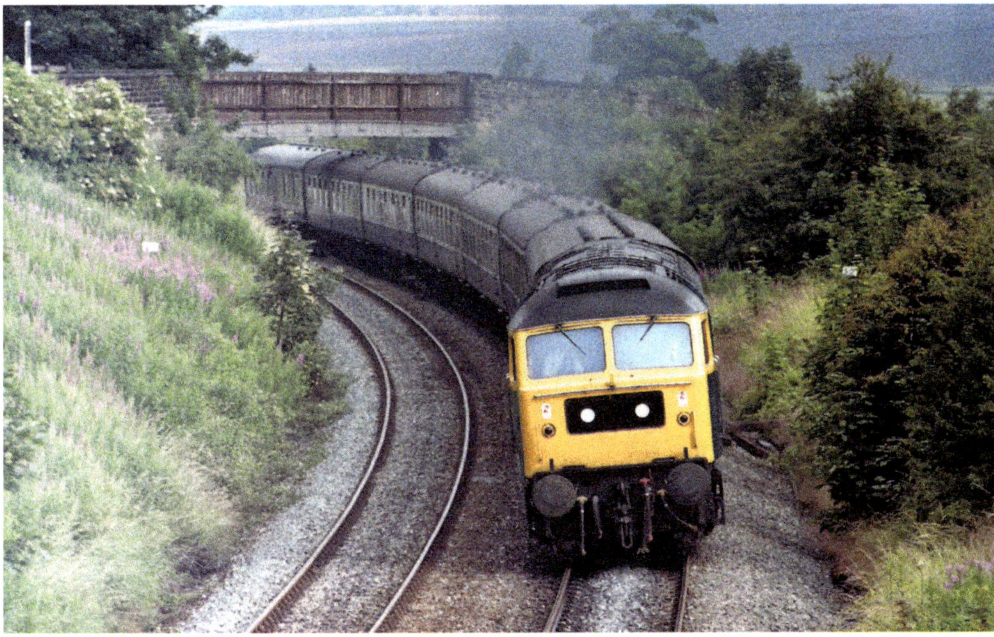

Summer Saturday power at Barnsley

In an image dating from July 1983, Crewe-built Class 47 No. 47273 powers up the grade from Darton to Barnsley with a summer Saturday holiday working. Seven Mk I coaches make up the load. The era of locomotive-hauled summer Saturday trains was coming to a close at this time. (Vaughan Hellam)

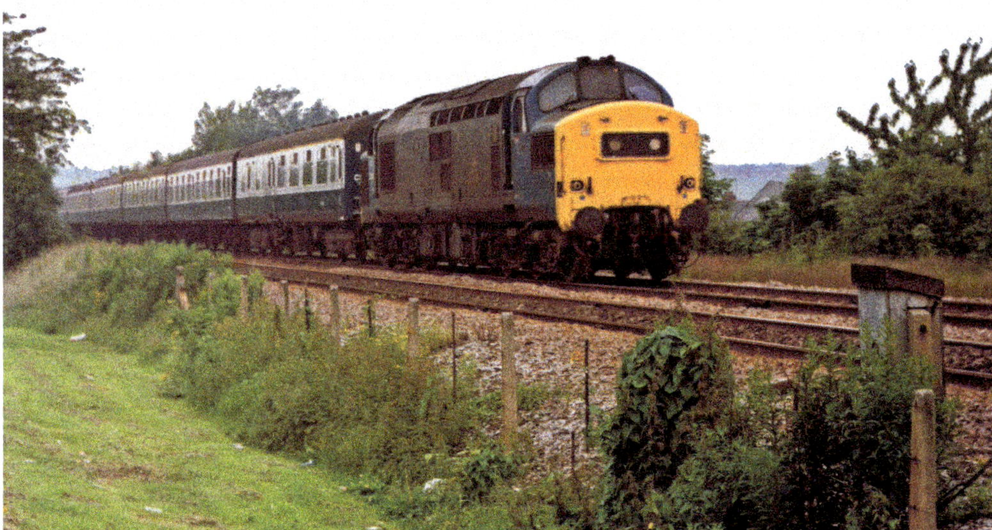

More weekend locomotive haulage, 1980 style

Tinsley's No. 37209 takes a break from its usual diet of freight haulage to bring a Saturday service into Barnsley in the summer of 1980. The motive power for these trains was remarkably varied, with half a dozen classes to be seen on some days. (Vaughan Hellam)

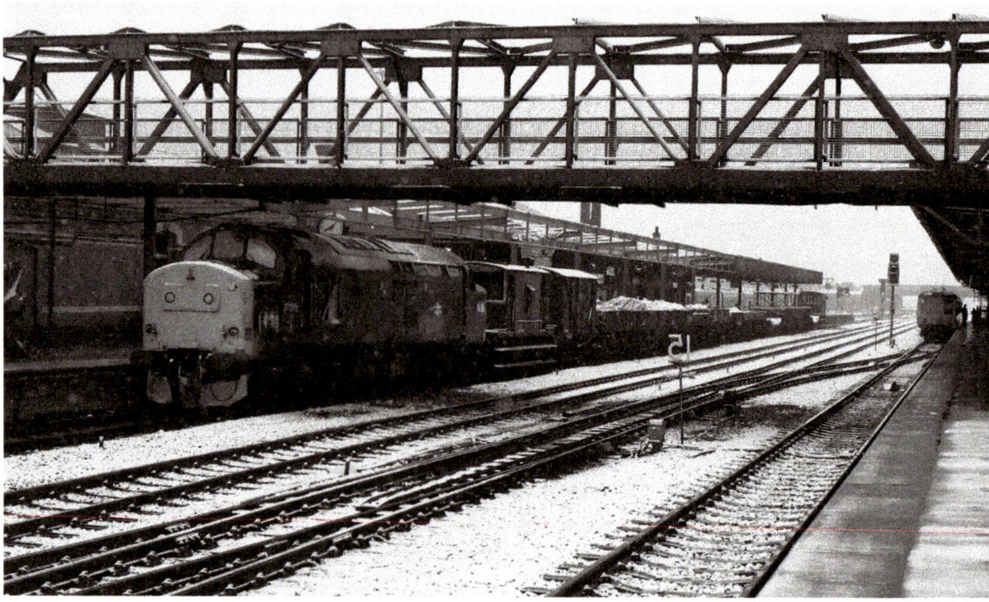

The snow comes down at Doncaster

The snow was falling thick and fast at Doncaster on 13 January 1985. Some maintenance work on the canopy of platform 4 required the attendance of Class 37 No. 37259, which is seen here occupying the Down line at the station. The footbridge seen here was subsequently raised to allow for electrification.

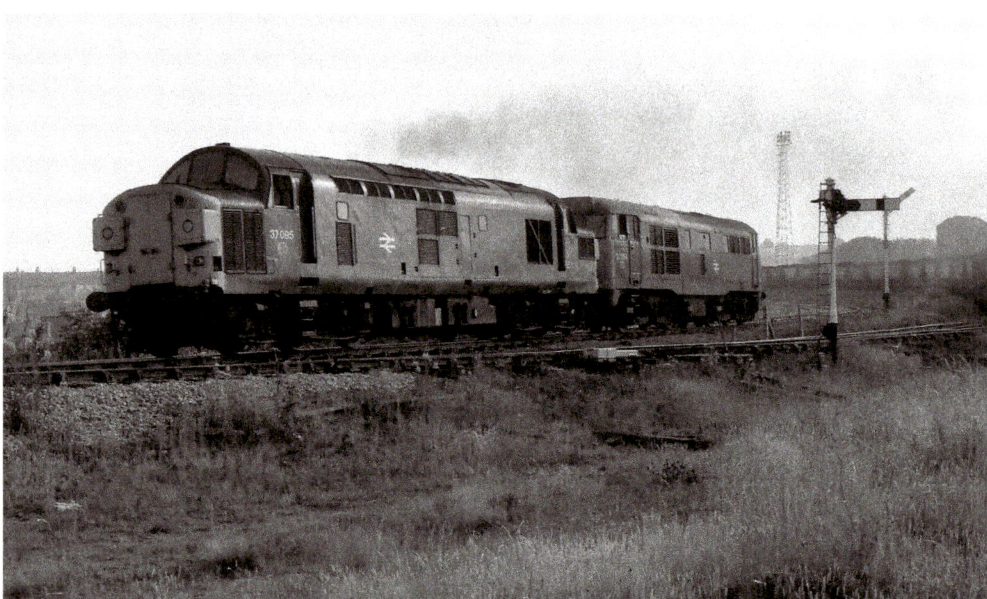

Manoeuvres at Dodworth colliery

The pit at Dodworth had less than three years' life ahead of it when this image was captured in the summer of 1983. Class 37 No. 37095 and Class 31 No. 31284 will take a loaded MGR rake away to Wath Yard after reversing back into the colliery yard. They are seen here moving off light engine after depositing an empty train in the sidings. (Vaughan Hellam)

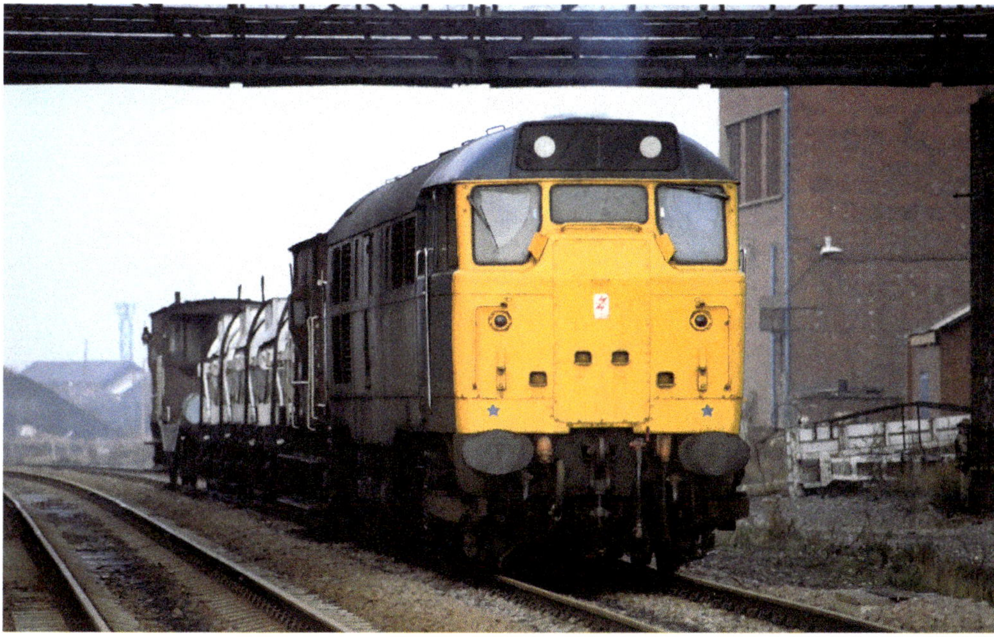

Engineering work at Wath

This view is looking towards Wath from Adwick Crossing, which was close to Manvers Colliery and coking plant on the line to Mexborough. Class 31 No. 31221 is in charge of an engineers' train on 23 January 1983, the day that Wath shed closed.

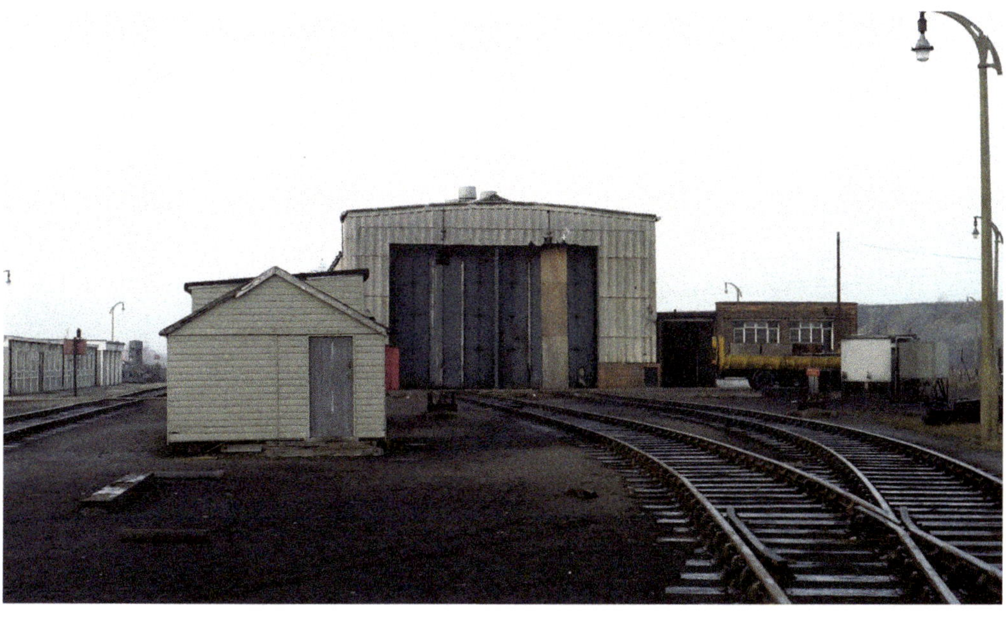

Lonely Wath, 23 January 1983

The contraction of the coal industry in South Yorkshire, compounded by the closure of the Woodhead route, spelled the end for Wath depot, which is seen here on the day of closure. The adjacent marshalling yard lasted for a few more years, but now there is no railway here at all.

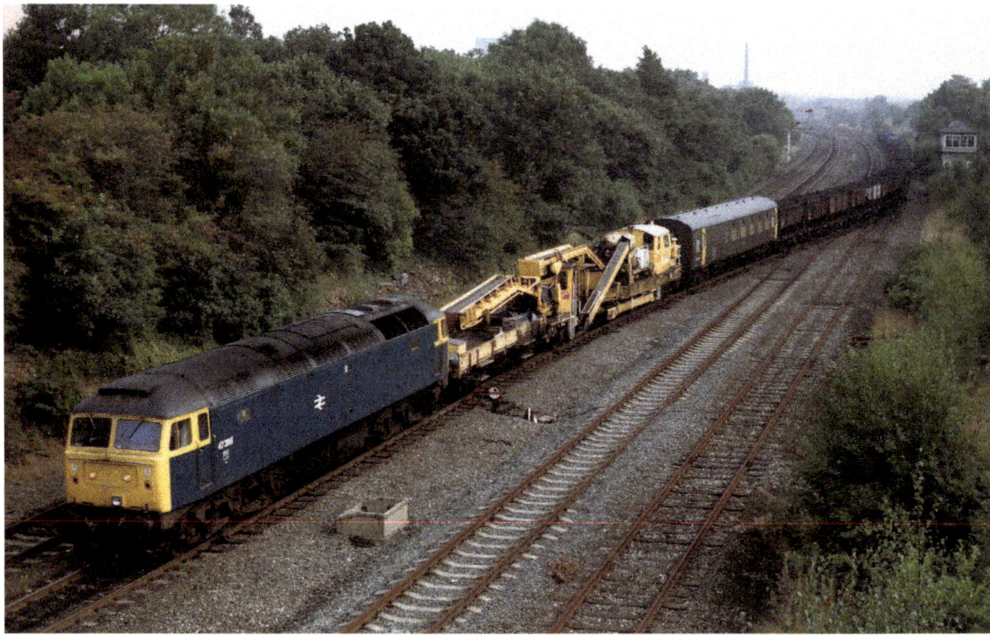

An enforced meander for No. 47288

Royston Junction, on the Swinton to Normanton section of the Midland Main Line, is seen here in September 1983, with Class 47 No. 47288 weaving across from fast to slow lines to avoid a section of subsidence-affected track. The junction itself, where a line diverged to Dewsbury, had long since closed. (Vaughan Hellam)

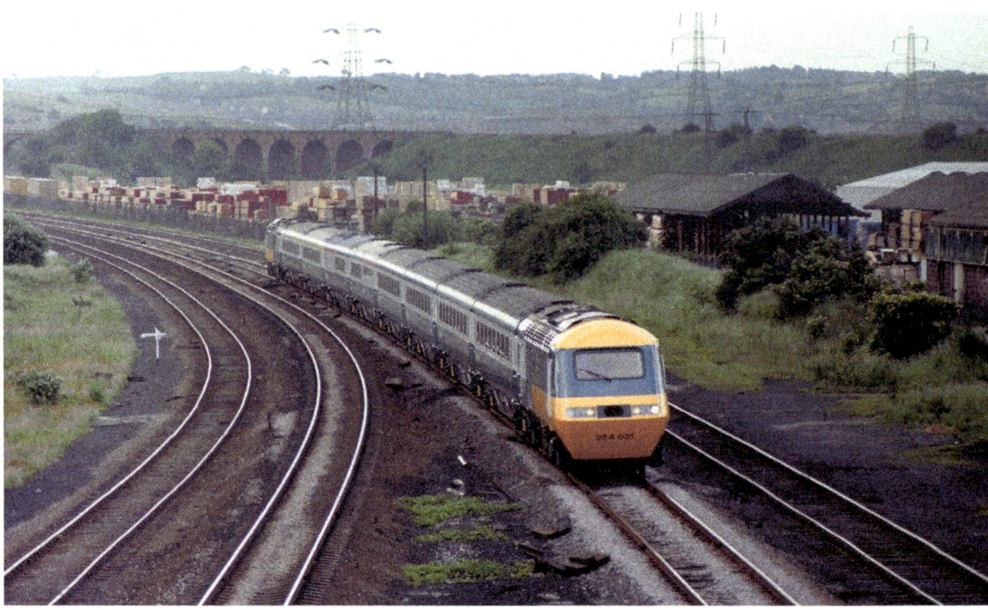

Brand new HST on test

Looking south at Woodhouse Mill, on the former Midland Railway Chesterfield to Rotherham route, a brand new HST set approaches at speed on a test run, probably from Derby. In the background the viaduct marks the location of the Sheffield to Worksop line.

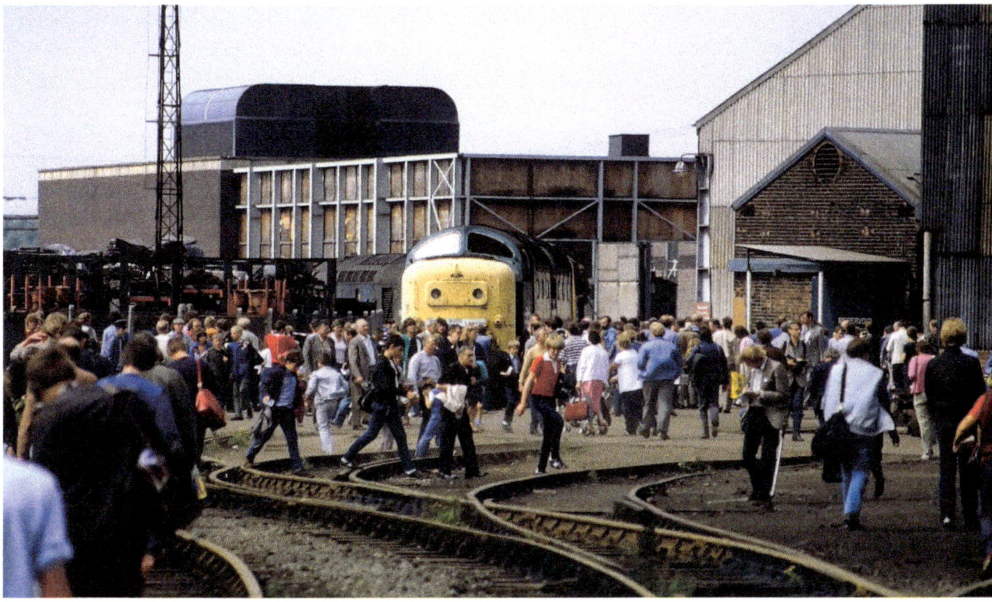

Thousands flock to 'the Plant'

A withdrawn Deltic makes a somewhat forlorn sight at the centre of the bustling crowd at Doncaster's Works Open Day in July 1984. For this machine though, there was a happy outcome as No. 55016 *Gordon Highlander* was saved for preservation. The infrastructure in this picture has all since disappeared.

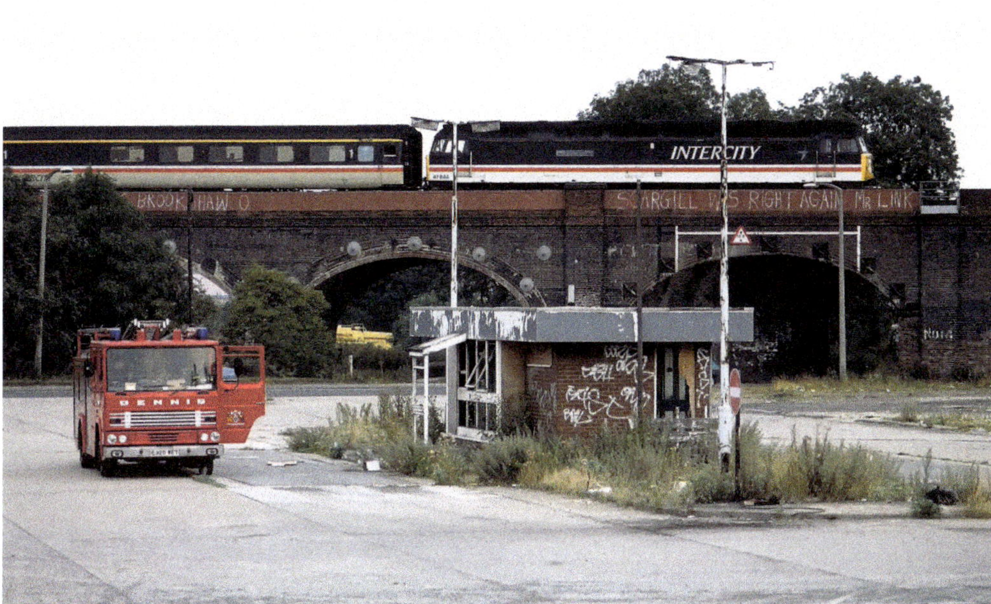

Abandoned infrastructure at Manvers

The area around the giant Manvers coal and coke installation was in transition to new economic purposes at the time of this image in September 1993. Heading off the Bolton-on-Dearne line, Class 47 No. 47844 speeds towards Sheffield with a passenger service, passing a redundant weighbridge.

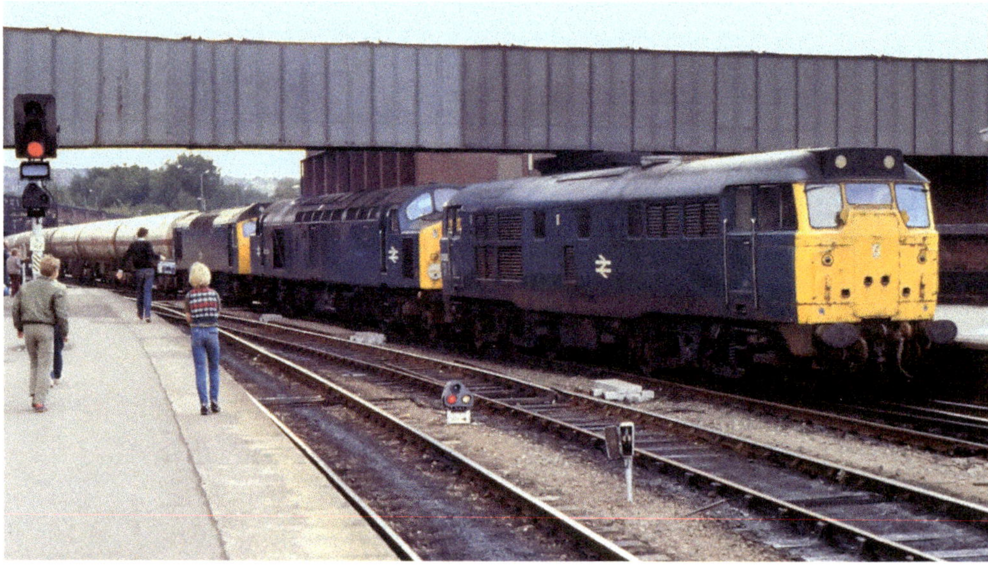

Helping hand for the Broughton Lane BOC tanks

A Class 40/25 combination was relatively common on the Ditton to Broughton Lane oxygen tanks service, but something must have gone awry here, as the two train engines are given some additional tractive effort in the form of Class 31 No. 31235. The trio is seen entering Sheffield station on 17 September 1983.

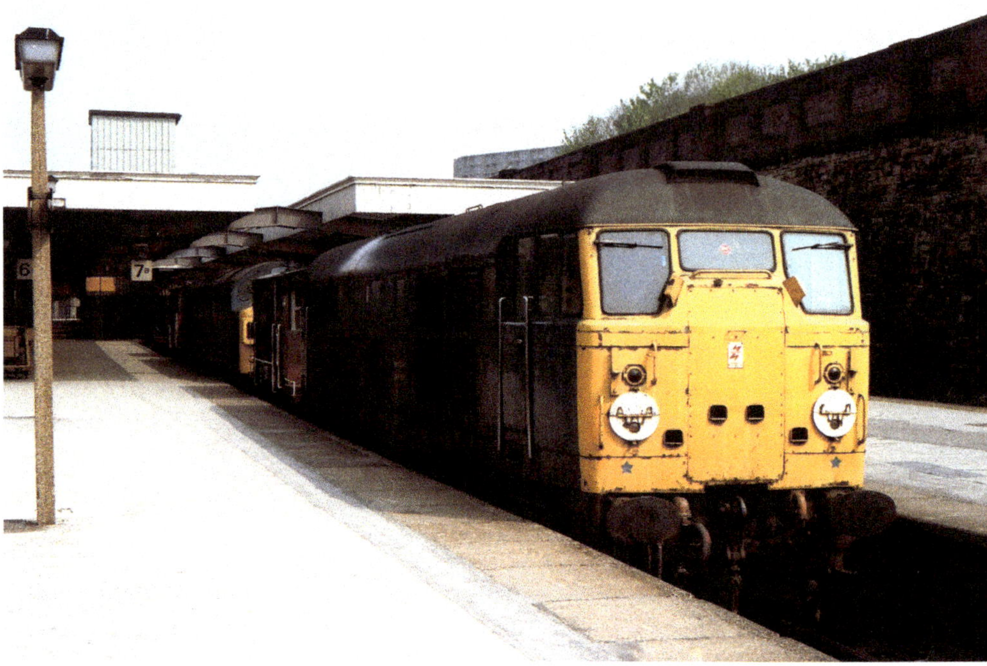

Unusual occupants for Sheffield's bay platform

Class 31 No. 31134 and Class 40 No. 40135 are temporarily occupying Sheffield's platform 7a in this image from May 1985. The Type 4 has recently been withdrawn from main line service and is en route to Crewe where it will be recruited to the ranks of the Civil Engineer's departmental fleet. (Vaughan Hellam)

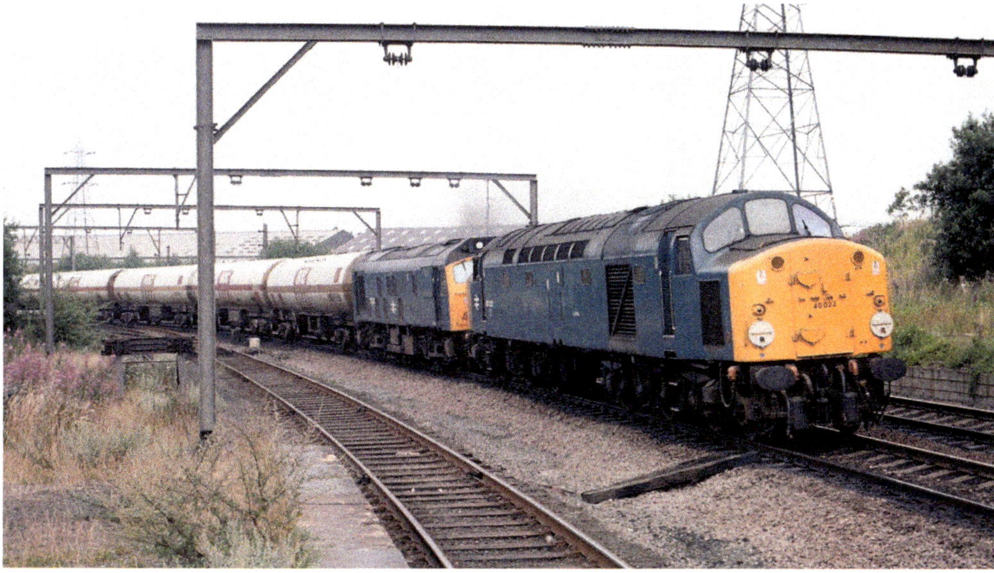

BOC tanks head past Broughton Lane

This August 1983 view was taken from the disused platform at Sheffield's Broughton Lane station as the BOC tank train to Ditton pulls away from the terminal with Nos 40022 and 25230 in charge. At this stage all the Woodhead route catenary was gone but many of the overhead gantries were still in situ. This stretch of line was on the 1960s electrification extension from Woodburn Junction to Tinsley Yard.

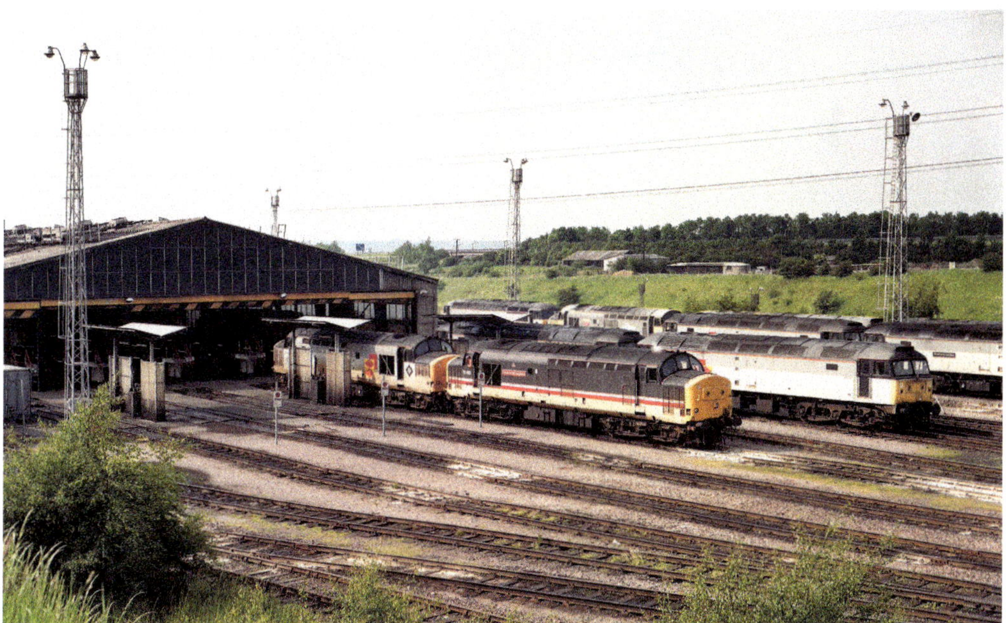

Type 3 and 4 gathering at Tinsley

Tinsley depot would soon close, but here in June 1993 it was still a relatively busy depot with a substantial allocation of locomotives. There is a single Class 56 just visible in this view, but otherwise Class 37s and 47s dominate. In the foreground is No. 37420 *The Scottish Hosteller*.

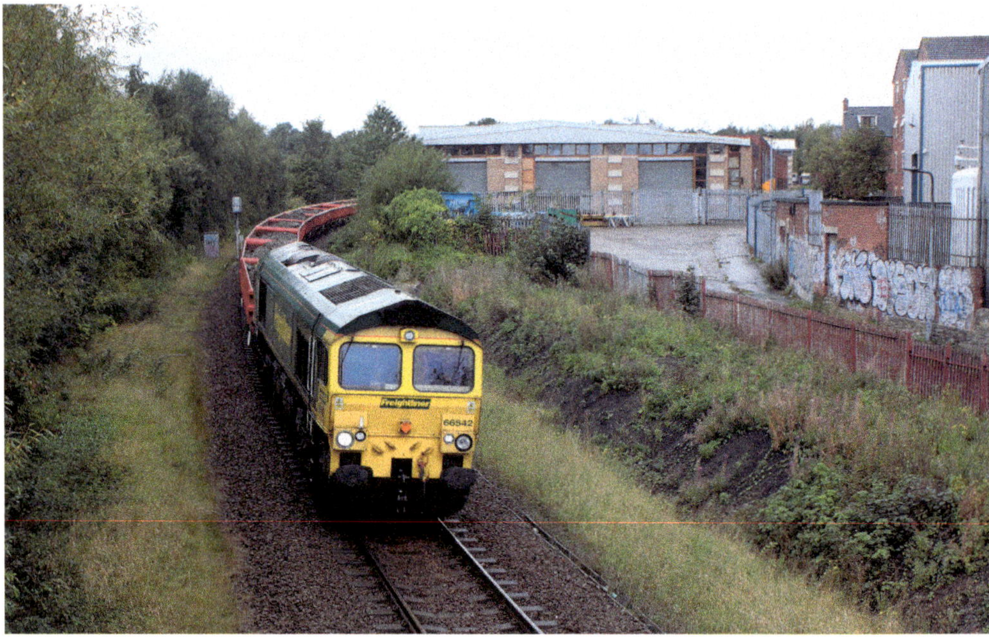

Resurgent woodland thrives on railway land

A Class 66 locomotive brings an engineers' train down the steeply graded Penistone to Barnsley branch in September 2017. It is approaching the site of Summer Lane station, where on the left was once a signalbox and extensive sidings serving the Barnsley Co-op's warehouse.

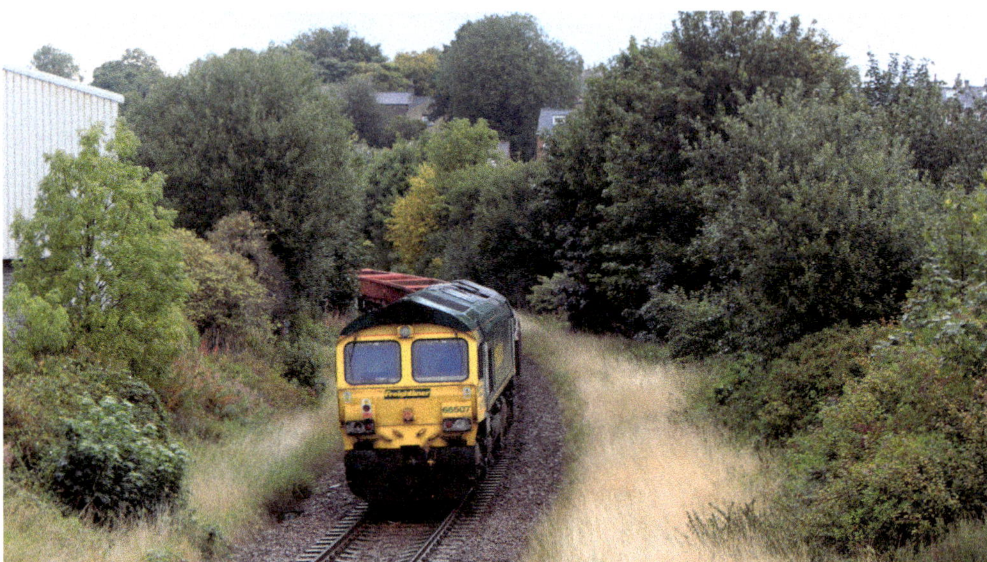

Where a Great Central station once stood

Britain's railway landscape is changing rapidly, particularly in urban locations where trees and shrubs are encroaching where sidings and other infrastructure once stood. Here at Summer Lane in Barnsley in September 2017, a Class 66 passes the site of the former Great Central passenger station of the same name, closed in 1959.

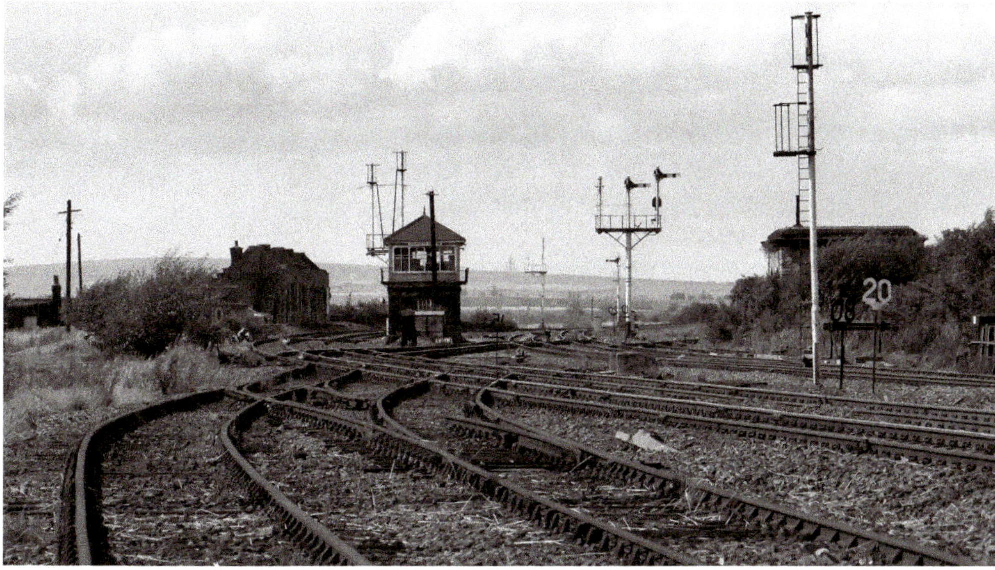

Gradual dismantling of a once great main line

A panorama of Cudworth Station Junction, once such a busy interchange on the Midland's main route north of Sheffield but seen here in August 1984 with little more than the status of a colliery branch line. Three forlorn semaphore arms remain visible and the tracks of the Stairfoot line in the foreground lie rusting. Soon there would be no railway here at all.

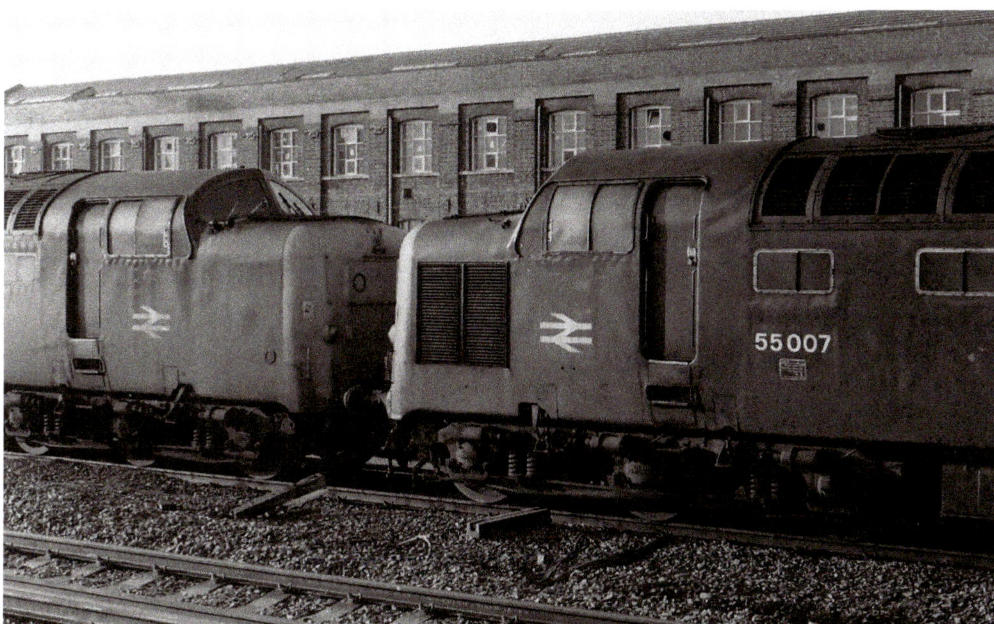

Arriving at the last resting place

Two days prior to this photograph, No. 55015 *Tulyar* had hauled the final train of the BR Deltic era. On 4 January 1982, classmates Nos 55021 *Argyll & Sutherland Highlander* and 55007 *Pinza* were brought to Doncaster for scrapping. They are seen here standing alongside the famous plant.

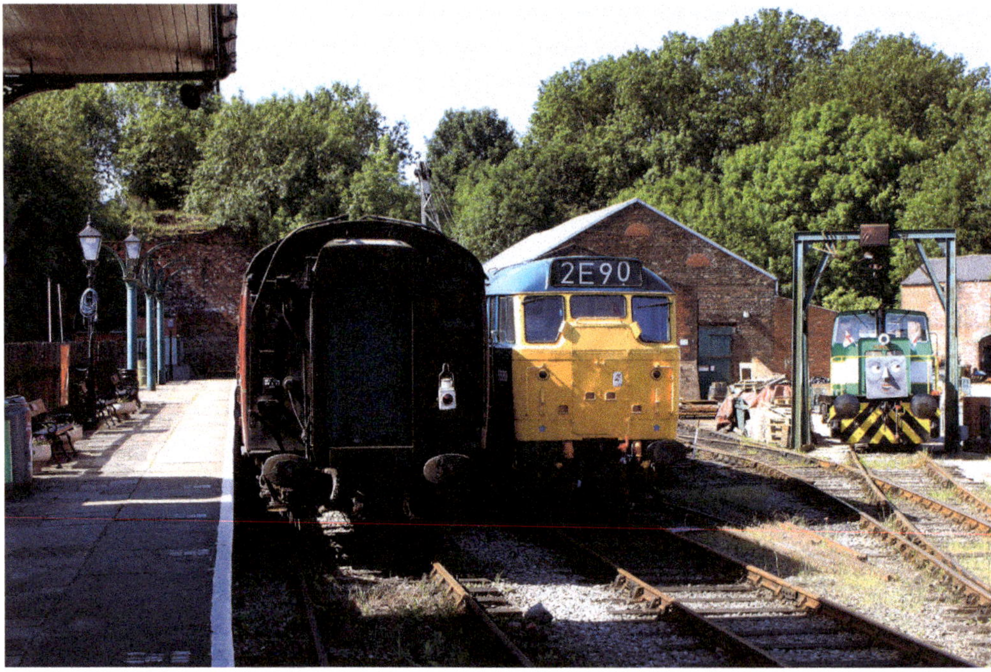

A colliery terminus is now a visitor centre

This is the Elsecar Heritage Centre near Barnsley, at the terminus of the former colliery branch from Wath, seen in June 2010. At the neatly kept visitor centre station, Class 31 No. 5580 (31162) keeps company with an industrial diesel and a Mk I coach.

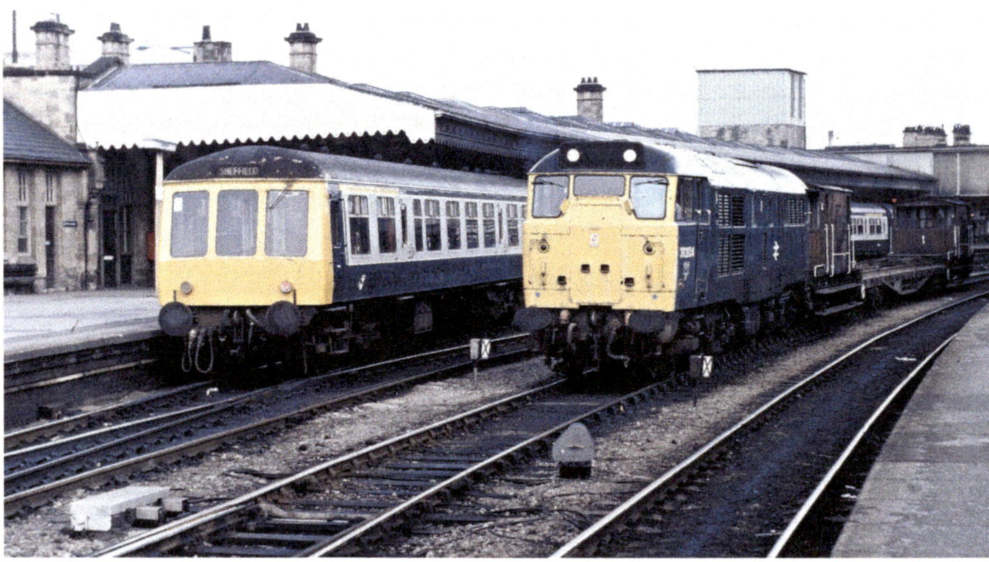

Days of BR blue at Sheffield

An everyday scene that is now part of history – a refurbished DMU stands at Sheffield's platform 1, while Class 31 No. 31204 passes on a short engineer's train. The date was November 1981. (Vaughan Hellam)

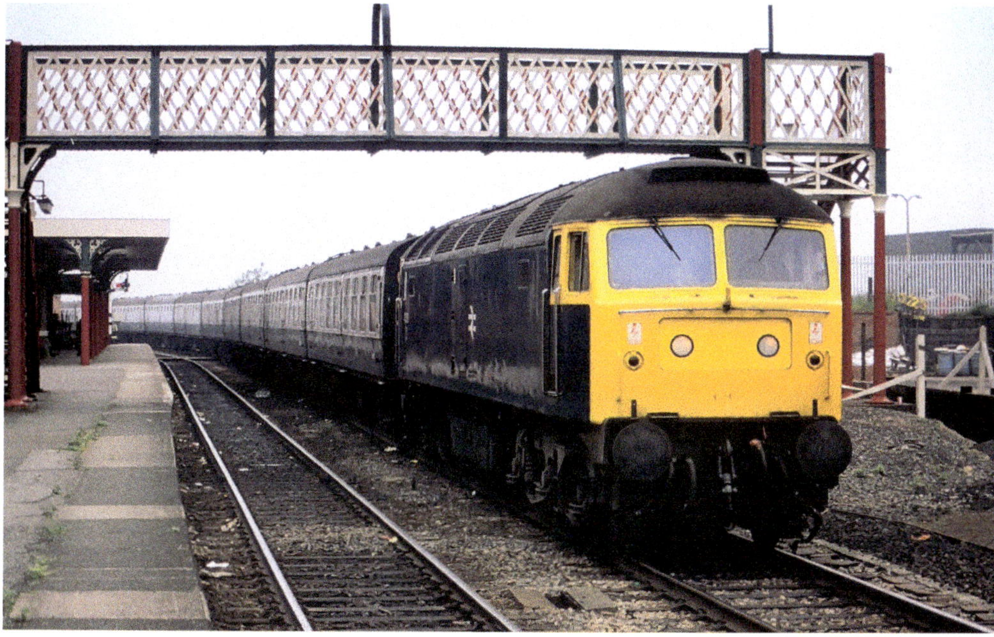

Not surprisingly, the train is longer than the platform

The ten-coach Bradford to Weymouth summer Saturday service is seen here at Barnsley's modest Sheffield platform on 18 June 1983. This was a regular Class 47 turn, and on this occasion, No. 47281 does the honours. Train lengths would soon diminish to far smaller typical consists across the national network.

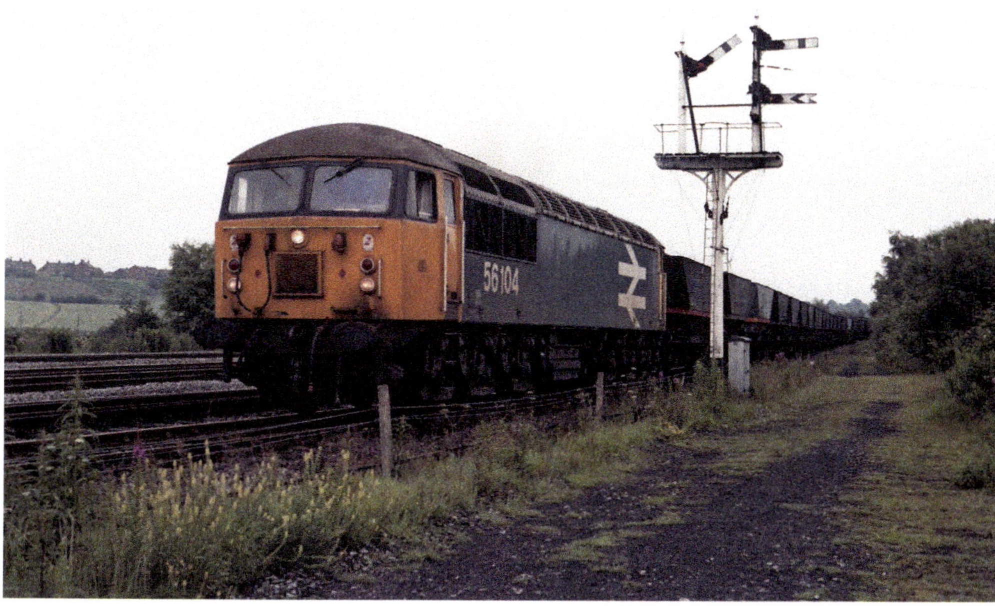

No. 56104 joins the Midland main line

Large-logo-liveried Class 56 No. 56104 brings an empty MGR service off the Stairfoot branch and onto the main line at Cudworth in this image from July 1982. Despite being just a few months old in this picture, the 56 is already showing the effects of working colliery traffic, as the grimy roof demonstrates. (Vaughan Hellam)

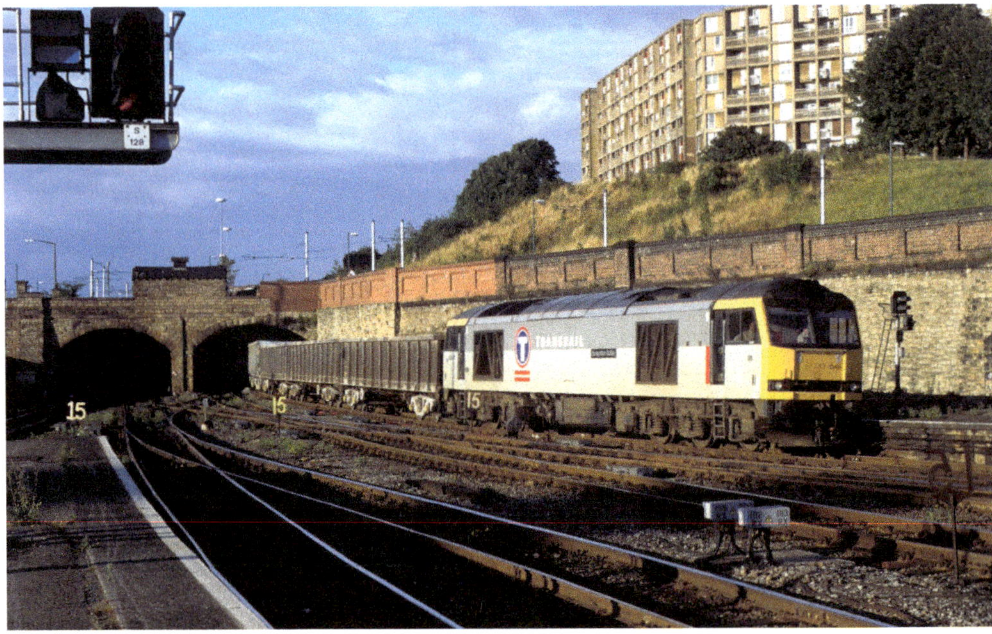

Short-lived branding for Class 60

Wearing Transrail decals applied over its original two-tone Railfreight grey livery, five-year-old Class 60 No. 60045 *Josephine Butler* passes Sheffield station on a southbound freight service on 30 August 1996.

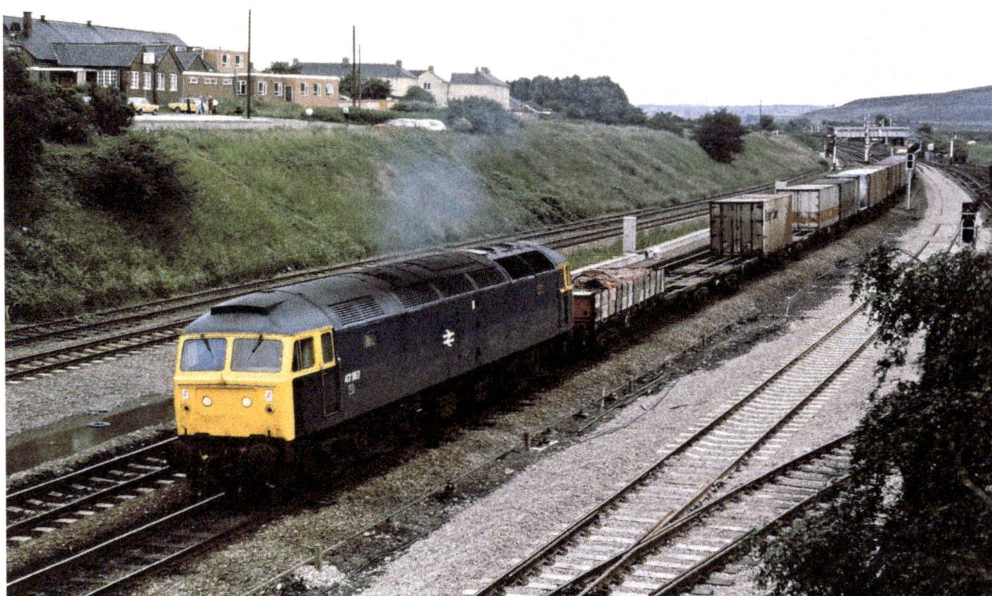

Treeton modernisation progresses, 1982

This view of Treeton South Junction shows Class 47 No. 47367 going north with a container service. A line diverged here to Tinsley Yard, with the main route going ahead to Rotherham Masborough. The Tinsley line is now closed, but the main line is still a through freight route for services heading to and from the Midlands via Chesterfield. (Vaughan Hellam)

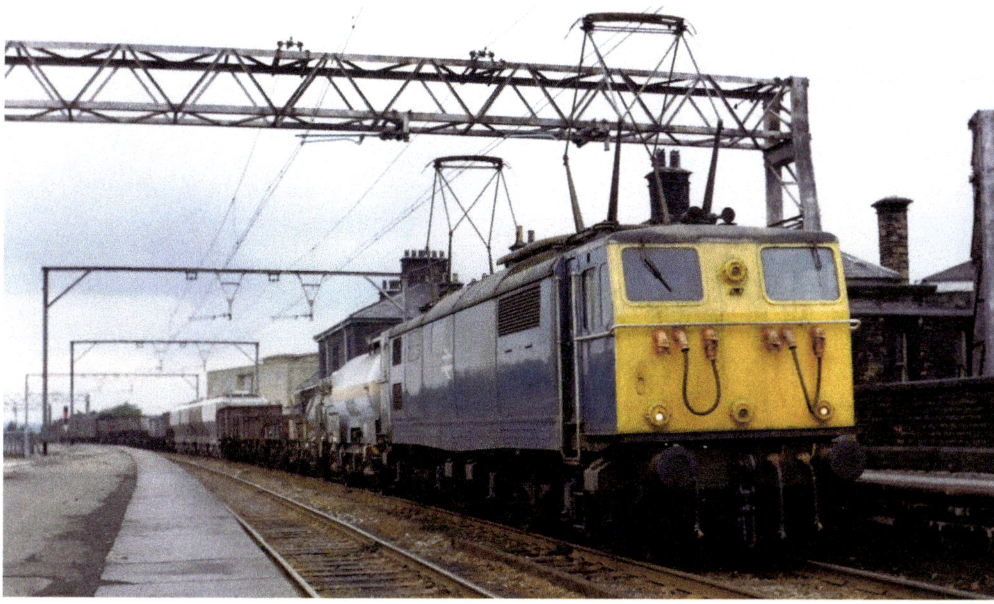

Mixed freight at Penistone as the end approaches

With just one month to go before the closure of the Woodhead route, Class 76 No. 76035 waits for a path at Penistone with a mixed freight bound for Tinsley Yard. Making a change from the usual diet of MGR traffic, this varied consist even includes a couple of parcels vans for good measure. The date was 18 June 1981.

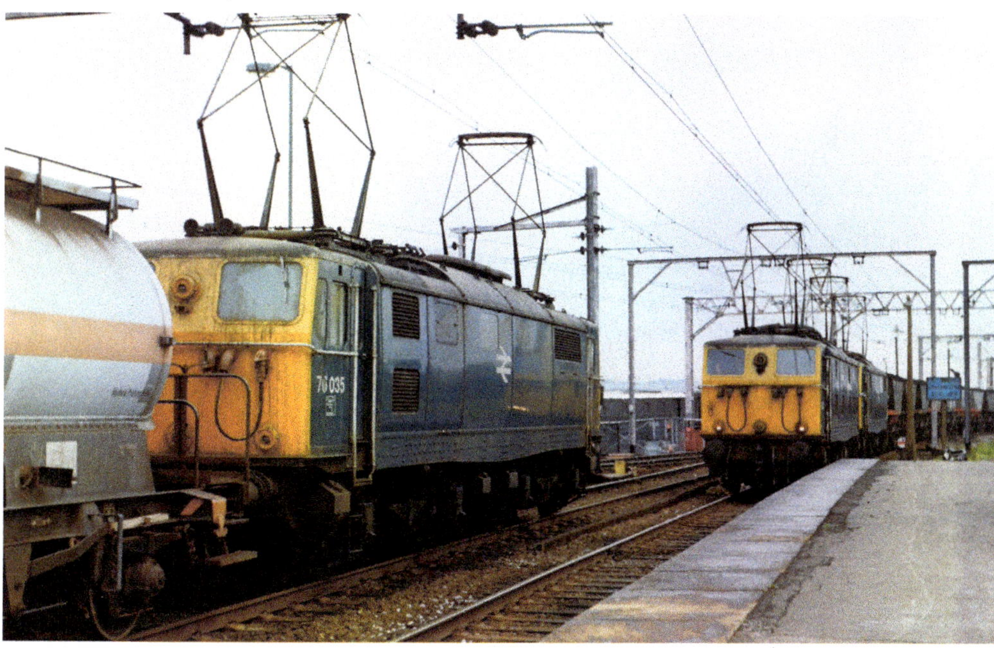

EM1s meet on freight at Penistone

In the dying weeks of the Woodhead route, there were still busy moments like this at Penistone. On 18 June 1981, a pair of dual-braked Class 76s approaches the station with a loaded MGR service while No. 76035 waits for a path with a mixed load bound for Tinsley. A month later, and it was all over.

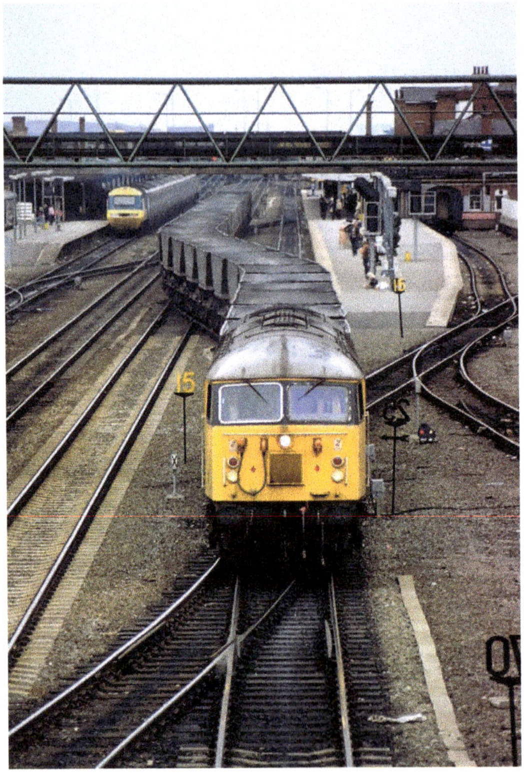

Snaking through Doncaster

A telephoto lens is used to good effect in this powerful image of Class 56 No. 56101 crossing from Up fast to slow lines with a returning empty MGR service at Doncaster in August 1983. One of the later Doncaster-built examples, it is less than two years old at this point. The loco is carrying the large logo livery, which featured an all-yellow cab with black window surrounds.

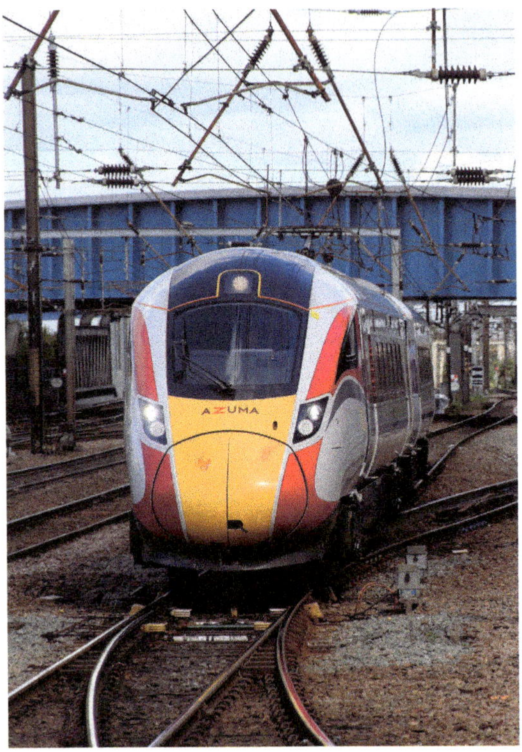

New order on the East Coast Main Line

A new 'Azuma' multiple unit approaches Doncaster with a King's Cross service in the summer of 2019. These new bi-modal trains began to replace both the Class 91-hauled and HST services on the East Coast earlier in the year.